TURNING POINTS

Other books by Paul Moon

Hobson: Governor of New Zealand 1840–1842

The Sealord Deal

Muldoon: A Study in Public Leadership

FitzRoy: Governor in Crisis 1843-1845

Hone Heke: Nga Puhi Warrior

Te Ara Ki Te Tiriti: The Path to the Treaty of Waitangi

Tohunga: Hohepa Kereopa

The Treaty and its Times 1840–1845

A Tohunga's Natural World: Plants, Gardening, and Food

Ngapua: The Political Life of Hone Heke Ngapua, MHR

Fatal Frontiers: A New History of New Zealand in the Decade Before the Treaty

The Newest Country in the World: A History of New Zealand in the Decade of the Treaty

The Struggle for Tamaki Makaurau: Auckland to 1820

The Tohunga Journal: Hohepa Kereopa, Rua Kenana and Maungapohatu

This Horrid Practice: The Myth and the Reality of Traditional Maori Cannibalism

The Edges of Empires: New Zealand in the Middle of the Nineteenth Century

New Zealand Birth Certificates: 50 of New Zealand's Founding Documents

Victoria Cross at Takrouna: The Haane Manahi Story

New Zealand in the Twentieth Century: The Nation, The People

Framing the World: The Life and Art of Augustus Earle

A Savage Country: The Untold Story of New Zealand in the 1820s

TURNING POINTS

EVENTS THAT CHANGED THE COURSE
OF NEW ZEALAND HISTORY

PAUL MOON

First published in 2013 by New Holland Publishers (NZ) Ltd
Auckland • Sydney • London • Cape Town

www.newhollandpublishers.co.nz

218 Lake Road, Northcote, Auckland 0627, New Zealand
Unit 1, 66 Gibbes Street, Chatswood, NSW 2067, Australia
86–88 Edgware Road, London W2 2EA, United Kingdom
Wembley Square, First Floor, Solan Road, Gardens, Cape Town 8001, South Africa

The publisher wishes to thank Jenifer Curnow and Auckland University Press for permission to reproduce the excerpt on page 10 from *Landfall in Unknown Seas* by Allen Curnow.

Publishing manager: Christine Thomson
Editor: Geoff Walker
Design: Camille Lowe / Undercover

Front cover top: The first signing of the Treaty of Waitangi; bottom, from left to right; Presentation of petition against homosexual law reform; Anti-Springbok tour demonstrators overturn a car in Auckland; A flock of Border Leicester ewes and lambs in a sheep pen. Back cover, from left to right; Pro-MMP advertising, November 1993; Crowd at Aotea Quay, Wellington, as K-Force troops leave New Zealand; A group of young Maori on the steps of Parliament in 1972.

National Library of New Zealand Cataloguing-in-Publication Data

Moon, Paul.
Turning points : events that changed the course of
New Zealand history / Paul Moon.
Includes bibliographical references and index.
ISBN 978-1-86966-379-7
1. New Zealand—History. 2. New Zealand—Social conditions.
I. Title.
993—dc 23

10 9 8 7 6 5 4 3 2 1

Colour reproduction by Image Centre, Auckland
Printed in China by Toppan Leefung Printing Ltd, on paper sourced from sustainable forests.

CONTENTS

Plate XXV

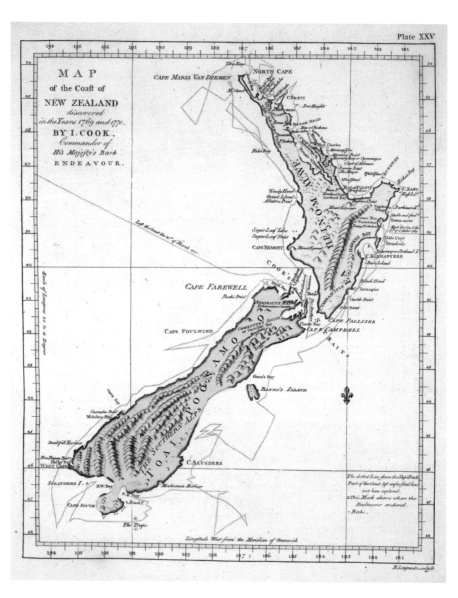

An engraving of Captain James Cook's map of the coast of New Zealand, printed in 1773.

INTRODUCTION

WHAT MAKES A PORTION of the past a 'turning point' in a nation's history? To a considerable extent, it is an arbitrary decision, but the primary criterion relied on in this book is that the chosen events have left their mark on the country in some way, or have affected subsequent developments in the nation. Such peaks in the historical landscape have long been the standard fare for chroniclers of the past, but the episodes included in this book are not so much the obvious highlights of New Zealand's history as those that have had consequences beyond the radius of their immediate occurrence.

This emphasis here on events of enduring significance reveals history as the highly disruptive force that it can sometimes be, in which change is more likely to be the result of convulsions than of tranquil transitions. Any attempts at straightening out the bends and altering the course of the meandering flow of the country's history would end up in misrepresenting the essentially organic nature of New Zealand's periods of development.

Of course, when neatly laid out in chronological sequence, historical events can have the appearance of an ordered progression of which the present is its inevitable culmination. However, such a view relies on looking back at the past from the convenient outcrop of hindsight – a position denied to those living through an event. There is certainly seldom anything inevitable about the way in which history unfurls. The earliest Polynesian arrivals in New Zealand, for example, and those European explorers who followed in their wake centuries later, were focused on survival in a turbulent and unpredictable world. Whatever sense of distant destiny they may have momentarily pondered on was limited by the much more urgent demands of the present and the recognition that the future is unknowable.

From the moment that the first migrants from the apocryphal homeland of Hawaiki dragged their weather-beaten waka up onto a New Zealand beach around the thirteenth century, nothing about the course of events in the country has been preordained. And it is precisely this capricious nature of history that is revealed in the turning points that are explored in this book.

It can be tempting, though, when the nominated turning points in the country's history have been assembled, to look for common threads. This is the sort of 'grand narrative' approach which downplays historical chance and the relative insularity of some episodes in favour of deference to an overarching theme. Such themes can range from the country being a leader in social reform or race relations, to the depiction of New Zealand as an egalitarian utopia or agrarian arcadia. The reality is that most events are often more entangled in concerns of the moment rather than entwined around any notion of a national destiny. Indeed, certain episodes included in this book, such as the violent protests which occurred in reaction to the 1981 Springbok tour, abruptly dispel some of the more dilatory stereotypes about the nation.

This is not to say that there are no connections at all. Supporters of the Maori renaissance in the 1970s evoked previous Maori leaders in their rhetoric, and the economic reforms of the following decade which became known as Rogernomics were often compared with earlier approaches to managing the economy. However, such associations with past events are often more rhetorical than substantial, with their similarities not sufficiently strong to overshadow their distinctive character and the specific environments from which they are born.

The selection of episodes that appear in this volume has no pretensions to being definitive, and many more events could rightly have vied for inclusion. New Zealand's involvement in the First World War, for example, is regarded as a crucial turning point because of its lasting effects on the country's relationship with Britain, on the way New Zealand perceived wars, and on the need to commemorate annually the fallen. The Second World War is not included precisely because in many ways its impact on the way New Zealand society viewed wars was not as profound. This in no way diminishes the importance of the country's involvement in the Second World War, but in the context of a turning point in the nation's history the First World War was the more significant of the two.

For similar reasons, great disasters, such as the Napier earthquake in 1931 or the Air New Zealand crash at Mt Erebus in 1979, have been omitted because although they were undoubtedly traumatic for the country, they did not lead to lasting changes to the society. Indeed, considered from one angle, great national disasters generally result in the population doing its best to return things to normal, not allowing the consequences of the calamity to result in too much abrupt change.

Choosing which turning points would be included in this book, and those which would be culled, was thus inevitably a subjective exercise. However, the individual topics that feature in this volume are sufficiently varied, and encompass a broad enough historical range, to give the reader some impression of some of the routes by which New Zealand has advanced over the centuries. A quick glance through the book will reveal, though, that the scope of some of these points varies enormously. The chapter on discovery, for example, stretches over a period of several centuries, for reasons that are made evident, while other episodes, such as the Maketu execution, are largely confined to a single event which occurred in a relatively short space of time.

It is the long shadows cast by many of these turning points that have partly dictated the dimensions of some chapters. If some episodes have a longer trail of consequences than others, or a more deeply contoured historical topography, then that generous inheritance is dealt with as much as the constraints of space allow. The result is not a neatly trimmed, evenly apportioned inventory of events but an exploration of a series of incidents whose repercussions justify their claim to being turning points in New Zealand's history.

1

DISCOVERY

Now do I direct the bow of my canoe
To the opening whence arises the sun god,
Tama-nui-te-ra, Great-son-of-the-sun.
Let me not deviate from the course.
   —Polynesian migration chant, transcribed by Te Rangi
   Hiroa (P. Buck), *Vikings of the Sunrise*, 1938

you launched the whole
On a fine morning, the best time of year,
Skies widening and the oceanic furies
Subdued by summer illumination; time
To go and be gazed at going
On a fine morning, in the Name of God
Into the nameless waters of the world.
   —Allen Curnow, *Landfall in Unknown Seas*, 1942

NEW ZEALAND IS ONE of the few nations in the world which can claim the distinction of having been discovered twice. It was not a case of flimsy communications between competing ships racing to reach the country's coast first, though, but the encounter of two entirely different civilisations with New Zealand that led to this twice-discovered status.

The first humans to set foot on New Zealand soil were Polynesians.

Exactly when this took place was subject to over a century of debate until 2010, when an analysis of more than 1400 radiocarbon dates from across the South Pacific confirmed that the earliest human presence in the country could be dated to between 1210 and 1385 AD.

Such certainty in establishing dates was beyond the hopes of earlier generations of New Zealanders. In the nineteenth and early twentieth centuries suggestions that the country had initially been populated by pre-Polynesian peoples periodically gained some ground in the popular imagination. Amateur anthropologists and ethnologists speculated, for example, that a society known as the Maruiwi had been the country's original occupants. The ethnologist Elsdon Best claimed that there were 'certain customs, implements, and arts' in New Zealand that were 'not traceable, apparently, to the kindred peoples of Polynesia'. This led him to the deduction that 'the first inhabitants of New Zealand were a people of unknown origin, whose racial or tribal name, if any, has not been preserved'. Best then leapt to imaginative conclusions about their origins and ethnicity: 'Their home-land . . . was a hot country – a much warmer land than this. In appearance these folk are said to have been tall and slim-built, dark-skinned, having big or protuberant bones, flat-faced and flat-nosed, with upturned nostrils. Their eyes were curiously restless, and they had a habit of glancing sideways without turning the head. Their hair in some cases stood upright, in others it was bushy.' Through intermarriage with the recently arrived Polynesians, followed by wars of annihilation, asserted Best, the Maruiwi were wiped out and in their place Maori society evolved.

The flimsy props supporting such theories easily collapsed when the slightest pressure of evidentiary scrutiny was applied to them. More difficult to dislodge were the related notions that the first arrivals to New Zealand – though probably Polynesian – were variously the descendants of Aryans, Persians, Druids, Jews, Indians and other imagined ethnic candidates. It was only in the early twentieth century that a general consensus settled among academics that the Polynesians were the first to reach New Zealand. However, this raised three other crucial and contentious questions: where did they come from, why did they leave, and how did they get here?

According to Maori oral traditions, the answer to the first question was simple: Hawaiki. Only it was not quite that straightforward. To Maori, Hawaiki was more a mythical homeland than a geographical location, and by the mid-twentieth century frustration had set in among scholars trying to pinpoint its position – so much so that in 1945 an exasperated Te Rangi Hiroa (Sir Peter Buck) concluded that if Maori had once known where Hawaiki was, that knowledge now lay 'buried under the accretions of time'. One Victorian writer had gone further, insisting that 'we must not search for historical truth in those traditions, as we thereby involve ourselves in a labyrinth of mythical fancies, out of which only the thread of mythical analysis can point the way to light'.

Yet even if Hawaiki had been reduced to an idea rather than a fixed geographical location, its repeated occurrence in Maori migratory legends gave it a prominence that scholars could not ignore. One way to resolve this dilemma was a compromise theory. Instead of Hawaiki being one place, it was several – a metaphor for the most recent point of departure. And with each migration to a new destination, the mythology of the Hawaiki that was left behind was added to.

As the twentieth century came to a close, the view among academics (with a few exceptions) was that there was little point in probing the Hawaiki myth as it appeared too unreliable. However, although Hawaiki assumed mythical status for Maori, both as a place of departure, and in death, as the location where the spirits returned, it is now accepted that Hawaiki was probably a reference in Maori tradition to the Tahitian island of Ra'iatea (Rangiatea, in Maori).

The reasons for these migrants leaving to establish a community in New Zealand have been similarly rendered opaque through centuries of oral histories, but a possible combination of over-crowding, wars and food shortages are all likely reasons. However, above all, migrations occurred because they could – because ancient Polynesians possessed the means to navigate their way across the Pacific Ocean and create settlements in new locations.

But were the Polynesian navigators really this skilled – especially at the same time as most European mariners were still sailing close to coasts for fear of falling off the edge of the earth? Well into the twentieth century, academics agreed that the arrival of the first humans in New Zealand had been accidental. Without compasses and sextants, there was evidently no way that ancient Polynesians could have deliberately made their way to New Zealand. The most likely explanation for the presence of Maori in the country was that their ancestors had been caught in a storm while out fishing and had drifted until reaching New Zealand. On finding three Tahitian castaways on the island of Atiu – about 1100 kilometres from their home island – in 1777, a British captain concluded that these survivors proved 'better than a thousand conjectures of speculative reasoners, how the detached parts of the earth may have first been peopled: especially those that lie remote from any inhabited continent, or from each other'.

This accidental drift theory was modified slightly at the end of the nineteenth century into the notion of the Polynesian discovery of New Zealand having taken the form of the arrival of a great fleet. The Great Fleet theory was championed by the amateur historian Stephenson Percy Smith, and centred on the premise that a large assembly of Polynesian migrants departed Tahiti for New Zealand in a migratory armada in 1350 AD. Smith even went to the trouble of ensuring that each tribal account of its past that he subsequently recorded matched this theory.

However, although the Great Fleet theory gained widespread public acceptance – thanks in large part to a painting on the theme, *The Arrival of the Maoris in New Zealand* by Louis John Steele and Charles Goldie, completed in 1898 – it was still difficult to ignore the fact that this fleet could not have carried the Polynesian discoverers of New Zealand because most Maori whakapapa (genealogies) extended back before 1350 AD. According to Maori histories, Kupe was the first to find the country, and based on a calculation of generations Te Rangi Hiroa estimated that this legendary navigator must have arrived around 925 AD. Kupe was a problematic figure for scholars, though, because his accomplishments, and even his very identity, were all braided with myths and legends, making it almost impossible to separate the fact from the embellishment.

Not that any of this mattered to Andrew Sharp. Any suggestion that New Zealand was deliberately discovered and colonised by Poly-nesians was discounted from the late 1950s in Sharp's detailed study of traditional Polynesian navigation techniques, which drew him to the conclusion that the existence of New Zealand's Maori population was the result of sailors being marooned after being blown off course during a journey between islands in the Pacific, or of fishermen being caught in a storm and blown to the New Zealand coast.

Sharp's thesis drew criticism from a number of quarters, most of which concentrated on a few elemental flaws. Firstly, if the castaways who reached New Zealand were part of a fishing expedition which had been blown off course, how did Sharp account for the presence of women on these vessels when women almost never accompanied men when fishing? And how was it possible for such a sizeable population to have been established in New Zealand without the knowledge of how to navigate back and forth from the country?

Tucked away in Sharp's rejection of the idea of planned discovery and migrations was the concession that 'deliberate exploration could have been a factor'. It was only towards the end of the twentieth century, though, that science caught up with this century of speculation about the first human discovery of New Zealand. Advances in linguistics, biology, genetics, archaeology and numerous other disciplines enabled the routes of Polynesian migration across the Pacific – ending up in New Zealand – to be traced with much more certainty. The name of the first Polynesian to set foot in the country, along with the precise date, will never be known, but for Maori, science finally moved closer to what their own histories had always confirmed – that their ancestors discovered New Zealand, and were able to navigate back to their homeland and organise for the country to be settled.

Several marae locations around the country are said to be close to where ancestral canoes alighted, and legends about the precise routes of migrating waka as they sailed along the coast of New Zealand were shared by most hapu and iwi. At some point, however, the migrations stopped, and possibly within two centuries of Polynesians having discovered New Zealand, travel back and forth to Hawaiki ceased. For centuries thereafter, Maori society became sealed off from the rest of the world until another civilisation began to extend its reach into the South Pacific in the seventeenth century.

And here lies the quandary which was mentioned at the opening of this chapter: can there have been two discoveries of New Zealand? The answer relies on a particular racial and cultural perspective being taken. Assertions of discovery are as much political gestures as they are geographical undertakings. In any age, bringing together the resources needed for exploratory ventures was expensive and was undertaken with some notion of benefits eventually accruing. Discovery also carried with it an implicit claim of ownership of the territory that the explorer finally stumbled across. Of course if the territory in question was devoid of other people, such claims were usually more straightforward. However, in the case of New Zealand the first Europeans to reach its shores invariably came across Maori communities. So is it even possible to speak of the European discovery of New Zealand? Clearly yes if you look at an older generation of books on the topic. On the issue of who discovered the country, Bishop George Selwyn had a blind spot when it came to the Maori. In 1844, he wrote that 'The islands of New Zealand, the inhabitants of which are almost our exact antipodes, were first discovered by Tasman, the Dutch navigator, in 1642.'

For the historian Arthur Thomson, writing in the mid-nineteenth century, the matter was not even one of conjecture: 'The honour of discovering New Zealand is, therefore, justly bestowed on Tasman', was his unequivocal conclusion on who had found the country. In his 1883 history of New Zealand, George Rusden was similarly clear that it had been the Dutch explorer Abel Tasman who had 'discovered' New Zealand. The association of Tasman with the discovery of New Zealand had become received knowledge, with even some Maori apparently untroubled by such views.

Such attitudes can too easily be dismissed as Victorian and Edwardian chauvinism, yet even as recently as 1961 one historian was unworried about the paradox of asserting that the country was

15

Abel Janszoon Tasman, the first recorded European discoverer of New Zealand, in 1642.

REF: A-044-006. ALEXANDER TURNBULL LIBRARY, WELLINGTON, NEW ZEALAND. HTTP://BETA.NATLIB.GOVT. NZ/RECORDS/23168841

'again discovered' by Tasman. Evidently, the hold on the imagination of 'discoverer' status is a powerful and enduring one.

What is intriguing about these claims that Europeans discovered New Zealand is that they carry with them strong implications about how the status of Maori was perceived. The idea that Europe and European identity were superior in comparison with all the non-European peoples and cultures was breathtakingly self-assured and even arrogant, and yet its effects lingered until comparatively recently. Certainly in the eighteenth and nineteenth centuries the popular view among colonists in New Zealand was that 'their' country had been discovered by Europe. It is little wonder, then, that the idea of Maori having arrived by accident was so quickly absorbed into the nation's popular history. It confirmed that the 'real' act of discovery, and therefore the corresponding right to claim sovereignty over the territory, lay with Europeans. Any historical evidence that got in the way was dismissed accordingly. And if all else failed, colonists could always point to the fact that there was documentary evidence about which of their compatriots arrived in New Zealand first, while

16

all Maori communities seemed to have was a semi-mythical figure about whom details had long since been forgotten. For Polynesian communities, the exacting precision of historical dates had never been of overriding concern – that was one of the many things that Europeans introduced into the culture.

However, European confidence about the 'white' discovery of New Zealand was not the neatly trimmed narrative that it was later portrayed as. China, France, Portugal and Spain have all been suggested at one time or another as candidates for the first countries to visit New Zealand in the period after the Polynesian migrations concluded, with the Portuguese being the most likely contenders to have beaten the Dutch to New Zealand's shores. But in the absence of documentation verifying that any of these potential arrivals actually reached the country before 1642, the line that 'Tasman had discovered and named New Zealand' stuck.

The first account of a European encounter with New Zealand that can be confirmed with certainty is the Dutch one written in December 1642. Holland's mercantile expansion in the seventeenth century had created a geographically enormous commercial emporium which survived and grew on an escalating volume of both imports and exports. The accompanying need to find new markets and new sources of raw materials coincided with advances in the West's understanding of the shape of the world. For a start, by this time it was known to be spherical, and so with the risk of sailing off into oblivion now cast into the ignorance of a previous era, explorers were much more confident in penetrating the unknown parts of the world, especially if there was a prospect of riches to be found.

The other shift in Western knowledge about the Southern Hemisphere at this time was the increasingly confident presumption that there lay somewhere in the vast tracts of the Pacific Ocean a Great Southern Continent. If this was true – and there were all manner of hypotheses to say that it was – then the opportunities for a sudden expansion in trade and wealth in an even more enlarged Dutch capitalist empire were incentive enough for enterprising business owners to fund exploratory expeditions to locate the Great Southern Continent.

Since the 1630s Tasman had been based in Jakarta and was employed by the Dutch East India Company, whose fortunes were on the rise at this time. Tasman sailed the waters around Indonesia, patrolling Company routes and fending off any potential intruders.

In August 1642 the Company's directors decided to put Tasman's maritime skills to use in an exploratory venture that they had conceived. The purpose was to chart unexplored areas, with the intention of a more invasive mission to be despatched at some point in the future, depending on what Tasman reported back.

There had been rumours of lands in the South Pacific, mainly from those who had been washed up on coasts after being blown off course in storms, so with the hydrographer Franz Jacobszoon Visscher (who served as chief pilot) Tasman commanded two diminutive vessels – his flagship, the yacht *Heemskerck*, and an armed transport ship, *Zeehaen* – to undertake this voyage of discovery.

Contrary to some popular stereotypes, though, this was no flag-waving quest for national glory by passionate, furrow-browed explorers. Instead, it more resembled a speculative business venture – the chance to discover possible resources and to report back to his superiors on his finds. However, at some point, there must have been a sense of excitement at encountering territories that up until that time had been unknown to Europe.

On departure, the existing knowledge that Tasman had at his disposal about what lay ahead amounted essentially to the awareness of the 'provinces of Beach' – a section of the northern coast of Australia. The nature of knowledge at this time was not that precise, though. As an example, in addition to the provinces of Beach, Tasman was also reliably informed that there was an immense continent somewhere further south which stretched on the charts from the southern tip of South America across the entire South Pacific Ocean and further west, in the direction of Africa. Tasman was probably able to discern between a confirmed area of coast and an imagined continent, but as he set out on his mission the line distinguishing the two was blurred. Similarly, the knowledge of the type of animals and peoples he might come across was uncertain and subject to imaginative exaggeration. Wherever there was mystery about a region, speculation and a measure of terror easily filled the gaps in knowledge.

The boundaries of Europe's knowledge of the world were literally expanded as a result of Tasman's voyage into the South Pacific, the climax of which was his sighting of what was later to become known as New Zealand. On 13 December 1642, having been tormented by a strong south-westerly wind since departing Tasmania, the crews of the *Heemskerck* and *Zeehaen* sighted a range of mountains rising on the eastern horizon. Their first thoughts must have been that this was part of the Great Southern Continent – especially as they had been led to believe that such a land mass lay in this vicinity. However, from this distance there was no way of being certain.

Over the next four days the vessels followed the coast, pausing where necessary to calculate their bearings. The thought that this was the fabled undiscovered continent was put to the back of their minds when their attention was caught by smoke rising from a fire on the beach: proof of human habitation. The captain ordered his ships to approach cautiously. As they neared the shore, they saw a gathering of Maori, gesturing, shouting and blowing 'a strange trumpet', which was responded to by one of the Dutch sailors playing a tune on a trumpet.

The next day a group of Maori paddled out to the ships and attacked some Dutch sailors who were rowing from one of their vessels to the other. Three of the sailors were beaten to death with patu and their corpses thrown into the water, and another Dutchman on the boat later died from the wounds he received in the assault.

Tasman later noted down his rendition of these events in a way that conveys something of the terror he and his crew felt: 'The canoes of natives which were between our two ships made furiously towards her, and ran with their beaks violently against her, so as to make her heel and take in water; and the foremost of these villains, with a blunted pointed pike, gave the quarter-master a violent blow in his neck which made him fall overboard. The others then attacked the rest of our boat's crew with their paddles, and with short thick clubs . . . and overcame them . . . After the fight, these murderers

19

Captain James Cook, the first European known to have set foot in New Zealand.

took one of our dead people into their canoe: another of our dead men fell overboard and sunk.'

The crew of the *Heemskerck* responded by aiming their artillery at the Maori in their waka, forcing them to retreat to shore. For this episode in the European discovery of New Zealand, the location of the skirmish was given the name 'De Moordenaars Baay' – Murderers' Bay – by the Dutch. The act of naming this place assumed greater significance in that it was appended to Visscher's sketch of a portion of New Zealand's coast – the first certain map of a part of the country. Having produced this fragment of a chart of this length of coast, Tasman and his men sailed away from New Zealand in the early days of 1643. His boss, Anthony van Diemen, concluded that Tasman had 'left everything to be more closely inquired into by more industrious successors'.

By the turn of the twentieth century, predominantly Anglo-Saxon New Zealand paid polite homage to Tasman being the first

(European) to discover New Zealand, but the real hero was (and in a way had to be) an Englishman. It suited New Zealand, as a loyal member of the British imperial family, that Captain James Cook took the honour of having somehow been the 'proper' discoverer of the country.

Yet there was even less cause for James Cook being awarded the distinction of having discovered New Zealand, arriving almost 130 years after the Dutch explorer. Except that there was one niggling fact that irked with Tasman's 'discovery' of New Zealand: neither he nor any of his crew actually set foot in the country, and Cook did. It was a detail that one nineteenth-century historian snidely commented on, insisting that Tasman's 'countrymen could scarcely lay claim to the territory on which he did not set foot, and where

Ship Cove, Queen Charlotte Sound. The events depicted occurred in February 1777, during Captain Cook's third voyage to New Zealand.

Ref: B-098-015. Alexander Turnbull Library, Wellington, New Zealand. http://beta.natlib.govt.nz/records/22664325

21

he did not even endeavour to plant his country's flag, – the cheap pretence recognized by Europeans as giving them titles to foreign lands'.

Cook's 'discovery' of the country on 6 October 1769 grew in significance to the point where it quickly overshadowed the fact that New Zealand had been known to Maori for centuries by the time the English captain landed on shore, and that its general location had been commonly known by those in Europe with an interest in the region for over a century. Patriotism accounts in part for the sustenance of this conceit, but hindsight also made Cook's arrival appear like a type of discovery. The paternity of the country's subsequent evolution into a fully fledged British colony, and its later maturation into a British-inspired parliamentary democracy, can be traced to an act Cook undertook on 31 January 1770, and which he proudly described in his journal: 'After I had thus prepare'd the way for seting [sic] up the post we took it up to the highest part of the Island and after fixing it fast in the ground hoisted thereon the Union flag and I dignified this Inlet with the name of Queen Charlottes Sound and took formal possession [sic] of it and the adjacent lands in the name and for the use of his Majesty'. It was a piece of theatre with no immediate constitutional significance, but it set in motion a series of events which would determine profoundly the future of the country.

2

HONGI'S VISIT TO ENGLAND, 1820

WHENEVER COLONISATION IS MENTIONED it is typically portrayed as an unequal relationship between the (usually European) colonising power and the (usually non-European) people they are subjugating. For the most part this is a fair assessment, with the debate mainly focused on the character and extent of the subjugation. So when one of the subjugated takes the initiative and successfully obtains ideas and – in this case – weapons from the colonising power, the potential exists for dramatic change to occur in the status and influence of the person involved. Such was the case in New Zealand when a Maori chief, Hongi Hika, visited England in 1820.

Hongi was one of the most important Maori leaders in the country at this time. He was a descendant of Rahiri – the legendary founder of the Ngapuhi tribe – and was born around 1780 near Kaikohe, the son of Te Hotete, chief of Te Tahuna, and Tuhikura. Hongi was a feared military leader, and had long been encouraging Europeans to settle in the vicinity of his settlements as a means of boosting trade and education for his people.

The background to what would be a hugely influential visit involved the fortuitous meeting of Hongi and the sometimes errant Anglican missionary Thomas Kendall. Kendall's interest in Maori culture had blossomed since he had arrived in New Zealand in 1814, to the point where it exceeded the levels that his colleagues felt were acceptable. In hindsight, the signs of this enthusiasm were there as early as 1808, when Kendall had written to Josiah Pratt, the Secretary of the Church Missionary Society (CMS), about his desire to become fluent in Maori.

Like other missionaries, Kendall, together with his colleague William Hall, initially struggled to familiarise himself with the language, and at first could manage only a few basic sentences. However, one of the results of Kendall's immersion in Maori society was that he soon rapidly picked up the language and, in 1815, published a small textbook on it – *A Korao no New Zealand; or, the New Zealander's First Book*.

But Kendall's affection for New Zealand waned at some moments, and he experienced intermittent nostalgic longings to be back in England. No doubt his wife's infidelity, coupled with the daily privations of missionary life in this remote field of Christian outreach, did little to endear him to his posting, despite his growing obsession with Maori culture and religion.

With his marriage collapsing and his faith sometimes wavering, Kendall decided that he needed a rest from the demanding work of being a missionary. He submitted a request to the Church Missionary Society to have a break in New South Wales. Taking a missionary out of the field was not a decision made lightly, and it took months until the request filtered its way up through the CMS hierarchy, and for a decision finally to be reached. By the time that the organisation approved the request, in late 1819, Kendall seemed to have lost interest in New South Wales. Instead, his thoughts had turned to England as a preferred destination. Only in his homeland did he feel that he would be able to rest and to recover some of his lost enthusiasm for his vocation.

Despite the fact that Kendall had no specific approval to return to England, he made plans to travel there regardless. The response from at least one of his colleagues was hardly favourable. John Gare Butler, who took up residence in Kerikeri in late December 1819, was infuriated by Kendall's apparently self-indulgent attitude. 'I think your journey to England is very ill-timed on many accounts,' he advised Kendall in February the following year. 'Several of us are just arrived in the country, and our settlement is in its very infancy, and we, of course, can have no knowledge of the language, and, therefore, require every assistance.' This was merely the start of Butler's concerns. 'Moreover', he continued, 'there is no object can justify you, in leaving your family unprotected in a heathen land. I should have thought you have suffered enough in your family heretofore to prevent you ever leaving them.'

Kendall was not bothered by such barbed comments. A week later, he was on his way to England, but with two fellow-travellers whom he took probably from a mix of motives: to assist in his plans to produce a Maori dictionary; to act as an alibi for his unauthorised trip; and as a novelty gesture which might deflect attention from his act of disobedience. The two men in question were Hongi and a junior chief, Waikato.

Hongi's departure from the country sent ripples through the missionary community, not least because at times the chief acted as the sole guardian of the small and frightened missionary communities, which otherwise felt themselves besieged by hostile Maori. 'By taking away Shunghee [Hongi], you take from us all our protection,' Butler complained, adding that to take the chief to England 'would be to act in direct opposition to the instructions of the Society, and I very much doubt whether he or yourself will live to return; I well know how very prejudicial the climate of England is to the health of a New Zealander'. The founder of the New Zealand mission, the Reverend Samuel Marsden, was if anything even more annoyed that Kendall was disobeying his orders and that this errant missionary was taking one of the most important chiefs in the country to the other end of the world.

It would be a mistake, however, to presume that Hongi was merely some witless pawn in Kendall's scheme to leave New Zealand for a while. The confluence of a series of circumstances was already directing the thoughts of the chief towards England. Kendall's freely expressed desire to return home was the sort of fortunate chance that Hongi needed.

One of the chief's main reasons for wanting to travel to England had roots that were sunk deep in tribal history and nourished by generations of animosity. In particular, the constant tension

The Reverend Samuel
Marsden, who oversaw
the establishment of the
first Christian mission in
the country.
REF: A-039-038. ALEXANDER TURNBULL
LIBRARY, WELLINGTON, NEW ZEALAND.
HTTP://BETA.NATLIB.GOVT.NZ/
RECORDS/22298069

– interrupted only by the intermittent eruptions of war – between
Hongi's tribe of Ngapuhi and those tribes that lay to the south
(especially Ngati Whatua and Waikato, although several others were
contenders as enemies) had scarred the Maori political landscape
for centuries and had left Hongi desperate for some sort of strategic
advantage against these age-old enemies. With each new attempt to
bring balance to bruised reputations by one side launching an assault
against another, the cycle of attack and retribution only continued,
resulting in animosities spilling over into each new generation.

The latest in this tit-for-tat approach to intertribal relations had
occurred in the spring of 1819, when the Ngapuhi chiefs Patuone
and Tuwhare assembled troops and weapons (including the much-
valued but still scarce muskets) for a campaign to strike at Waikato
and then Taranaki, with the aim to 'settle old scores'. Although the
political motives behind the raid were predictable, it is significant
that Hongi was not leading this raid. He may have helped in the
planning but he did not command the expedition, leaving it to the

two other chiefs to gain whatever glory might be on offer if a victory for Ngapuhi was secured.

It is possible that Hongi – who was close to Kendall – was more interested in the prospects of a visit to England than in another military campaign. This could give him the opportunity to secure muskets on a scale that would give him an unbeatable military advantage over his many enemies and the chance to wreak unparalleled revenge on them. Not participating in the 1819 campaign being mounted by his fellow chiefs was a small price to pay in return for the hugely greater strategic advantage that lay for him in visiting England.

Perhaps in compensation for missing out on this confrontation, Hongi stirred up a small skirmish in Kerikeri with a neighbouring chief, Te Morenga. The pretext was largely a fabricated one, and the total of only ten fatalities (of which just two were on Hongi's side) suggests that it was a case of the chief going through the motions of a battle rather than launching a conflict that served any greater purpose. There was no question, though, of Hongi putting his aggressive tendencies into hibernation while he was out of the country. As he made his plans to depart, he urged his colleagues to launch an assault against Ngati Whatua. The order was carried out in his absence, resulting in a substantial loss of life.

England remained his principal focus, but not simply as an exotic destination. There was one extraordinary aspect of the visit that was more than enough motivation for Hongi: Kendall's promise that he would have an audience with the King. Kendall, for his part, had been doing everything within his powers to ensure that his plans to take Hongi to England worked out as he intended. Kendall cited an agreement that Marsden had allegedly made with Hongi in 1819 in which the chief had been promised a trip to England (and possibly even a chance to see the King) as part of the deal of selling some land to the missionaries. The prospect of breaking this alleged promise to Hongi could have seriously jeopardized the future of the missionary movement in the country. This was probably sufficient reason for Marsden to have given his reluctant and hesitating approval to the journey to England of the missionary he disliked and the chief he feared.

At the beginning of March 1820, Hongi and his entourage crowded the decks of the vessel that would take him to England. It was a prolonged and emotional farewell, but the sense of the moment did nothing to cloud Hongi's grand vision for this voyage to the centre of the British Empire. The chief got Kendall to write down some of his thoughts as they prepared to depart. This record offers a very clear insight into Hongi's expectations at this time: 'I wish to see King George, the multitude of his people, what they are doing, and the goodness of the land. My desire is to stay one month in England, and then to come back.' It was the list of assets he expected in return that revealed Hongi's ambition: 'I want a party to dig for iron, a number of blacksmiths, a number of carpenters, and a number of preachers who will try to speak in the New Zealand tongue, so that I may understand them. I want twenty soldiers to protect the settlers, and three officers to keep the soldiers in order. The settlers are to take cattle over with them.' There was an inducement of sorts at the end of this inventory: 'There is plenty of spare land in New Zealand, which will be readily granted to the settlers.'

Conveniently for Kendall, who was transcribing this, Hongi avoided mentioning his desire for weapons and ammunition, possibly in order to avoid putting his host in a morally awkward position. However, it is highly likely that Kendall had more than just an inkling of what this great Maori warlord intended to acquire once in England.

Although Kendall must surely have had at least a suspicion about Hongi's interest in muskets, the missionary's main concern was that his own projects in England would receive a boost from Hongi's presence. In Kendall's mind, the novelty of a tattooed 'native' – the epitome of the exotic – would help in his scheme to raise funds for a mission school and might even assist in his more ambitious desire to finally become fully ordained as a minister. And Hongi would certainly be useful for another of Kendall's plans: to work on a book which would form the basis of a written form of the Maori language.

Kendall organised the project, but he admitted that he lacked the necessary skills to undertake it. This task was left to Professor Samuel Lee, an Oriental linguist at Cambridge University, who with

The Reverend Thomas Kendall, with the chiefs Hongi and Waikato in 1820.
REF: G-618. ALEXANDER TURNBULL LIBRARY, WELLINGTON, NEW ZEALAND. HTTP://BETA.NATLIB.GOVT.NZ/
RECORDS/23241174

the support of the Church Missionary Society took Kendall's rough efforts at producing a written form of Maori and polished them as much as time and the limits of knowledge allowed. And while the CMS was still outwardly annoyed at Kendall's unauthorised departure from his vocation (it 'highly disapprove[d] of his conduct in returning'), they nonetheless welcomed the fact that he had brought Hongi to London – something that they viewed as a fundraising opportunity.

Of the two Maori visitors, Waikato apparently had a better command of English than Hongi, but both men were of interest to their English hosts. One churchman observed that 'these interesting Strangers have little notion of our Holy Religion. They are the subjects of a subtle and deeply rooted Superstition . . . but with the nature and influence of which, we hope, through Mr. Kendall, to obtain such an acquaintance as will enable us to place the affecting condition of this Noble Race in its true light – the finest natural dispositions, abused and held in bondage, under the dark and cruel tyranny of the God of this World!' There was always the hope – probably misplaced as it turned out in Hongi's case – that these chiefs would see the 'light' and convert to Christianity.

Hongi suffered from fluctuating bouts of sickness throughout his time in England, although this was probably never life-threatening and it certainly did not interfere with Kendall's ambitious itinerary for his guests. Cambridge was the first important venue for the chiefs, and it is there that Hongi got a taste of the sort of attention his appearance would generate throughout his stay in England. Their habits did nothing to diminish their novelty value to titillated English onlookers. The chiefs slept on floors, and wore an odd hybrid of fashionable English garments and their traditional dress. One churchman recorded how Hongi 'was remarkably sensitive. Whenever he was recognised as a great chief, and treated with that deference and respect which he considered due to his official dignity, he assumed the attitude and spoke with the authority of a prince. But where he was regarded only as an object of curiosity, he became sullen and indignant.'

Those with an eye on New Zealand as a mission field were eager to sound out Hongi on what sort of protection and maybe even patronage he could offer. One of the would-be missionaries who saw such opportunities was the Wesleyan Reverend Samuel Leigh. Leigh had already been undertaking planning for a mission station at Whangaroa and took Hongi and Waikato to London for a week to give him a good chance to sound out the senior chief on his thoughts about the Whangaroa proposal – something that Hongi eventually came to support whole-heartedly. To more casual onlookers Hongi, with his 'savage' looks, was the epitome of the brutish savage of popular imagination. But appearances were only skin deep, and in his behaviour he earned respect and even admiration from those members of the English establishment with whom he came into contact.

One of Hongi's main purposes in visiting England was to meet King George IV. A journalist present at this august encounter left an account of the chief's audience with the King. Hongi and Waikato were wearing 'European raiment covered with their own native costume. Bowing as gracefully as they could, "How do you do Mr. King George?" said the chiefs. "How do you do Mr. King Shunghee? How do you do Mr. King Waikato?" replied His Majesty.' With this immediate formality over, Hongi and Waikato took off their 'native costume' (which they had obviously been advised to wear for effect) and walked with the King through part of the palace, chatting with him on a number of topics.

The image of a Maori chief, far removed from his people and homeland, meeting one of the most influential world leaders of the day, has a surreal air to it. Yet it was not as though Hongi and the King had nothing in common. Both men seemed to have an appreciation of military issues, and at the culmination of this extraordinary meeting, George IV gave a helmet and a gun to Waikato and a coat of chain-mail and two guns to Hongi.

Thereafter, the visit to England became something of an anticlimax for the chiefs. An element of fatigue set in with the constant attention that was being lavished on them. There was only so much adulation that they could take before it became repetitive and boring. Still, Hongi did his best to play his part, knowing full well that his mission to obtain a haul of weapons could be upset if he caused undue offence to anyone.

But where did the weapons come from and how did Hongi manage to sneak them under the noses of what would have certainly been disapproving missionaries? Conventional wisdom has it that Hongi simply purchased the muskets and ammunition in England and took them back with him to Northland; or, alternatively, that he acquired his weapons in Sydney while en route home. The chief had described England as a 'country of great muskets and great ships', but he bemoaned the fact that his hosts had refused to sell or make available to him any weapons at all. Given the strength of opposition to Hongi's plans, it is not surprising that the trail of documents about this aspect of Hongi's visit falls away almost completely, leaving a few frayed circumstances from which some explanation can be stitched together.

Sydney is the more probable source of Hongi's muskets, being out of the scrutiny of too many English officials, and unencumbered by the close public gaze which followed the chief's every movement in England. The story goes that the chief, with Kendall's complicity, off-loaded the various gifts that had been bestowed on Hongi during his English tour and used the money they received to buy arms.

However, there is at least one aspect of this account that poses a significant problem. Why would Hongi not purchase weapons in England, where the supply was so much more plentiful, on the off chance of acquiring weapons in Sydney in the few days that he was due to stop over there, particularly when there was no guarantee that there would be any muskets available for purchase? Then there is the issue of how could Hongi afford the 500 guns he ended up acquiring when the gifts he received from England were not worth anywhere near that value.

What is most likely is that the weapons Hongi wanted were already waiting for him when he arrived in Sydney. This consignment of muskets and ammunition had been arranged by Baron Charles de Thierry – a Frenchman who had been introduced to Hongi in Cambridge, and who had his own plans for the establishment of a settlement in New Zealand. He probably thought that earning the favour of a powerful chief such as Hongi was a way to win Maori support for his scheme. De Thierry paid for the cache and arranged for Hongi to pick them up in Sydney.

Hongi and Waikato returned to the Bay of Islands on the *Westmoreland* with Kendall on 12 July 1821, completing a journey that had taken 457 days. Despite the heavy exposure to English culture that both chiefs had endured, their thoughts were focused firmly on future military campaigns in New Zealand, as Butler regretfully acknowledged: 'Shunghee and Wykato have returned from England with a great quantity of guns, swords, powder, balls, daggers, etc . . . and thus they are fully armed to murder, kill and destroy, without reserve, which is the highest pitch of glory to a savage of New Zealand! ! !'

Having lived by the musket, it was fitting that Hongi should die by it as well. In January 1827, during a small battle at Mangamuka beach near Hokianga, he was wounded, with shot entering at least one lung. He returned to Whangaroa, where he slowly succumbed to his injury, finally passing away on 6 March 1828. In November 1827 the English artist Augustus Earle had visited Hongi and later produced an oil painting of the scene: *Meeting of the artist and Hongi at the Bay of Islands.*

The consequences of Hongi's visit to England remained with the country for decades. The weapons he acquired enabled him and his allies to wreak havoc among their enemies, which in turn led to an arms race that fuelled even more lethal wars among Maori. There were an estimated 20,000 fatalities from the hundreds of battles in what became known as the Musket Wars. Hongi's English journey precipitated the greatest spree of killing in the country at any time in its history. His subsequent reputation as the most feared warlord in the nation remained fixed in the popular imagination – and justifiably so.

This is what Hongi tends to be principally remembered for – his monumental military campaigns which inflicted unprecedented losses on his enemies. However, what this notoriety has tended to overshadow is another lasting consequence of the chief's visit to England: his assistance with the embryonic attempts at developing a written version of Maori. The dissemination of Christianity and of European culture and knowledge was assisted enormously by the use of Maori in a printed and mass-produced form. The work that Kendall and Lee carried out with the Maori language – with Hongi's aid – reverberated for decades afterwards and formed the basis of more sophisticated and standardised attempts at producing a Maori orthography.

3

APPOINTMENT OF JAMES
BUSBY AS RESIDENT, 1832

FORGET THE FLAG-WAVING CROWDS, the military bands pumping out patriotic tunes and images of a Union Jack-draped Britannia symbolically ruling the waves. Until the tail-end of the Victorian era, Britain's imperial project was far removed from such popular shows of enthusiasm for the Empire. For most of the century, the British Empire was an undertaking driven by two often conflicting imperatives: to develop what was in effect a multinational commercial enterprise with its headquarters in London; and to bring about the improvement of indigenous colonial populations through introducing them to civilisation, and in some cases inflicting it on them.

In the early decades of the 1800s these competing roles of the Empire – as both business and benefactor – helped to ingrain in the minds of senior colonial officials a healthy reluctance to intervene in any new territories unless there was a very compelling reason to do so. In New Zealand's case there was no evident justification for official involvement, and so the country was kept safely at arm's length by British authorities.

However, several interlocking circumstances in the region were, from the 1810s, slowly forcing Britain's hand in New Zealand. The first of these was that the country lay within the gravitational pull of New South Wales, which was a fast-growing British colony, built on farming, trade and a string of penal settlements.

Because New Zealand was so close to New South Wales, there

was a steady, if small, drift of undesirables from Sydney mainly to Northland. Former convicts, escaped convicts still serving their sentences, ship-jumping sailors and other men (they were nearly always men) of dubious stature made their way to New Zealand, partly to flee the impositions of their present circumstances and partly attracted by the freedom New Zealand appeared to offer. That living beyond the reach of British law was an inducement testifies to the moral calibre of many of these European (mainly British) arrivals.

Efforts were made by the authorities in New South Wales to extend British jurisdiction to New Zealand, but in practice these tended to be ineffectual. Child prostitution organised mainly by visiting European sailors was rife in the 1820s; there was a lingering trade in shrunken Maori heads; convicts from Australian penal settlements were fleeing to the freedom of New Zealand; and there were even accounts of Britons fighting for Maori communities and partaking in cannibalism.

It was not all bad news. New Zealand's healthy supply of high-quality flax together with its untapped stands of timber were among its main redeeming features in the eyes of Europeans at this time. Experiments were undertaken in the 1820s proving the superior strength of rope made from the country's flax, and reports were made on the suitability of kauri in particular as a timber for ship masts. There is no doubt that these resources were useful, but cheaper alternatives could still be obtained elsewhere with great ease. And that was the problem. New Zealand's relative isolation, and the difficulty at times in negotiating with Maori to acquire these resources, put the country in the category of 'potentially useful' rather than 'necessary' in the list of potential colonial acquisitions.

Of course if New Zealand was the repository of valuable resources, as some were claiming, then it was possible that other nations apart from Britain might start taking an interest in the country. It was the possibility of the French, in particular, poking around New Zealand's coast that prompted the CMS missionary William Yate to write a petition to King William IV on this and related issues. The petition, written in the name of the thirteen Ngapuhi chiefs who signed it, suggested that the French were 'coming to take away our land', and hence requested the King 'to become our friend and guardian of all these islands'. It further requested that some official British presence be established in New Zealand to manage 'any of thy people [who] should be troublesome or vicious towards us'. The French threat was nothing but a mirage, but for the embattled missionaries in New Zealand at the start of the 1830s any assistance from British authorities would have been welcomed.

The weight of these various considerations placed British colonial officials in a dilemma. On the one hand, the lawlessness of their fellow countrymen, the accompanying need to rescue Maori from the depredation of undesirable Europeans, the potential economic benefits of the country's flax and timber resources and the plight of New Zealand's morally besieged missionaries were all sound justifications for intervention. On the other hand, the substantial and ongoing expense of establishing a fully-fledged colony enforced a sense of restraint for any enthusiasm for grand colonial enterprises.

However, New Zealand was hardly a unique challenge in this respect. Over the preceding century, the Empire had devised a remarkably effective compromise – one which gave the impression of colonial rule, but without the encumbrance, commitment and cost: the Resident system. The Resident was an official placed in a country of economic or political interest to the Empire. The rank was lower than a consul, and typically came without any legislative, taxation or judicial authority. Residents often ruled through affixing themselves onto existing indigenous political structures, giving the appearance of the traditional system remaining intact and in power, while out of public gaze the Resident could whisper 'advice' in the ears of local rulers.

This system, which had first been enacted in India in the 1700s, was widespread in the Empire by the beginning of the nineteenth century and allowed for a reasonable semblance of rule without the need for full territorial and political annexation. Indeed, so successful was the Resident system in India that it was held up as an example whenever justification was needed in London for subsequent imperial expansion in other parts of the world.

The personally precocious but professionally persistent James

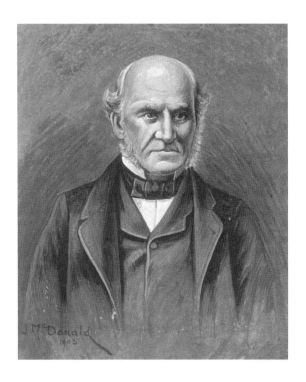

James Busby, the British
Resident in New Zealand
from 1833 to 1840.
Ref: A-044-008. Alexander Turnbull
Library, Wellington, New Zealand.
http://beta.natlib.govt.nz/
records/23133573

Busby had written to the Colonial Office (the British Government
Department responsible for managing the affairs of the Empire) in
1832, suggesting that a political agent or Resident be appointed to
New Zealand, even though this thirty-one-year-old had never been to
the country. Along with his parents Busby had moved to Australia in
1824, filling a variety of minor clerical posts in the New South Wales
Government. Clearly, his ambition soared above his achievements
to date: a precursor to either eminent success or protracted failure.
In Busby's case, his career over the next eight years would contain a
roughly equal measure of both.

   With Yate's petition, the intimation of French interest in New
Zealand and the distressingly ceaseless flow of accounts of the
objectionable behaviour of Britons in New Zealand, Lord Goderich,
the Secretary of State for War and the Colonies, acceded to Busby's
suggestion. In 1832 Busby was appointed Resident to New Zealand,
in what officials ambiguously specified would be an experimental
role, with no police force and with no authority to tax or legislate.

Busby took up his appointment on 5 May 1833 when he sailed into the Bay of Islands. One of his first official actions was to read out a letter Goderich had written for the benefit of local chiefs in response to Yate's petition. The relevant section of the letter relating to Busby's appointment explained that 'In order to afford better protection to all classes, both natives of the island of New Zealand and the British subjects who may proceed, or be already established there, for purposes of trade, the King has sent the bearer of this letter, James Busby, Esq., to reside among you as His Majesty's Resident, whose duties will be to investigate all complaints made to him.'

Busby would also be responsible for preventing the arrival of convicts in the country and for apprehending those who managed to reach its shores. All the Resident would require, in return, was 'assistance and support' from Maori. The deliberately simplistic prose – aimed at Maori who had acquired some English, and easily translated for those who had not – nonetheless did little to clarify exactly *how* Busby was expected single-handedly to bring peace and order to New Zealand, patrol its borders, expel undesirable Britons and so forth.

The considerable flexibility of the Resident system made it adaptable to the uniqueness of the various territories in which it was installed. However, the distinct challenges thrown up by New Zealand, together with the modest abilities that Busby possessed, meant that some difficulties with the country's Residency were almost preordained.

For his part, Busby did his best to advance official British interests in the country. One of his first accomplishments was to organise for New Zealand-owned ships that were involved mainly in trade between the country and Australia to carry their own ensign. In the process of confirming this flag, Busby had assembled twenty-five chiefs, most of them in the immediate vicinity of Waitangi, to announce to them the decision and to use this opportunity to convey to these hapu leaders an impression of British authority that Busby believed he represented. It had all the appearances of a piece of political theatre, but in the Resident's mind this gathering of chiefs was 'the first step towards the formation of a permanent confederation of the chiefs which may prove the basis of civilised institutions in this country'.

This hint of some form of government based on an unorthodox partnership between Busby and various Maori chiefs worried the Governor of New South Wales, Sir Richard Bourke. Bourke's relations with Busby had never been easy, and the Resident's latest suggestion prompted the Governor to advise Busby that there was a need to proceed with caution and restraint in his functions.

Busby may well have complied with this request, but his panicky nature was inflamed from 1834 by the possibility that the French might have plans to lay claim to New Zealand. It was a preposterous suggestion, but one that had become real for Busby when he was confronted with the eccentric designs of Baron Charles de Thierry. De Thierry, a Frenchman, had purchased a small tract of land in the Hokianga in 1822 and had announced his intention to establish a settlement in the country, with himself as its 'Sovereign Chief' and 'Lord and Governor'. For Busby, this was all the evidence that was needed that Catholic France was on the verge of establishing a colonial outpost in New Zealand. He was growing increasingly apprehensive about what he believed was 'the intervention of foreign interests'. He proposed to Bourke a complex and costly series of land deals, bound up in a treaty, that would supposedly secure New Zealand as an exclusively British field of interest (and presumably also secure Busby's ambition for a position with far more authority than he currently exercised).

Bourke not only rejected Busby's schemes, but recommended to his superiors in London that the Resident be dismissed as he had proven to be a failure in his post. So on top of the French 'threat' Busby had to contend with the fragile state of his career. In October 1835 these two pressing considerations converged with the idea of a confederation of chiefs – a concept that had been germinating in his mind for at least a year. The result was the Declaration of Independence, whose grand title raised expectations that remained unfulfilled in its text.

The Declaration was signed at Waitangi on 28 October 1835 by Busby and thirty-five chiefs who had gathered for the occasion.

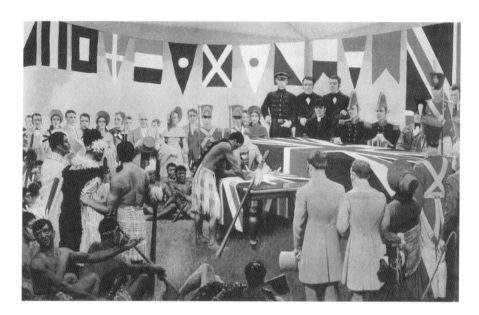

An artist's impression of the first signing of the Treaty of Waitangi.
REF: C-033-007. ALEXANDER TURNBULL LIBRARY, WELLINGTON, NEW ZEALAND. HTTP://BETA.NATLIB.GOVT.NZ/
RECORDS/23183602

It was a simple document that was divided into four articles: the first declaring New Zealand an independent country 'under the designation of the United Tribes of New Zealand'; the second asserting that 'All sovereign power and authority within the territories of the United Tribes of New Zealand' would reside exclusively in the hands of the chiefs; the third proposing that the signatories meet at Waitangi every autumn 'for the purpose of framing laws for the dispensation of justice, the preservation of peace and good order, and the regulation of trade'; the final article thanking the King for the acknowledgement of their flag and urging that 'he will continue to be the parent of their infant State, and that he will become its Protector from all attempts upon its independence'. It may have been a 'wild scheme' as one contemporary described it, and it had been undertaken without the permission of any of his superiors, but nevertheless Busby's Declaration required some official British response.

Bourke appeared ambivalent. He was wary of any additional costs the agreement might incur for the New South Wales Government, but at the same time he saw the Declaration as a move towards New Zealand's self-government; it could therefore be an opportunity to extend British law and order in the country. Back in London, Lord Glenelg, the new Colonial Secretary, initially warmed to the Declaration and responded by offering Maori continued British paternal friendship. However, this was not the same as endorsing the Declaration, or even recognising it as part of official British policy on New Zealand. On the contrary, the Colonial Office had been caught completely off guard by Busby's unilateral decision to forge a sovereign state from a British residency. It was a 'silly' and 'unauthorised' gesture in the opinion of Sir George Gipps, later Governor of New South Wales – a view that reflected colonial officials' hesitation about the Declaration's value.

However, the chilly reception the Declaration received in London was not nearly as threatening to its success as the situation on the ground in New Zealand. The convergence of various circumstances conspired to debilitate any chances of Busby's accord achieving lasting success. Firstly, there was the fact that the Declaration lacked a sufficient mandate from chiefs. With only thirty-five initial Maori signatories, it had attained fewer than 10 per cent of the 542 signatures that the Treaty of Waitangi received four and a half years later (and even that agreement did not get universal Maori endorsement). Sir Richard Bourke concluded that the Declaration's feeble mandate rendered it 'altogether primitive and imprudent'. Then there was the bigger issue of how the decisions that the Confederation of Chiefs made would be enforced. Without the means of carrying out its edicts, the Confederation was rendered impotent, and interest among its participants duly waned. But it was armed conflict among some of the signatories to the Declaration that terminally disrupted the collegial sentiment that Busby had hoped would be the bedrock of the Confederation of Chiefs.

The result was that Busby was as powerless as ever, and the lofty aims of his Declaration remained well out of reach. A visitor to the Bay of Islands in 1835 observed how the Resident was 'an isolated individual, not having even the authority of a magistrate, encircled by savages, and by a most troublesome class of his own countrymen'.

The Declaration did nothing to change these circumstances, and while Busby endeavoured to maintain the outward impression that all was well with his agreement, it was a facade that even the casual observer could easily see through.

The escalation of fighting between rival hapu in Northland from the beginning of 1837 was the subject of a slew of anxious despatches from Busby to his superiors in Sydney. Bourke was not entirely insensitive to what was portrayed by Busby as the deteriorating security situation in New Zealand, so he responded by sending a warship to the country with the dual purpose of making a show of British strength and for its captain, William Hobson, to report on what options there were for administering New Zealand in the future. The latter initiative, though kept reasonably confidential, was the clearest indication yet that Busby's period as a Resident was nearing its end.

Hobson arrived in the Bay of Islands on HMS *Rattlesnake* on 27 May 1837, and soon observed that the fighting that had so panicked Busby was not, in fact, the threat to British interest in New Zealand that Busby had claimed. Hobson reported that 'the hostile [Maori] forces have repeatedly passed through the very inclosures [sic] of the missionaries at Paihia, on their way to and from the field of battle, without molesting a single article belonging to the whites; and in one instance the two parties by mutual consent removed the scene of action to a greater distance from our settlements lest a white man should by accident be injured'. At once Busby's anxieties took on the appearance of little more than paranoia. According to Hobson there was no need to fear for the safety of British settlements in the Bay of Islands as a result of Maori military actions.

Hobson's report on the prospects for New Zealand made no provision whatsoever for Busby's future in the country. The captain was guided by the need to have some form of British authority applying to British settlements, but any grandiose plans he might have entertained about a large administration being established in New Zealand with sweeping powers were curtailed by the tight financial pressures that were bearing down on the Colonial Office. London could afford only the minimum of expense, and so was

William Hobson, who
became New Zealand's
first Governor.
REF: G-826-1. ALEXANDER TURNBULL
LIBRARY, WELLINGTON, NEW
ZEALAND. HTTP://BETA.NATLIB.GOVT.
NZ/RECORDS/22725431

looking for a solution to the 'New Zealand problem' that would be
effective yet affordable.

The most notable feature of New Zealand society in Hobson's
eyes was the unsavoury type of European who was settling in the
country. They were the 'ruffians from our own country', he advised
Bourke, and while the missionaries had been partially successful in
introducing civilised habits into some Maori communities, Hobson
lamented that 'the dissolute conduct of the lower orders of our
countrymen not only tends to diminish that holy influence, but to
provoke the resentment of the natives, which, if once excited, would
produce the most disastrous consequences'.

Busby maintained his belief that Maori ought to play a central
role in governing the country, but Hobson favoured adapting a

model of rule that had been applied by the East India and Hudson Bay Companies in other parts of the British Empire. His report favoured the formation of a factory system, initially to be established in three Northland locations, where British law would apply to all those residing within the confines of the factory and its surrounds. The factories would be run by magistrates, and all British subjects in the area would be required to register themselves and their land holdings. There was even a suggestion that prisons be erected in each factory area to ensure that the facility existed to punish crimes according to British law.

Hobson's vision for British jurisdiction in New Zealand hinged on the commercial success of his planned factories, while Busby favoured encouraging a more home-grown model of law and order to evolve as a product of cooperation between settlers and Maori. But because Hobson's commercially inspired model would need greater levels of official British protection, the captain recommended that a treaty be concluded with those chiefs in the vicinity of each of the factory areas, 'for the recognition of the factories and the protection of British subjects and property'.

Busby sensed that his career in New Zealand was under threat and decided to pre-empt Hobson's report by sending one of his own to Sydney. Conceding that his Confederation of Chiefs was by now practically defunct, Busby suggested that a replacement body be formed that would serve as some vague peace-conserving organisation. Other suggestions included establishing a system for educating Maori; the formation of a Maori newspaper; the establishment of settler and missionary councils to advise the Resident; the implementation of land titles and registration; the setting aside of reserves of land for those Maori who had sold ancestral territories; and the imposition of duties on shipping and transactions in alcohol and tobacco.

However, Busby's recommendations were passed over without consideration. Not only were his hopeful suggestions redundant as far as colonial officials were concerned but their idealism was at odds with accounts from New Zealand of the country's apparent descent into anarchy. In March 1837, for example, the New Zealand missionary Henry Williams wrote to a relative in England that it was 'high time something be done to check the progress of iniquity committed by a lawless band daringly advancing in wickedness and outrage, under the assurance that "there is no law in New Zealand". Without some immediate interposition on the part of the Government for our protection, our position will become very desperate, as we may expect to be surrounded ere long by a swarm of rogues and vagabonds . . .' Williams was not alone in this fear of declining order. As such sentiments trickled their way back to London, Busby's schemes and promises for establishing a settled government and society looked increasingly implausible.

As a result, it was largely on the strength of Hobson's 1837 report on New Zealand that two years later Hobson was selected by the Colonial Office to arrange a cession of sovereignty from Maori to the Crown, and thereafter to be Lieutenant-Governor (later Governor) of the country. He was issued with instructions for this undertaking by the Colonial Office in London in August 1839, with the 'principal object' of his mission being to implement 'effective measures for establishing . . . a settled form of civil Government' in New Zealand. No mention was made of Busby and the Residency, signifying that it was to be replaced.

Hobson's arrival in New Zealand on 29 January 1840 made Busby's position as Resident superfluous, but in the crucial first week that followed, Busby played a central role in the creation of the Treaty of Waitangi. The extent of that role is difficult to fathom. Busby claimed that because of Hobson's illness at the time, which prevented him from leaving his ship anchored in the Bay of Islands, draft notes of the Treaty were handed to Busby for his consideration. The outgoing Resident looked at the draft and later wrote that he did 'not consider the propositions contained in those notes as calculated to accomplish the object', and that he then 'offered to prepare a draft of the Treaty for Captain Hobson's consideration', which according to Busby's recollection, 'was precisely what Captain Hobson desired'.

In fact Busby did far more than simply tamper with the draft – he effectively produced a new version 'almost from scratch'. In particular, the references in the final version of the Treaty to 'The Chiefs of the Confederation of the United Tribes of New Zealand' was a direct attempt by Busby to breathe life into his 1835 Declaration. Busby's amendments to the text also gave the impression that there were two categories of Maori signatories to the Treaty: those who were members of his now-defunct Confederation and the rest who were not. Hobson and his clerk, James Freeman, then made substantial alterations to Busby's text before the final version of the Treaty was sent to Williams for translation into Maori. Busby's later assertions that he had been almost solely responsible for the Treaty's text do not match the documentary evidence.

From the moment that Hobson returned to New Zealand in 1840, Busby's tenure as Resident officially came to an end. Although he was magnanimous in assisting the Lieutenant-Governor, he later declined a position in the colonial administration and persevered, with fluctuating success, in a career in farming and as a politician in the Auckland Provincial Council. But it is the first seven years of his presence in New Zealand, in his capacity as Resident, that represented a turning point in the way the British Government viewed New Zealand and set in train the course of events and decisions that culminated with the conclusion of the Treaty of Waitangi.

4

MAKETU EXECUTION, 1842

THE EXECUTION OF a minor chief in 1842 in the grim confines of Auckland's prison for the crime of murder hardly seems to warrant the status of a turning point in the nation's history. But the background to the event and the symbolism of the decision by the Governor to execute the criminal was of lasting significance to the country, particularly in the way that the Crown's authority was applied to Maori at a very early stage in its tenure in New Zealand.

Within a matter of months of the first signatures being inscribed on the Treaty of Waitangi, Hobson was on the lookout for a new capital for the country. The de facto capital at Russell was a ramshackle settlement that was unsuitable for a rapidly expanding settler population and was still marred by its reputation as the 'hellhole of the Pacific'. In late 1840 Hobson made plans to shift the fledgling seat of government to Auckland, around 180 kilometres south of Russell. In the wake of this move there was an exodus of settlers from the Bay of Islands to the new capital, although the region was not completely drained of its European presence. Most of those settlers who had established farms in the Bay of Islands area found that there were few buyers for their land and so, unable to afford to move to a new location, they had little option but to stay put and make the best of their circumstances.

One of these farming families was the Robertons. John Roberton had been a sailor, but had decided to change career and in September 1839 purchased the island of Motuarohia in the Bay of Islands. The island covered an area of around 66 hectares and was about one and

47

a half kilometres from the mainland. The island was purchased from a consortium of chiefs comprising Wharerahi, Moko and Rewa for £213, paid with a combination of cash and goods.

Using nearby boulders, Roberton and his wife Elizabeth built the foundations of a small wooden house on a piece of flat land between the beach and the hills on the south-eastern side of the island. They commenced farming, and their son was soon joined by a daughter. But prospects for the young family were shattered when Roberton died in 1840. He had been sailing 'merely for his own amusement' as his wife put it, in a new boat that a local builder had made, when a gust of wind capsized the vessel and Roberton and the other person on board drowned.

Elizabeth was now widowed, with two small children and a farm that still had £100 owing on it. It might have been best for her to sell the farm and take her children and whatever profits remained back to Britain, except that the colonial government was in the slow process of investigating all land purchases that had occurred prior to 1840, which had the effect of freezing any land transactions in the interim.

By the end of the year the surrounding area was slowly sinking into an economic slump as Auckland replaced Russell as the country's main port and trading centre. To make matters worse the house was not finished, and Elizabeth described herself and her children living on an 'inhospitable island in a cannibal country'. Elizabeth had no option but to try to make the best out of a bad situation. She had the aid of one servant (whom she struggled to pay), and barely enough livestock, but from this impoverished situation she began to try to grind out a living from the farm.

In Elizabeth's mind she owned the island because her husband had paid for it at a price agreed to by the vendors. However, as John had been the actual purchaser, and as John was now dead, traditional Maori custom dictated that the land be returned to its former owners. During 1841 hints, accusations and threats were directed against Elizabeth by some Maori, who were becoming increasingly militant in their insistence that the island be 'returned' to them. Ironically the vendors themselves, who according to traditional practices would have been the ones to make such demands, did not do so and appear to have accepted that the land they sold was now permanently in possession of the Robertons.

Elizabeth's anxiety was hardly eased by this technicality. On 11 November 1841 she attended a hearing in Russell held by the Land Commissioner to investigate her claim to the island. The Land Claims Commission had been established on the principle, as Hobson had explained it, that Maori 'never were in a condition to treat with Europeans for the sale of their lands, any more than a minor w[oul]d be who knows not the consequences of his own Acts'. The New South Wales administration had agreed; Governor Gipps had introduced the New Zealand Land Claims Bill to the New South Wales Legislative Council in July 1840, which was based on the principle 'that the uncivilized inhabitants of any country have but a qualified dominion over it, or a right of occupancy only; and that, until they establish among themselves a settled form of government, and subjugate the ground to their own uses, by the cultivation of it, they cannot grant to individuals, not of their own tribe, any portion of it, for the simple reason, that they have not themselves any property in it'.

Elizabeth was hardly an exception in turning to the Land Claims Commission to clarify her ownership. As William Swainson, the colony's Attorney-General, noted, 'At that time nearly the whole European population of the North Island were claimants of land alleged to have been purchased from the natives before the proclamation of the Queen's authority: the number of claims, in addition to the gigantic claims of the New Zealand Company, amounted to upwards of twelve hundred; and, in extent, they varied from a single rood to more than a million and a quarter of acres. Three of these claims exceeded a million of acres each; three of them comprised more than half a million of acres each, three others exceeded a quarter of a million of acres, and upwards of thirty of the claims comprised more than twenty thousand acres each. For some of these claims, the claimants had nothing to show but the ornamental scrawl or signature of one or more.'

The result of the hearing into the Robertons' purchase was in

Elizabeth's favour. The deed of purchase for Motuarohia was examined by the Commissioner, as was the will of John Roberton, in which the island was left to his wife. Moreover, Wharerahi and Rewa – as the original vendors – both attended the hearing and attested to the fact that they signed the deed of sale with full understanding of its provisions, and that they had entertained no expectation of the island reverting to their ownership if John Roberton died. The matter now seemed settled, and Elizabeth continued to salvage some sort of business from the struggling farm, safe in the knowledge that there was no chance that the land on which it lay would be pulled away from her by the Crown.

To help with work on the farm, Elizabeth enlisted the help of another settler, Thomas Bull (aged probably in his mid-thirties). A short time afterwards she got additional assistance from 'a remarkably powerful' local sixteen-year-old named Maketu Wharetotara, the son of Ruhe, a minor chief from Waimate. The missionary George Clarke junior was suspicious of this latter addition to the island. 'There was madness in Maketu's family of a homicidal character,' he later wrote. 'His brother and sister were both deranged, his aunt strangled herself in a paroxysm of rage, and his father Ruhe was subject to fits of frenzy, that made it dangerous for his best friends to go near him.' This assessment, it must be said, was written with the benefit of hindsight. There are no records of any warning being given to Elizabeth Roberton at the time she hired the youth.

The complement of people on the farm was augmented with the arrival of three-year-old Isabella Brind, who was described five years later as 'the natural daughter of a Captain Brind, by a native woman – the daughter of Rewa, the head of the Ngapuhis, who principally inhabit Kororarika [sic]'. It is most probable that this addition to Elizabeth's family was made to earn favour with the Maori community closest to her farm.

Bull and Maketu possessed characters that were inflamed almost every time they came into contact with each other. Bull allegedly provoked Maketu on several occasions, and threatened the latter that 'he should have little or no food unless he worked better for Mrs. Roberton'. Bull threatened Maketu's source of employment and

Maketu Wharetotara, executed in Auckland in March 1842 for murder.

belittled his mana as the son of a chief. In return, Maketu became sullen, which Bull mistook for laziness, thus exacerbating the ill-will between them.

Maketu's mind turned to justice – at least as he saw it. If his job was in jeopardy and his status was being demeaned then utu, or revenge, had to be exacted. So on the evening of Saturday 30 November, Maketu grabbed an axe, crept up to where Bull lay sleeping and split his head open. It was a gesture that would possibly have found some acceptance in traditional Maori communities, but to European eyes it was an outrage.

A near-contemporary account neatly laid out the sequence of events which occurred next: 'Mrs. Roberton having accidentally happened to come upon him [Maketu] when in the act of doing so, he judged it advisable to despatch her also with the same instrument, and then the two female children. Mrs. Roberton's son seeing what was going on, fled to a mountain close by, but the monster overtook him, and threw him headlong over the rock, two hundred feet high, so that he was literally dashed to pieces.'

51

The press was more indignant in its reporting of the murders. One journalist wrote in graphic terms of how Elizabeth's body was 'horribly mangled and mutilated', Bull had been 'decapitated' and 'the remains of a child were found burnt in the ashes of a house'. The result was a 'most shocking and inhuman atrocity'. Yet Maketu was not at first a suspect. He had fled the scene, perhaps acknowledging that his transgression was bound to reap repercussions; and the authorities in Russell apprehended three Europeans whom they initially suspected of the crime. Initially, as one Victorian historian noted, 'No human being could now bear witness against Maketu; he fired the house where the murdered lay, [and] paddled in a canoe to his father's village.' Once there he confessed to his actions, and reports of his guilt spread swiftly throughout the region.

When news of the killings on the island reached Russell, two local merchants – Mr Wilson and Mr Spicer – sent messages to the three British naval ships which happened to be in the Bay at that time. They also sent an urgent note to the town's police magistrate, but in the panic it was mis-addressed and ended up on one of the naval ships. The captains on the vessels agreed not to act unless they were formally warranted to do so by the magistrate, so, sensing that valuable time could be lost in gaining the necessary approval, the two merchants engaged a small boat with a crew of five and headed towards the island.

As they approached the shore a group of Maori who had moved onto the island threatened to kill them, but these seasoned residents were not so easily put off by such bluffing. Without flinching they demanded that Maketu be handed over to them. A settler recorded the astonishing course of events which followed: 'The merchants then spoke of the enormity of the crime which the prisoner had been guilty of; and many of the chiefs said it was very wicked to do such a thing as murder a woman. The merchants, finding there was no chance of obtaining the prisoner by fair means, went amongst the whole of the natives, 1500 in number, although the latter threatened to kill them with their tomahawks. But they, being assured from their knowledge of native manners and customs that this threat would not be put into execution, did not hesitate to seize the prisoner, and, with the assistance of their crew, put him into their boat, the natives all the while looking on with astonishment, but afraid to attack the Europeans, as they knew the prisoner had been guilty of murder.' However, a further confrontation forced Spicer and Wilson to leave the island late that evening without Maketu.

It was nonetheless a brave gesture, and it was made all the more remarkable because, on the face of it, it was unnecessary. At Russell there were police constables as well as a detachment of troops from the 81st Regiment and the crews of three naval ships. However, the magistrate was adamant that troops would not be used, believing that any show of force on behalf of the British would prompt aggression from those Maori protecting Maketu. He was prepared to wait for official permission from Hobson before committing troops, and so the cause of tension in the region – the failure by the British to apprehend Maketu – remained.

Henry Williams' wife Marianne recorded on 23 November 1841 how the situation was revealed to her family, and the sense of apprehension that the event instilled in them. 'Just as we were going to bed,' she wrote, 'a note brought from Mr. Busby, mentioning that the murderer was discovered to be a son or brother of Ruhe; that upwards of three hundred natives were assembled at Motu Apohia, generally called Robertson's [sic] island, and refused to give the murderer up; that one of Rewa's sons was sitting with him . . . altogether, it was more alarming than anything he [Busby] had known in New Zealand; that Mr. King thinks the natives ripe for an outbreak, and that Mr. Mair had intimations of the same nature. That Mr. Beckham, the police magistrate, was to go to Kerikeri for Mr. Clarke, and to write to Auckland for all the disposable force. We shuddered as we talked over it.'

There was a fear among the local European community that capturing and arresting the suspect could lead to a sudden eruption in violence in the region, with vulnerable settlers bearing the brunt of any conflagration. The local magistrate initially refused to seize the suspect, fearing that the consequences would outweigh the merits in apprehending a criminal. Eventually Henry Williams applied the pressure of diplomacy to yield the desired result, but it was a delicate and risky process, as Williams wrote in April 1842: 'The disturbance arising from the arrest of Maketu was happily suppressed, but I do not hesitate to say, that had not the grandchild of Rewa been one of the victims, thus bringing all the Ngapuhi tribes as auxiliaries to the Europeans in the event of war, the result would have been far otherwise. The assertion of the Colonial Secretary, that the natives never did entertain an opinion of distrust, as far as regards the Government, required more reflection than perhaps was given to it; for the fact is too palpable to be refuted. I must say that I do not know a chief who has not expressed his "distrust" in the Europeans generally; and it has required all my energies and influence, in common with other Missionaries, amongst the natives, to set their minds at rest upon these subjects.'

The suspect was finally delivered into the hands of the police magistrate by his own community, 'partly from a sense of justice, and partly from terror of the relations of the murdered half-caste infant, a powerful tribe in the Bay of Islands', as a writer in the 1850s put it. Missionary pleading also played a major part in the crisis reaching a peaceful resolution.

As the weeks passed, however, the peace in Northland in the wake of Maketu's capture looked increasingly brittle. The threat that British law would apply to Maori was at the heart of the mounting fury of some Maori in the region. Henry Williams reported that 'The Missionaries were threatened, it having been stated that Mr. Clarke and I had taken Maketu as a prisoner on board the Government brig. A large party had been met on the road, fully equipped for mischief, and threatening the Mission. As soon as this intelligence was received at Paihia, I paid an especial visit to the chiefs around the Bay, who all regarded the affair as most serious, and advised me to call a general meeting for the following Thursday, to be held at Paihia, as no time was to be lost.'

The meeting was held, but to begin with 'much angry language was used by Pomare, Heke, and others, against the Government and the *pakeha*'. However, as the afternoon drew on, the 'angry feeling began to subside, and the conduct of the opponents to order and justice condemned by the well-disposed. At sunset, all dispersed quietly to their places. Ruhe, the father of the culprit, fully approved that the law should be carried out, though months passed before quietness was fully established.'

The result was a resolution signed by around twenty chiefs on 16 December 1841. Here, for the first time, was a document endorsed by a number of tribal leaders supporting the extension of British (criminal) law to their communities, at least in the case of capital offences: 'Sir, Maketu's work is his alone, his own; we have nothing to say for him. That man is with you; leave him there. Do not bring him back here to us, lest there be a disturbance: leave him there. Governor, do not listen to the reports that have flown about in the wind . . . Sir, Governor, let your regard be great for us, the children of the Queen Victoria, the Queen of England, of Europe also. Now, this is the word of the book: "Love one another." This is a good word. Shew us the greatness of your regard to us and our children, and we shall all turn without one exception to Victoria to be her children. But if not, what shall we do? Governor, here we are sitting in ignorance; we have no thoughts; you are our parent.'

The murder of Europeans by Maori was an extremely rare occurrence at this time, but as the country had recently become a British colony there was in the minds of settlers an expectation that British justice would somehow be enforced. The emphasis, however, was on 'somehow'. Although British rule had been formally established in the colony through the provisions of the Treaty of Waitangi, in practice Maori sovereignty still prevailed over the majority of the country's territory. And to complicate matters further, official policy on the jurisdiction of British law in New Zealand was still far from clear.

During 1839, when the final touches were being put to the British policy to annex New Zealand, consideration turned to the issue of over whom British sovereignty would apply. The decision boiled down to two options: either the sovereignty of the Crown would blanket everyone in the country, or it would apply just to British subjects living there. The Colonial Office went for the latter (cheaper) option. Glenelg, the Colonial Secretary, wanted British rule to prevail only in 'certain well-defined portions of the country . . . where the British

These are the thoughts of Maketu Waretotara just before his death.

These are my words, Maketu Waretotara on the morning of the 7th of March just before my death. I say it is true, it is right that I should die, it is my own doing, and for my sins I am going to to the place that is burning with everlasting fire, If I dont repent of my Sins, but I have prayed to God to wash my sins away, with the blood of Jesus Christ, my thoughts are these, He can wash my sins away; I have prayed to God to pardon all my past sins, O, yes, He can wash my sins away

I forgive every man that has sinned against me, I hold no enmity against man.

I commit my Soul into the hands of Jesus Christ; You that I have after me my — countrymen or (Pakeha's) foreigners, all of you be — careful of sin — Murder — for it is that, that has — brought me to death

This is my speech
Maketu Wareotara

A transcript of a statement made by Maketu immediately prior to his execution.

are already settled'. In March 1839 Sir James Stephen, the sagacious permanent head of the Colonial Office, expressed a preference for the establishment of a ruling body in New Zealand which would govern 'the Anglo Saxon Race'.

By June 1839 British policy had firmed, with officials desiring the appointment of a consul in New Zealand who would exercise 'some competent control over British subjects in the New Zealand Islands' – a policy endorsed by the British Treasury, which agreed to fund the annexation of New Zealand on this basis. Hobson's decision to put Maketu on trial stretched the elasticity of Colonial Office policy to an extreme degree, making the law that was supposed to govern settlers now apply to the country's Maori population.

On 1 March 1842 Maketu made his appearance in the Supreme Court in Auckland. He was found guilty and was executed on 7 March. The gossip in Auckland was that Maketu's execution would take place in the Bay of Islands, as close as possible to the scene of his murders. However, Hobson and his Executive Council immediately sensed that this would be one provocation too far and prudently decided that the convicted youth would be executed in Auckland, where British authority was at its strongest.

At first light on the 7th, carpenters and smiths worked on erecting the gallows. At the same time, an apparently deeply penitent Maketu requested the presence of a minister, and the Reverend Churton attended to him, baptising the prisoner under the name William King. Then at midday Maketu, dressed in a blue blanket, was brought from his cell. He exhibited 'the peculiarly dignified demeanour and appearance for which the native chiefs are so peculiarly distinguished', as one observer wrote. The prison bell tolled, and Maketu was led to the scaffold, which was surrounded by a large military guard in case there was any last-minute attempt by a sympathetic group of Maori to rescue the prisoner. As it turned out, however, there were few Maori present (although around a thousand Europeans turned up to witness the spectacle). A few minutes after twelve noon, Maketu was cast off, the noose snapped his neck and he died 'almost instantly'.

It was the ultimate penalty that could be exacted against a criminal under British law. The fact that it was a Maori who was sentenced, convicted and executed set in motion the extension of British jurisdiction throughout the country, most importantly in its application to Maori, who made up the vast majority of New Zealand's population at the time. Prior to the Maketu case they were considered by almost everyone to exist beyond the reach of British law.

In 1842 Swainson wrote to the Colonial Office querying this usurpation of Maori sovereignty, which in his legal opinion went beyond the provisions of the Treaty of Waitangi. Stephen wrote a minute on the matter in 1843 which concluded: 'Mr Swainson may think this is unjust or impolitic or inconsistent with former Acts, but still it is done.' As far as Britain was concerned, the decision to try and convict a Maori on a serious charge was a major evolutionary step in the jurisprudential history of the colony.

5

NEW ZEALAND COMPANY SETTLEMENTS

> Two elements of order and civilisation were thus at last
> introduced into the beautiful wilderness where nature
> had done so much and man so little – the Colonial Office
> missionary-government in the north, the Colonising-
> Company in the south; and the sad history of New Zealand
> for the next five years is but the history of the successful
> intrigues of the former institution to destroy the latter.
>
> —Charles Hursthouse, *New Zealand; or Zealandia,
> the Britain of the South*, 1857, p43.

THE PEOPLING OF BRITISH colonies in the nineteenth century was typically a haphazard affair. Communities were formed where enough settlers happened to coalesce at a common point; while the sort of people who emigrated from Britain were a mixture of classes and skills, motivated by a chaotic concoction of ambitions. In one way, this was the great strength of British colonisation: its ability to operate organically, free from the restrictive bureaucracy and unworkable ideology of any state-backed settlement scheme. It was also its great weakness. As the case of New Zealand demonstrated in the 1820s and 1830s, unrestrained immigration may not have lead to overcrowding (the flow was far too slight for that) but it did lead to the coagulation of small pockets of crime and immorality, nourished by the specific calibre of Europeans who made their way to New Zealand. They included escaped convicts, sailors who had jumped ship, would-be farmers fallen on hard times, grog dealers and all the other flotsam and jetsam that could be found in most imperial frontier settlements in this era.

Yet in almost all instances in the nineteenth century the British Government turned its back on any suggestions that it somehow take responsibility for the flow of its citizens to other parts of the world. At best, it endeavoured to offer these emigrants the protection (as well as the penalties) of British law in any location they settled that was unclaimed by another European power.

In the 1830s and 1840s, however, New Zealand was subject to an ambitious plan which its creator – the ambitiously named Edward Gibbon Wakefield – called 'systematic colonisation'. The scheme was notable not only because of its grandiose aims but because its backers succeeded in forcing the hand of colonial officials, who until the late 1830s had displayed a marked reluctance to intervene in New Zealand; and because it resulted in the creation of sizeable settlements in the colony in the following decade.

Wakefield's vision of systematic colonisation germinated during the late 1820s when he was serving time in Newgate Prison for abduction. A series of correspondence and minor publications were succeeded in 1837 by one of his more important works, *The British Colonization of New Zealand*. In its 423 pages he sketched out in often minute detail the architecture of his scheme.

Wakefield saw himself as reviving the spirit of colonisation, which he suggested had nearly expired by the beginning of the nineteenth century. In doing so, he placed himself in the league of some of the great British explorers and pioneers going back to Elizabethan times. But where Wakefield differed from most of his self-identified predecessors was in his view of land. His innate hostility to state involvement in colonisation surfaced repeatedly. The claim of colonial governments to waste lands had the effect of distorting the price of land, constricting the supply of capital and therefore making it harder for settlements to prosper. Central to Wakefield's approach to planned colonisation was 'a sufficient, but no more

Edward Gibbon Wakefield,
the architect of the systematic
colonisation of New Zealand.
Ref: 1/2-031744-F. Alexander Turnbull
Library, Wellington, New Zealand. http://
beta.natlib.govt.nz/records/22559033

than sufficient, price for all new land . . . It obviates every species of bondage; by providing combinable labour, it renders industry very productive, and maintains both high wages and high profits'. And the advantages did not stop there. Such a system would make the colony 'as attractive as possible, both to capitalists and to labourers . . . and to those who have a distaste for the primitive condition of new colonies heretofore'. The profits obtained from selling cheaply (or even freely) acquired land at a modest price to settlers would be ploughed back into the scheme. This would ensure that the young settlements would be peopled by a healthy cross-section of British society, and that they would be furnished with the sorts of public amenities they would have been accustomed to back in Britain.

As a by-product of the scheme, there would also be 'a deliberate and systematic plan for preserving and civilizing the native race'. It was, for the era, a noble intention, but as it turned out it was one more honoured in the breach than the observance. Maori tended to exist only on the periphery of Wakefield's vision, and it was not until later conflicts broke out that they briefly became the focal point in his scheme. In general, Wakefield was content to allow Maori to exercise full sovereignty over their own territories, provided that they accepted the imported sovereignty of the settlements that were to be established, often in their midst.

The process by which the scheme would operate was fairly straightforward in Wakefield's mind. 'The first step,' he explained, 'will be to obtain from those tribes which are already disposed to part with their land and their sovereign rights, certain portions of territory, which would become part of Her Majesty's foreign possessions.' At this time Wakefield clearly anticipated working in partnership with the British Government to achieve his objectives. With the assistance of the Crown, 'British settlements would be formed, with regular government'. Everyone living in the territories acquired in the name of Britain (but at the hands of Wakefield and his organisation) would have the same rights and privileges as British subjects anywhere else. And as for Maori, they would be parting with land 'which they scarcely know how to cultivate, and with a dominion which they are incapable of exercising beneficially'. There were advantages for everyone, it seemed.

After a lengthy analysis of the geography of the country (to the limits of which it was known at this time), *The British Colonization of New Zealand* drew readers' attention to the descent into lawlessness that the country was experiencing – made all the more graphic by the provision of numerous examples, which made Wakefield's scheme seem so compelling. The confluence of other circumstances – apparently acquiescent Maori; the growth in trade and favourable climate and soils – added strength to the case for this particular form of planned settlement.

Wakefield's vehicle for achieving his goal of systematic colonisation was the New Zealand Association (later called the New Zealand Company). The labyrinthine trail along which various incarnations of this venture emerged and then subsided to be replaced by an alternative is less important here than its underlying ideology, which remained remarkably consistent in its main tenets throughout.

It was during the 1830s that New Zealand had appeared on the horizon to Wakefield as the ideal territory where his scheme for planned settlement – which he had rehearsed in his mind countless times – could finally be acted out. In 1837 he wrote to his brother-in-law describing New Zealand as 'one of the finest countries in the world for British settlement'.

The biggest obstacle to Wakefield's plan being put into practice in New Zealand was Sir James Stephen, who was unyielding in his opposition to the association and its goals. Part of the reason for Stephen's strenuous objection was what he saw as the association's repeated failure to live up to its own doctrine. Stephen wrote a minute on the matter, observing that 'it is at least curious to see how . . . abstract theories supposed to be of universal application are made to bend to practical difficulties of which the mere theorist was ignorant or heedless'. His fear was that, left unchecked, the Association would have 'unlimited power of incurring expenses, multiplying Offices, and granting Salaries', which might lead to a 'form of dynasty as absolute, and as completely exempt from control, as can possibly exist within the British Dominions'.

Wakefield's backers naturally saw things in a very different light. A group of them wrote to Lord John Russell, the Secretary of State for the Colonies, in 1841, arguing that 'Colonization Companies in good hands would be the best possible instruments for effecting . . . the end in view'. Such organisations could operate without the need to uphold 'official dignity', and would possess 'all the hardihood and effrontery of commercial enterprize [sic]'. Such pleas were met increasingly with stony silence from colonial officials, which led to the association resolving in 1839 to proceed with its plans for the systematic colonisation of New Zealand in spite of unfavourable British policy towards its ambitions.

Sensing (correctly as it turned out) that the Crown was coming around to the idea that it should annex New Zealand, Wakefield decided to get a head start over the Colonial Office. From May 1839 his soon-to-be-renamed New Zealand Company began despatching ships to the country. The first was the *Tory*, which sailed from England under cover of darkness to escape observation (based on a rumour that the Government might wish to prevent the Company undertaking such a venture). Indeed, so clandestine was the operation that only after the *Tory* was already en route for New Zealand did the company make a public announcement of formation and purpose.

On 22 May 1839 Lord Durham, who had been appointed to the committee of the Company as its titular head, sought an interview with Lord Normanby. He informed the Colonial Secretary that 'preparations for a very extensive emigration were in progress in various parts of England and Scotland. Under these circumstances, the gentlemen whom I represent trust that Her Majesty's Government will be convinced of the expediency, or rather the necessity, of affording to British settlers in New Zealand better securities for law and government than have hitherto been established amongst Her Majesty's subjects there.'

The British Government was caught off guard by the Company's plans to send the *Tory* off to New Zealand. Normanby refused to sanction the mission and all but ruled out the chances of the Company acquiring letters patent from the Crown for its undertaking. What it feared was that the Company's agents would soon establish a system of government whose authority was entirely independent from the Crown. Normanby wanted his wish to be 'further understood that no pledge can be given for the future recognition of Her Majesty of any proprietary titles to land within New Zealand which the company or any other persons may obtain by grant or by purchase from the natives', and that it was likely that the Queen would be 'advised to take measures without delay to obtain cession in sovereignty' of lands occupied by British subjects in the islands.

Ironically, what the Government feared would happen was being hastened by its very actions. The immediate victory belonged to Wakefield, as one nineteenth-century historian wryly observed: 'deluded settlers were drawing lots in London for selection of New Zealand lands, which the Company affected to be able to sell. But Governors in ships of war did not move so rapidly as Colonel Wakefield, the principal agent for the company, in the "Tory", despatched with a celerity which confounded the Colonial Office. In the race for priority Colonel Wakefield was the winner.' The *Tory*'s departure in May 1839 was followed in August by the *Cuba* and, from September, by a succession of vessels transporting settlers to the newly founded Company colony in Port Nicholson.

Henry Petre, the son of a director of the New Zealand Company, expressed wide-eyed optimism at the possibilities that Port Nicholson presented. Arriving in the harbour on the *Oriental* on 22 January 1840, he was one of the earliest crop of Company settlers deposited at this location. His record of this time suggests that Port Nicholson was pregnant with possibilities: 'The business of establishing the settlement, the choosing of the Town Sections, and getting the population housed, have hitherto very much confined the agricultural operations of the Colonists. Enough had been done, however, in the way of experiment to prove that agriculture will rank high among the resources of the Port Nicholson district. The wheat grown upon the banks of the Hutt from seed obtained from the Cape of Good Hope yielded well, and was of excellent quality; and bailey [*sic*] grown from some seed which I brought from New South Wales, where it had been raised from Cape seed, also turned out remarkably well. Oats yield abundantly, and Indian corn or maize is universally cultivated by the natives. Potatoes are produced in great abundance, as the climate admits of two crops in the course of a year. The native potatoes are very good, but those which have been raised by the settlers are as fine as those of any part of the world.'

Potatoes from the embryonic settlement were already being exported to New South Wales, and wheat promised to follow a similar route of commercial success. Indeed, despite what is now known about Wellington's setting and climate, all the omens Petre encountered pointed to a fruitful future: 'All the vegetables of this country have succeeded remarkably well at Port Nicholson. When we arrived, we found turnips, cabbages, and other garden stuff in great perfection. They had been raised from seed taken out by the *Tory*. They were grown between the present site of Wellington and the Hutt; and as some of them were left to seed, every one who chose to do so, helped himself in passing, by which means excellent sorts of every species have been spread over the Colony. There were, when I left Wellington, several well stocked gardens within the precincts of the town; and now that the Colonists are fully in possession of their town lands, a considerable portion of the future town will no doubt be converted into garden grounds.'

John Bidwell, who visited the settlement in 1840, offered an independent assessment of its circumstances, noting that 'At Port Nicholson there is an excellent harbour; a navigable river, the Hutt; a great extent of very rich land; an admirable site for the town; with a population at present of between two and three thousand persons, among whom are many of high family connexions and respectability from England, who have brought considerable capital with them, and a consequent demand for labour.'

The artist, explorer and later colonial administrator Charles Heaphy was equally ebullient, arguing that 'The selection of the site of the principal settlement on so fine a harbour as Port Nicholson gave great satisfaction to all the settlers on their arrival, and experience has since confirmed their opinion of its eligibility, in proving that it is a harbour of easy access as well as of accommodation and security.'

Not everyone was enthused about the conditions they confronted on arrival. Having been promised a pastoral idyll, abundant in land, temperate in climate and ripe for farming, first impressions were bound to disappoint even the more moderately expectant migrant.

In April 1840 Dr Samuel Martin (who later in the year was to be appointed a magistrate by Governor Hobson) jotted down his disparaging observations of this flagship New Zealand Company settlement. 'That the settlement of Port Nicholson will be a failure,' he wrote, 'I strongly suspect and fear. A sad mistake has been committed in sending the emigrants out so soon, before any proper preparations had been made for their reception. Neither the town nor country lands have been yet surveyed, and it will be a long time before they are so. The immigrants and purchasers of land are left in the meantime to shift for themselves the best they can: that they should under such circumstances feel disappointed, and even disgusted, is not to be wondered at. They have paid their money in England in the hope of obtaining land immediately on their arrival, but they now discover that the hope was a delusion.'

A chromolithograph of the settlement of Port Nicholson (Wellington) in 1840.
REF: C-033-005. ALEXANDER TURNBULL LIBRARY, WELLINGTON, NEW ZEALAND. HTTP://BETA.NATLIB.GOVT.NZ/
RECORDS/22898001

Apparently some of the immigrants were so discouraged with the struggling town on arrival that they made loud murmurs about leaving to go to South America, but the fact that all their funds were tied up in Port Nicholson was all the incentive they needed to stay put.

Martin complained about the settlement's mediocre harbour, the 'strong gales of wind which almost always blow through Cook's Straits' and the fact that apart from 'a small valley at the head of the bay, containing certainly not more than 10,000 acres, there is no other available agricultural land near the harbour, which is on both sides bounded by steep and impassable hills, or rather mountains, rising abruptly from the water's edge'.

As Martin surveyed the terrain, clues to Port Nicholson's hesitant start as a town were evident. 'Judging by the immense quantities of stores and agricultural implements which are lying about and being destroyed on the beach,' he noted, 'there must also be several men of property among the immigrants. It is a great pity and a loss to the Colony that they should not be enabled to carry out their intentions of becoming settlers and cultivators of the soil.'

Even two years later, the situation had hardly improved, as one settler wrote to his parents: 'I travelled for days and found nothing but mountains for miles, which could not be cultivated whatsoever, by no means. There were at a distance two farms; Francis Molesworth and another gentleman had many acres of wheat tilled and looking well; but I thought we were ruined, to hear so many complaints that of this island the great parts were mountains, which could not be cultivated by no means.'

Yet despite Port Nicholson not living up to the heightened expectations of all the settlers, Britons continued to pour into the town. Even after Auckland was made the country's capital, Port Nicholson's population continued to grow at a faster rate, thanks chiefly to the planning and marketing of the Wakefields, with siblings and other family members at the centre of a slew of officials in both Britain and New Zealand ensuring that the Company's intricate logistics functioned relatively effectively.

As far as the settlement's leaders were concerned, the only major fly in the ointment was Hobson, who from the outset was perceived as a rival to the Company's power, albeit an ineffectual one. Edward Jerningham Wakefield, the son of the Company's founder, wrote condescendingly of Hobson, indicating among other things that the presence of the Queen's representative in the colony was nothing to be deferential about.

When the Governor finally visited Port Nicholson, Wakefield junior's tone was heavily laden with derision: 'The whole audience was struck with the uncollected bearing of Captain Hobson. He looked timidly from one to the other of the speakers, and hesitated, and stammered, and gave vague unmeaning answers. When repeatedly pressed to explain himself, he tried in vain to "clothe himself with the power and dignity which became his station": and, throughout the interview, he reminded me of an offending school-boy who should have been brought up to be reproved, before an assemblage of scolding parents and teachers, unable to utter any remonstrance, or too humiliated and broken-spirited even to defend himself. To many in the room the exhibition was positively painful. I remember experiencing the same nervous feeling as though I were listening to the failure of a maiden speech, or the break-down of a middling singer in trying to execute a difficult passage.'

Hobson may have toyed with the idea of shifting the capital to the area in order to assert Crown authority over the largest European settlement in the country, but Stephen anticipated this possibility and wrote a cautionary note against such a move in December 1841, warning that if Hobson moved the seat of government to the Wellington area, the New Zealand Company 'would reduce him [Hobson] to the character of a mere Governor of their Settlements. I think he far more wisely asserted his independence of them. At Port Nicholson, he would have been their servant, not the servant of the Crown.'

Despite this official snub from London, along with the mutual resentment between Hobson and the Company and its settlement, Port Nicholson continued its boisterous growth, extending on the initial sale of 1100 lots, each of which consisted of one town acre and 100 country acres. By May 1845 the population of the settlement was 4047, supported by farming on 1070 acres of cultivated land. But this was no loose network of farms, knitted together by virtue of existing in a shared location. The settlement had its own administration, law enforcement, public buildings, mills, factories, banks, churches and all the other precocious trappings of an aspiring colony.

Above all it was the economic opportunities that Port Nicholson (soon to be known as Wellington) offered settlers that made the town such a tempting proposition to immigrants – something that Heaphy was quick to recognise and boast to readers. 'The happy effect of the "Wakefield system",' he proclaimed, 'has been to cause the supply of labour and the demand to be at all times equal, and neither have the rate of wages been high, or the labouring classes in want of employment. This was sufficiently proved by the failure of Capt. Hobson's attempts to induce the labouring population of Wellington to remove to his township of Auckland. It was singular and interesting, that neither the Auckland capitalists or government could offer better inducements in Wellington, than constant employment to labourers and mechanics, at wages one-third lower than what they were in the receipt of at that place.' It was little wonder then that while Auckland struggled with intermittent bouts of economic depression in the early 1840s, Wellington continued its muscular advance in both size and prosperity.

There can be no doubt that New Zealand's colonisation would never have been so rapid, so organised or so prosperous had it not been for the formation of the New Zealand Company settlements. The template cast in Wellington was subsequently imprinted by the Company and its various off-shoots (sometimes with minor changes) in other settlements, including Nelson, New Plymouth, Whanganui, Christchurch and Dunedin. Of the 18,000 British immigrants who settled in New Zealand between 1840 and 1852, around 14,000, or 78 per cent, were brought in under Wakefield's schemes of systematic colonisation. In that twelve-year period, Wakefield's vision for the colony materialised (although not every detail was in the form he envisaged), and by the end of the century many of New Zealand's largest cities were the descendants of settlements he was either directly or indirectly responsible for founding.

6

THE NEW ZEALAND CONSTITUTION ACT, 1852

FOR A COLONY WITH a European population at the beginning of 1840 of around just 2000 – many of whom were huddled in small settlements which lacked even the barest protection afforded by British law – the Treaty of Waitangi was (on paper at least) a useful device for establishing some semblance of order in the country. The Treaty's roughly-hewn articles may have lacked the polished precision that a legal mind could have brought to bear on the agreement, but overall it served the purposes of the nascent colonial government, and gradually allowed (as the Maketu case demonstrated) for the British system of justice to extend throughout the country.

However, the substantial influx of settlers in the decade following the conclusion of the Treaty imposed a new set of circumstances and constitutional burdens on the government, which the Treaty was manifestly inadequate to deal with. Two aspects of the status quo in the colony in particular were ripe for constitutional change by 1850: the essentially dictatorial Crown colony system of government; and the rapid demographic changes that were occurring in the colony.

The Crown colony system of government which the Treaty ushered into New Zealand from 1840 comprised the Governor and the Executive Council, which consisted of the Colonial Secretary, the Attorney-General and the Colonial Treasurer. It was supposed to serve as an advice-giving body, but in practice it met irregularly and infrequently. The accompanying Legislative Council, which was responsible for enacting the Governor's ordinances, was comprised of the same members as the Executive Council, but with the addition of three senior Justices of the Peace.

Members of the Legislative Council could be suspended at the Governor's whim (subject to consent from the Colonial Office), and they were all obliged to vote with the Governor on any issue he declared to be of sufficient importance. Swainson neatly encapsulated the essence of this system: 'Before parliamentary, or "responsible", government is established in a Colony, the representative of the Crown both reigns and governs: he fills up all appointments to vacant offices, determines upon the policy and measures of the Government, and his officers carry them into effect. He is entitled to command their advice, but he is not bound to act upon it; and in the exercise of his powers he is responsible to her Majesty alone.'

Yet despite having almost unfettered power in the colony, the role of a governor was hardly an enviable one, especially if New Zealand's experience was anything to go by. 'So long as the Colonial form of Government continues to be that of an absolute Monarchy,' Swainson observed, 'the Governor has an arduous and harassing duty to perform: he is at all times, almost unavoidably, in a state of unpleasant relations with some portion of the community; and he is personally made the principal object of attack by the Colonial Press. In the ordinary discharge of his duty, he has frequently to thwart the projects of those who, regardless of the public interests, seek to promote their own aggrandizement; and even in the disposal of the patronage of the Government, he makes more enemies than friends; and, however popular he may have been at the commencement of his reign, he is soon surprised to find himself pursued with unrelenting malignity by a host of bitter enemies.' Lack of representation was at least part of the reason for such deeply rooted hostility towards the Governor. As the population changed, so too did the need for a democratic system of government become more pressing.

Whereas in 1840 Europeans made up about 2 per cent of the country's population, provincial statistics in 1853 show that there were 31,272 Europeans in the country and around 56,400 Maori, meaning that the European portion of the population had risen to

35 per cent of the total. However, this shift was not due entirely to rising immigration rates. The Maori population at the same time was tilting towards a steep decline, which also had political implications.

In 1859 the magistrate Francis Fenton churned through the available official statistics on the Maori population and suggested that the population decline could be attributed to the 'want of fecundity of the females ... the extreme mortality among the children, the great paucity of births, together with a rate of mortality of both adults and non-adults far higher than any average known in temperate climates'. Fenton was worried that 'the decline of the numbers of the people appears at the present rate of decrease to be very rapid, there is reason to fear that a population which has once reached such a state of decrepitude as that exhibited by the Maori inhabitants of this country will, from causes strictly intrinsic, proceed to its final catastrophe at a greatly accelerated pace, unless, indeed, the causes of decay be ascertained and removed'. Yet it was precisely the colony's rapidly changing demographic patterns – particularly the decreasing Maori population, together with the burgeoning number of immigrants – that was making the existing system of rule-by-governor increasingly cumbersome.

The idea of New Zealand having a constitution and a democracy required a shift in how the colony viewed the purpose of its government. The role of the country's administration would go, theoretically at least, from being an instrument restraining people to an instrument by which the people would be able to restrain the government. Colonies marching towards greater self-government was a comparatively new development in the British Empire at this time, and so precedent was still fairly thin on the ground. There were, however, some general themes for constitutional reform in the colonies that were finding favour with British officials by the 1850s. These included a bicameral legislature, a system of regional states or provinces and the primacy of a central government. To these elements were added specific consideration of New Zealand's circumstances – particularly the fact that the indigenous Maori population was still (just) the majority in the country, and the fact that there was no great popular chorus in the colony demanding more representative government at this time. The daily grind of forest-felling, farm-forming and struggling to put enough food on the table for the family occupied the minds of most settlers.

In 1846 an attempt had been made to introduce a constitution for New Zealand, and it failed. Admittedly it proposed a complex system of municipal councils, and provincial and general assemblies, all manned by a lumbering bureaucracy, but there was no sense of urgency for such an elaborate constitutional edifice. Although legislation for its creation was passed by the British Parliament in 1846, the New Zealand Governor at the time, George Grey, refused to bring it into effect in the colony.

Instead Grey lobbied for a simpler form of government – one more suited to the robust demands of the colony, and with less of the constitutional filigree that the 1846 Act possessed. In August 1851 he wrote to the Colonial Secretary in reply to earlier correspondence from London. Grey stated that he was convinced that the desire of the British Government to 'promote the welfare of the inhabitants of these Islands' was such that it was 'ready instantly to forgo the form of constitution proposed [in 1846] . . . if a better one can be presented'.

And a better constitution was not long in coming. The Governor had drafted a report for the Colonial Office on the sort of government institutions New Zealand required 'in order that the present state of these islands, and the condition of the several races inhabiting them, for whom representative institutions are to be provided, may be clearly understood'.

Grey's vision of representation for the 'several races' living in the country evidently excluded Maori. Indeed, New Zealand's indigenous population was portrayed almost as obstacles to the civilised advancement of the colony: 'The wide intervals between these European colonies [settlements] are occupied by a native race, estimated to consist of one hundred and twenty thousand (120,000) souls, a very large proportion of whom are males capable of bearing arms. These natives are . . . skilled in the use of their weapons, and take great care of them; they are addicted to war.' Grey went

Sir George Grey, who twice served
as Governor of New Zealand.
REF: 1/1-001345-G. ALEXANDER TURNBULL
LIBRARY, WELLINGTON, NEW ZEALAND. HTTP://
BETA.NATLIB.GOVT.NZ/RECORDS/22782578

on at length about the danger Maori supposedly posed to British
settlements in the country, but hoped that if assimilation continued
to occur, Maori could 'by prudent measures [be] brought under one
form of constitutional government, which might equally foster and
promote the really common interests of both races'.

Ironically only a few years earlier Grey had gone to some effort
to convince colonial officials in England that the colony's Maori
were turbulent and resistant to British rule. His new position – that
Maori might be brought relatively easily into the pale of civilisation
– was one that found quick favour with British politicians and
humanitarian groups.

New Zealand's geography was another major consideration
that Grey tackled in his recommendation to London. In parts of
the North Island, there was 'no overland communication, except
for foot passengers ... between the different settlements', with
mountain ranges and 'wide, parped, and dangerous rivers' posing 'an
almost insurmountable barrier'. Given the difficulties of transport,

any intricate system of government which required representatives to move frequently around the colony to attend meetings would be impractical.

Accordingly he advised the Colonial Secretary that any attempt to form a general legislature from such a widely dispersed set of communities as existed in New Zealand at the time would almost certainly fail 'because there are as yet no persons in these islands who have the means or leisure, to enable them to abandon their own affairs . . . to discharge their senatorial duties. Even if payment was made to such persons to remunerate them for their expenses whilst travelling and absent from home, they still could not afford to neglect their own affairs during so long an interval of time.' Grey's stated preference was for more powerful municipal institutions – ones which would exercise both considerable legislative and executive powers.

Much of this seems to have been a pretext by Grey to maintain his authority as Governor and to have as little of it as possible diluted by a representative body. He wrote in 1851 to his superiors that, by reserving substantial powers to the Governor, 'Great Britain would retain the means of promoting in every desirable way the interests and welfare of all Her Majesty's subjects' in New Zealand.

On receipt of Grey's lengthy suggestions, and with the backing of a sympathetic Colonial Office, on 30 June 1852 the New Zealand Constitution Act was passed in the British Parliament, and came into effect in New Zealand the following year. There was some opposition to the Act in the House of Commons, but as Sir William Molesworth observed, the only alternative to the proposed Constitution Act was to pass another piece of legislation which would suspend the 1846 Constitution Act for a further year – something that was becoming untenable given the growing settler population in New Zealand and the corresponding increase in trade between the 'Mother Country' and the colony.

The statute came into law with broad support in the House of Commons. It created six provincial councils based in Auckland, New Plymouth, Wellington, Nelson, Canterbury and Otago (two more were added later in the decade: Hawkes Bay in 1858 and

Marlborough the following year). These replaced the two provinces that had previously existed in the colony. The Act also brought into being a bicameral legislature comprising an elected House of Representatives and an appointed upper house: the Legislative Council.

The provincial councils were the most 'democratic' branch of government, in that they comprised a single house which consisted wholly of elected members drawn from the local province. However, this was far from a concession to valued democratic principles. On the contrary, as the British Colonial Secretary put it in a letter to Grey, democratic principles were extended so far to the provincial councils only because of 'the comparatively unimportant nature of the functions of these councils'. In a similar vein, the superintendents of provinces would be elected simply because this would 'be regarded by the colonists as a valuable concession'.

Such cynicism suggests that the tensions between settlers (particularly those in New Zealand Company settlements) and the new government was an issue that officials in London were well aware of. Certain elements of the Constitution Act were clearly designed to placate some of the more strident opposition the legislation was likely to encounter in the colony. Certainly there was mounting hostility in New Zealand to the Constitution Act even before it had been framed and passed into law, such was the sensitivity of some of the colony's residents to having the status quo disrupted to this extent.

As for the entitlement to vote, this was limited to males from the age of twenty-one who owned property with a net value of at least fifty pounds (or sufficient equity in a leasehold property, or owned a property in a town). Women were excluded from voting (as they were throughout the rest of the world at this time) and in practice so too were almost all Maori. The provision for land ownership as a prerequisite to the entitlement to vote excluded the vast majority of Maori, whose land was still in communal possession. So while Maori were still (just) the majority in the country, in the 1853 election – the first held under the provisions of the Constitution Act – of the 5849 voters enrolled throughout the colony, only 300 (approximately

The Provincial Council Building in Wellington, photographed around 1859.
REF: 1/2-003739-F. ALEXANDER TURNBULL LIBRARY, WELLINGTON, NEW ZEALAND. HTTP://BETA.NATLIB.GOVT.NZ/
RECORDS/22494909

5 per cent) were Maori. The only way by which Maori could be better enfranchised under the Act was if their lands were converted from communal ownership to individual title. This was part of Grey's assimilationist hope, despite the rupturing to the fabric of Maori society that such a shift would inevitably cause.

For the New Zealand Company settlements, nothing less than a replacement constitution would do. Company representatives feared that the power of the provinces (which they equated in the case of many of the provinces with the power of the Company) would eventually drain away as the central branch of government consolidated its influence in the colony. The Legislative Council – whose members would be appointed by the Governor – became the primary target of criticism by the Company. The Legislative Council had the power, according to one of the founders of the Canterbury settlement, John Godley, only of refusing to pass the Governor's laws. 'I leave you to imagine how much chance there was of *that* ever happening,' he suggested, 'when three out of the seven members were the Governor's own paid servants, and the other three nominated by him, and holding their seats at his pleasure, while he himself was to possess a casting vote.'

Godley's argument may have sounded technically correct, but he substantially overestimated the influence of the Legislative Council in the greater scheme of government. It was the House of Representatives where the Constitution Act vested the greatest measure of political power. This was not enough to stop the Company attacks, though. Newspaper editor and fellow founder of the Canterbury settlement, William Fox, was even less convinced than Godley that the new system of government would reflect the will of the colony's inhabitants. 'Pure unmixed despotism' would be the defining characteristic of the new regime, Fox predicted. Together with Godley's warnings, the Company settlements were roused in opposition to the proposed changes.

One of the most contentious aspects of the 1852 New Zealand Constitution Act was the way it dealt with how Maori should be accommodated in the new system of government – an issue that had polarised views both within the colony and back in Britain. Tucked away in sections 71 to 73 of the Act was the British Government's response to the fact that Maori still occupied an important demographic and territorial space in the country. The opening paragraph of section 71 set the tone for the way in which Maori would be regarded by the New Zealand state: 'And Whereas it may be expedient that the laws, customs, and usages of the aboriginal or native inhabitants of New Zealand, so far as they are not repugnant to the general principles of humanity, should for the present be maintained for the government of themselves, in all their relations to and dealings with each other, and that particular districts should be set apart within which such laws, customs, or usages should be so observed: It shall be lawful for her Majesty . . . from time to time to make provision for the purposes aforesaid, any repugnancy of any such native laws, customs, or usages to the law of England, or to any law, statute, or usage in force in New Zealand, or in any part thereof . . .'

At first glance it looked as though Maori would be permitted to live as they always had, provided that they did not commit any 'repugnant' acts (a reference principally to rape and murder). Sir John Parkington, the Secretary of State for the Colonies, stressed in a dispatch to Grey on 16 July 1852 that the Governor would maintain the authority to designate certain districts as places where 'the customs and usages of the natives may be preserved', where Maori would be exempted 'from the common law of the settled portions of New Zealand'. Far from usurping Maori sovereignty, the Act actually allowed for a degree of Maori political autonomy. This would not only hopefully nurture goodwill among Maori communities but also reduce the considerable costs likely to be incurred by a blanket imposition of colonial rule throughout the country.

Fox was critical of the provisions for Maori in the Act, however, claiming that the race was destined for 'extinction' and did not deserve any special treatment. The gradual process of Maori adapting to European ways would 'not rescue the race', he wrote. Before the benefits of European influence bore fruit, he suggested that 'scrofula and consumption, the drudgery and degradation of the women, will have done their work: the race will be gone . . . doom awaits the New Zealander [Maori]'. Godley pitched in with his conviction that Maori ought not to have any rights under the Constitution Act at all, insisting that they were 'wholly incapable of understanding the simplest rudiments of the questions on which their votes will be brought to bear'.

The counterpoint to such regressive views of Maori was found in England, where Parkington saw the future path of Maori heading in the direction of assimilation rather than extinction. 'Nearly the whole nation has now been converted to Christianity,' he pronounced to the House of Commons. 'They [Maori] are fond of agriculture, take great pleasure in cattle and horses; like the sea, and form good sailors; have now many coasting vessels of their own, manned with Maori crews; are attached to Europeans, and admire their customs and manners; are extremely ambitious of rising in civilisation and becoming skilled in European arts.'

This was soothing stuff for politicians and the public back in England, but settlers in the provinces in New Zealand were not buying it. Some even went as far as to claim that Maori lacked the 'social habits' to allow for amalgamation of the races to occur, and argued that the indigenous population possessed insufficient 'mental qualities' to make them fit members of civilised society.

Land, not social integration, however, was at the heart of the Constitution Act's application to Maori. Section 72 allowed for the Government to make laws for the regulation and sale of so-called 'waste lands'. This was any territory 'which Maori did not occupy or did not cultivate' – in effect, the majority of the country's terrain. Through this right to control such lands, the Government would be better positioned to 'promote colonization in New Zealand', which was clearly a consideration when the framers of the Act considered how Maori land ought to be dealt with.

The following section of the Act affirmed the Crown's authority (first established in the Treaty of Waitangi) to have the sole right to acquire land from Maori. It would then be the Crown's prerogative to sell this land to settlers or to use it as it saw fit. Ostensibly such a provision was intended to be a protective measure (as had been the intention with the Treaty), shielding Maori from the unscrupulous actions of land sharks. In practice, however, it put the Crown in the position of being the sole land trader in the colony and thus exposed its agents to future criticism for acts that were later perceived to be prejudicial to Maori vendors. It also failed to completely exclude land speculators, who in some instances bought former Maori-owned territories from the Crown with the intention of later selling them at a profit as settler demand for farming land continued to grow.

New Zealand did not achieve full self-government under the terms of the Constitution Act, and Crown-appointed governors continued to be vested with powers that could override the workings of some of the branches of government. However, the Act put in place the foundations of a system of government which has remained fundamentally very similar to that in operation at the start of the twenty-first century. Admittedly, there were numerous amendments to the legislation, and over time most of its sections were replaced or discarded, but the basic architecture of government that it established remained largely intact.

The Act was the next logical progression for a British colony with a growing settler population, and it signified a major turning point in the ability of the country to manage its own affairs with substantially less interference from London. However, the premise that Maori were fast on their way to becoming a people whose culture and values mimicked those of the colonisers was a mistaken one, and within a decade of the Constitution Act's passage into law, New Zealand was to discover just how misguided such a hope had been.

7

THOMAS GORE BROWNE'S WAITARA PURCHASE

W ITH THE NEW SYSTEM of government in place in the colony, politicians in Britain and New Zealand could reasonably expect to look forward to a long period of stability in the country – something that had been the experience in Australia and the Canadian colonies where similar constitutional developments had taken place. However, the one pivotal difference in New Zealand's case was the presence of a numerically strong indigenous people who were not prepared to yield unquestioningly to the dictates of a system of government in which they had practically no direct representation.

Yet even this political imbalance did not necessarily have to be incendiary. What made it so was the Crown's growing appetite for Maori land, which it in turn fed to incoming settlers who were eager to establish farms as soon as possible. This expanding demand for land, matched in some cases by the reluctance of Maori to sell territory to the Crown, was a potential point of friction and demanded of senior politicians and officials in the colony a heightened level of sensitivity and prudence when acquiring land.

However, despite the potentially volatile combination of circumstances that were concentrating around the Crown's acquisition of Maori land, for most of the 1850s there was no sense of apprehension about the possible consequences of such policies. Rather, Grey's comforting visions of Maori assimilation served as a palliative, reassuring the European population in New Zealand that all was

THOMAS GORE BROWNE'S WAITARA PURCHASE

well in the country and that with the assistance of the Crown the supply of Maori land would continue to flow in an uninterrupted stream into the possession of the settlers.

For at least a decade there had been one particular element in most land sales that Crown purchasers all too frequently averted their gaze from: who in a Maori community had the authority to sell tribal land? Traditionally the Maori view of land was that no one owned it; the community occupying it held the right to do so in perpetuity provided that they could defend their territory from the avarice of other communities.

This approach to land was entirely at odds with the European model; and in the early days of the colony there had been instances of confusion as the two understandings of what constituted land ownership collided. However, by the 1850s the notions of full, individual ownership and of vendors forfeiting the right to the land forever were gradually becoming recognised, if not accepted, in Maori society. Despite this, one of the problems at this time was that Maori and Europeans still had an imperfect understanding of each other; how each culture viewed land transactions applied unevenly across different parts of the country, and sometimes even within individual Maori communities.

The location from which this cultural distinction erupted into full-scale conflict was not a centre of European settlement, nor a site of strategic significance. Rather it was a small, remote, rain-swept stretch of land in the Taranaki region where a Crown purchase in 1859 turned rancid, then deadly. The place of this contentious purchase was Waitara, and the parcel of land concerned comprised a mere 600 acres.

Taranaki had already experienced hostilities between Maori and settlers, which were temporarily suppressed when on 19 August 1855 a detachment of the 58th Regiment from Auckland arrived in New Plymouth. The effect, as far as the local European population was concerned, was the desired one, with one local Maori leader watching 'in silent amazement', while another one, on seeing the soldiers disembarking, 'fled to the bush'. A reporter who was present expressed the hope that Maori would now 'be brought under the same civil restraints and responsibilities which control the rest of the community': a sort of assimilation by force.

The symptoms of rebellion may have been momentarily assuaged, but the underlying causes continued to nourish Maori resentment in the region. However, it was not as though Maori were thinking and acting as a single entity. Admittedly, many were desperate to prevent the Crown acquiring more of their territory, and some wanted land that they had already sold returned to them; but a smaller handful had even urged the Government to intervene in the region to uphold sales that had been made. And as if these factors did not complicate the situation enough, during 1856 there were skirmishes between rival hapu in the area, as previous offences were avenged and new causes for utu generated.

Such a chaotic situation made determining which Maori had the mandate to sell what land almost impossible for Crown land-purchasing agents. Yet as long as the Government could pretend that it held the military upper hand in the region (its military strength in Taranaki was still fragile), then it would be business as usual when it came to land sales.

Direct conflict with Maori was something that the Government was eager to avoid, almost at any cost. There had been previous fighting between Maori and the Crown, but it had occurred as a result of the truculent behaviour of the Ngapuhi chief Hone Heke and was eventually quashed by Crown troops with the support of hundreds of Heke's own tribesmen, led by his uncle, Tamati Waka Nene, who fought against and eventually defeated the rebel chief. Still, the financial costs had been considerable, and in political terms the then-Governor, Robert FitzRoy, had had his career severely damaged as a result of not stamping out the rebellion earlier.

What surprised some people in Taranaki – Maori and Europeans alike – was that in mid-1857 Crown agents decided to enter into negotiations with the chief Katatore, who put on offer 40,000 acres of land for sale. Katatore was regarded by some as an 'open enemy' of the European residents in parts of Taranaki, and as someone who had 'secretly planned a general massacre of the settlers'. As proof of his malevolent nature, when Rawiri, another local chief, announced his intention to sell to the Crown a disputed portion of land, Katatore 'shot him down in cold blood, unarmed'.

Some Europeans may have seen this chief as little more than a criminal and murderer, but with the tempting prospect of such a sizeable and potentially lucrative acquisition almost within reach, concerns relating to the vendor's morality easily slipped from view. However, those Taranaki chiefs who only recently worked with Katatore to create a land league as a means of forestalling further land sales were horrified by his duplicity, and they responded by ambushing and then killing him. This was an action that set in motion further rounds of revenge attacks in the region, which gave the embattled settlers even more reason to feel nervous.

With the Government pleading poverty it was left to the local European population to take responsibility for their own defence, which they did with the formation of the Taranaki Militia in February 1858. For its part, the Government responded with a small volley of legislation that aimed to achieve greater control over Maori living in Native Districts (which up until that time had enjoyed a degree of autonomy from the state).

The combination of these laws, the formation of a settler militia in Taranaki and general fatigue with the latest round of revenge attacks by factions of local Maori led to a cessation in hostilities by the close of 1858. For a few months it looked to everyone as though the storm had finally passed. In fact, it was only a lull before a much greater tempest hit the country – one whipped up by the Government's attempt to purchase the Waitara Block.

What entangled the Waitara episode with additional strands of complexity was the fact that much of the region had been part of a New Zealand Company purchase in 1839. The nature of this acquisition by the Company had been so dubious that FitzRoy had ordered the purchase examined in 1844 by one of his land commissioners, William Spain. But despite the evidence that Spain uncovered, he declared the New Zealand Company purchase valid. FitzRoy's assessment was entirely at odds with that of his official's. In 1846 he wrote that the 'substance of the case was this: the New Zealand Company's agents had endeavoured to buy a large tract of land from a few persons who owned about a thirtieth part of it, the great majority of the proprietors being then absent. When the absentees returned to their own places, after a few years, they found white men settled there and cultivating.'

FitzRoy also appreciated the consequences if the Company purchase was confirmed as legitimate: 'It appeared so clear . . . that the view taken by the land commissioner could not be adopted by the government without causing bloodshed, and the probable ruin of the settlement, – because the injustice of awarding land to the New Zealand Company, which was well known not to have been purchased by them, was apparent to every native, – that information was made known publicly at a large meeting of the settlers and natives, that the commissioner's award would not be confirmed by the governor'. It was a solution that proved unsatisfactory to all parties.

FitzRoy had devised a resolution of sorts by which settlers would be removed from the lands in question but paid compensation. It may have been a just gesture, but it upset not only the settlers concerned but also the Colonial Office, and in July 1846 the new Governor, George Grey, was instructed by the British Government to overturn FitzRoy's decision and uphold the propriety of the New Zealand Company's purchase.

Grey's edict to accept the validity of the Company acquisitions in Taranaki offered no lasting reprieve from the concerns Maori had over the way their territories had been appropriated by settlers. His decision 'quite paralysed the natives', as Land Purchase Agent Donald McLean noted, and the relationship between European and Maori in the area was only worsened by Grey's comment to one chief that if Maori did not obey his will, he would despatch a war steamer after them and destroy their canoes. Strong actions followed these strong words, with the Governor going as far as to allow European settlers effectively to become squatters on Maori land.

Grey was not oblivious to the truly scrambled mess of New Zealand Company and then Crown land acquisition in the region, and so when the chance for purchasing the Waitara Block arose, the Governor wisely side-stepped the opportunity and instead arranged for the Crown to buy land to the south at Tataraimaka.

Donald McLean, a
Government Land
Purchase Agent.

A decade later Maori sentiment on the issue had only hardened. James Richmond, the brother of Native Affairs Minister William Richmond, wrote on 6 June 1858 that the situation in Taranaki had grown 'pressing in its importance', and that it involved, 'in their fullest complexity the hardest riddles of the question [of] the contact of races & intestine quarrels', before adding in a slightly ominous tone that 'Vigorous handling of it ought to precede everything else'.

Enter Thomas Gore Browne, the stern-faced career soldier who had been appointed Governor of New Zealand in 1855. Although he initially expressed concerns about the complex issues that were knotted around the Taranaki region, he was increasingly convinced that the supremacy of British law could not be brought into question, observing threateningly in February 1858 that 'to show our teeth without biting would be imbecile'.

It was a sentiment that mirrored the feelings of many settlers in Taranaki. The same month the *Taranaki Herald* published a reader's letter which was just as defiant towards Maori: 'The time must come when the Maori will be differently ruled, when he will not be petted and coaxed and made like that most disagreeable of all animals, a spoiled child. The policy of elevating the savage and degrading the European must cease. Are we, the sons of the greatest nation of the earth, for ever to knuckle under to a parcel of savages? Or, rather, shall our rulers shew themselves possessed of that high moral courage as would make them execute judgment and justice alike upon Natives and Europeans?'

The impediment to European plans for the fertile land in Waitara was Wiremu Kingi (sometimes known by his anglicised name of William King) – the chief of the Te Ati Awa tribe for whom Taranaki was their ancestral homeland. Kingi was adamant that no more Maori land would be sold – possibly as a consequence of the misfortune that had afflicted his people in the wake of the New Zealand Company purchases in the area. By 1859 Kingi's insistence that there be no further land alienation in the Taranaki region was on a collision course with Browne's mounting intransigence on the matter.

On 11 February 1859 Kingi wrote to the Governor expressing his position on land sales, hoping to convince Browne of the rationale behind his stance. His language was deeply rooted in Maori culture, drawing on metaphors which may have seemed laboured to the Governor but which nonetheless conveyed the sentiment that lay behind Kingi's opposition to the sale of tribal land.

'These lands will not be given by us into . . . your hands', he wrote, 'lest we resemble the seabirds which perch upon a rock, when the tide flows the rock is covered by the sea, and the birds take flight for they have no resting place.' He then recited the list of previous governors to whom he had made similar pronouncements, emphasising that this was not a new message. Then, in keeping with the threatening tone of comments by so many Europeans who wrote on this matter, Kingi included a warning for his own people: if some Maori desired to sell land, then that would be the sort of action 'which causes the approach of death . . . If you hear of anyone desiring to sell land within these boundaries . . . do not pay

Sir Thomas Gore Browne,
Governor of New Zealand at
the outbreak of war in 1860.
Ref: PA2-0740. Alexander Turnbull
Library, Wellington, New Zealand.
http://beta.natlib.govt.nz/
records/23234339

any attention to it, because that land-selling system is not approved
of.' If it sounded heartfelt, it was. Kingi's father, Te Rere Ta
Whangawhanga, had specifically implored his son on his deathbed
not to sell Waitara; Kingi had no intention of violating a command
given at the point of a chief's death.

But Browne was in no mood to be dictated to by a chief, and
commenced moves to acquire the Waitara Block. At a meeting held
in Taranaki on 8 March 1859 the Native Secretary, speaking on
behalf of Browne, stated that: 'The Governor thought the Maories
would be wise to sell the land they cannot use themselves, as it would
make what they could use more valuable than the whole; but that
he never would consent to buy land without an indisputed title. He
would not permit any one to interfere in the sale of land, unless he
owned part of it; and, on the other hand, he would buy no man's

land without his consent.' At that point a (junior) Te Ati Awa chief, Teira Manuka, stood up and approached Browne. He announced that he wanted to offer the Governor a 600-acre block of land on the southern bank of the mouth of the Waitara River.

Kingi had two pa on the land in question, as well as paramount authority over its fate. Enraged by Teira's offer to Browne, he broke his silence at the meeting, saying, 'Listen, Governor. Notwithstanding Teira's offer, I will not permit the sale of Waitara to the Pakeha. Waitara is in my hands; I will not give it up. I will not. I will not. I will not.'

There the matter was left; but while Browne and his advisors contemplated their next move, a letter for the Governor dated 15 March arrived from Teira. In it the chief said, 'Friend. It is true I have given up Waitara to you; you were pleased with my words, I was pleased with your words. It is a piece of land belonging to Retimana and myself; if you are disposed to buy it, never mind if it is only sufficient for three or four tents to stand upon, let your authority settle on it, lest you should forget your child Teira.' It was the sort of written assurance that firmed the Governor's resolve.

The Assistant Native Secretary replied to Teira, confirming that 'The Governor consents to your word, that is, as regards your own individual piece, but be careful that your boundary does not encroach upon the land of any person who objects to sell; that is, let it not be included within the boundaries of that land which you publicly offered to the Governor in the presence of the Meeting held on the 8th day of March; but consent will be given to the purchase of land that belongs to yourself.' On the same day the official sent a letter off to Kingi, informing him of developments: 'Word has come from Te Teira, offering for sale his piece of land at Waitara. The Governor has consented to his word, that is as regards his own individual piece, not that which belongs to any other persons. The Governor's rule is, for each man to have the word (or say) as regards his own land; that of a man who has no claim will not be listened to.'

Browne repeated this proviso about ownership at a public meeting. Kingi had asked 'whether the resident land purchase Commissioner would be instructed to buy land from Native owners who could prove a clear right to sell, although parties having no interest in the land offered, might object to the sale'. Browne replied, 'most distinctly Yes. If you allude to William King's interference, I will not permit him to exercise his right of chieftainship for the purpose of deterring the rightful owners from selling their land, but if he should have a joint interest in any land offered for sale, his claim will receive due attention, and the land will not be purchased without his consent.'

Browne was still wavering on the issue of who possessed the right to sell the Waitara Block, but his officials seemed less bothered by considerations of right and wrong. For them, the sale had to go ahead and Kingi's objections had to be overridden. McLean sent a letter to Kingi clarifying the Government's position in a way that the chief would have unavoidably found offensive: 'Te Teira has the arrangement of his own piece [of land]. Another cannot interfere with his portions to obstruct his arrangements . . . This is a word to you. Do not you, without cause, interfere with Te Teira's . . . part.'

The purchase was temporarily put on hold in April to quell what officials thought might be a knee-jerk reaction from Taranaki Maori if the transaction proceeded immediately. But Browne was now committed to fulfilling his promise regarding the purchase, and so in August 1859 he instructed his officials to follow up on the agreement. It was not until November, however, that the wheels of government administration began to turn in Taranaki – accelerated to some degree by the fact that Teira had been bragging about the sale of 'his' land and the implicit fact that he had defied the great Wiremu Kingi.

On 12 December Browne wrote to Richmond insisting that the sale be finalised, but under the condition that the transaction take place 'when it can be done without danger of causing other troubles'. It was a vain and belated hope. Circumstances had already overtaken the chance of peace. The Crown had publicly committed itself to the purchase and would lose face by backing down. Teira had already received a guarantee that the Crown would buy his land and so had no cause to back away from the deal. Meanwhile, Kingi had staked his mana on being able to block the transaction and was about to

The main military camp at Waitara, 1860.
REF: A-032-008. ALEXANDER TURNBULL LIBRARY, WELLINGTON, NEW ZEALAND. HTTP://BETA.NATLIB.GOVT.NZ/
RECORDS/22870370

suffer the momentous indignity of seeing his will defied. Never had the prospects of war in the region been as great as they were now.

In January 1860 Teira complained to the Governor that he had still not received full payment for the land he had sold. Again the Crown was hurried into action and on this occasion commenced surveying. Kingi responded not with the expected show of force but with the opposite: he despatched elderly women from his hapu to pull out the surveyors' pegs. It was a form of what would later become known as 'passive resistance', but the effect was anything but calming. When the Executive Council met on 25 January it resolved that 'Should William King or any other native endeavor to prevent the survey, or in any way interfere with the prosecution of the work, in that case that the surveying party be protected during the whole performance of their work by an adequate Military Force under the command of the Senior Military Officer; with which view power to call out the Taranaki Militia and Volunteers and to proclaim Martial Law be transmitted to the Commanding Officer at New Plymouth.'

Martial law was imposed the following month, and soon afterwards vulnerable settlers in some of the more isolated parts of Taranaki began to gravitate towards the relative security that New Plymouth offered. Troops, armaments and other military supplies started to pour into the region in the first two weeks of March. The region was bristling with British military might and the atmosphere was stiff with tension. Kingi then occupied a pa inside the boundaries of the Waitara Block. The commander of the British troops, Colonel Charles Gold, responded by issuing a warning for Kingi and his people to evacuate the pa. Kingi refused even to receive the letter. The pa was bombarded by heavy artillery, but when the defences were finally blasted open and the British troops entered they 'were chagrined to find the pa abandoned'.

Meanwhile, Kingi's brinkmanship and his stealthy retreat from the besieged pa not only humiliated Gold but gained the chief a deluge of support from other Taranaki hapu and later from other Maori in various parts of the North Island. The scale and breadth of fighting soon escalated at a pace beyond the power of any individual to rein in: the Waikato region became the scene of even more intense combat. The conflagration affected several other areas in the country as well, and lasted until 1872, resulting in the deaths of around 2000 Maori and approximately 660 Europeans.

The bungling yet blindly defiant means by which Browne and his minions attempted to secure the Waitara purchase unleashed the most prolonged and widespread war fought in New Zealand history to that point. It also resulted in millions of acres of Maori land being confiscated or simply claimed by the Crown by right of conquest. And if the assertions of common citizenship for all stemming from the Treaty of Waitangi are to be accepted, this was also the country's only truly civil war.

8

MAORI GET THE VOTE, 1867

THE DEMAND BY THE New Zealand Government to have more control over its own structure and operation was relentless almost from the time that the 1852 Constitution Act was passed. The British Government was eventually persuaded of the need for a greater degree of autonomy in the colony and in 1857 passed the New Zealand Constitution Amendment Act, which gave the New Zealand Parliament authority to amend all but a few entrenched sections of the 1852 Act. In the administrative evolution that followed, responsibility for Maori affairs drifted from the British to the colonial government.

However, this shift to more localised authority over issues affecting Maori proved to be of little advantage for New Zealand's indigenous population. The passage of two Native Land Acts in the first half of the 1860s was part of a concerted effort by the colonial government to accelerate the process of placing Maori land under individual title. They were the prelude to a much more certain process of land alienation and also, as it happened, a setback for the unity of tribes and for the structures of authority in which they functioned. Technically speaking, Maori would be entitled to vote once they met the necessary land-owning requirements, but the process of land registration ground very slowly; as these Acts were passed during a period of war in many parts of the North Island, land registration as a prerequisite for qualifying to vote in general elections was at the bottom of the list of anyone's concerns.

The wars of the 1860s revealed another dimension to the place of Maori in the political landscape of the colony. Accompanying

Maori anxiety over the alienation of their land was a similarly acute sense that traditional tribal political authority was rapidly crumbling away. This decay had been underway since at least the early 1840s (and arguably before) but had become more noticeable by the late 1850s, resulting in a range of responses as some Maori communities attempted to grapple with complex shifts in the balance of power that were occurring in the colony.

In 1855 the Ngati Rangiwewehi chief Te Rangikaheke had expressed his doubts that the legislative process as it existed at that very early stage in the colony's self-government could ever meet the needs of Maori. 'There is no recognition of the authority of the native people,' he wrote, 'no meeting of the two authorities . . . Suggestions have been made (with a view to giving natives a share in the administration of affairs), but to what purpose? The reply is, this island has lost its independence, it is enslaved, and the chiefs with it.'

Te Rangikaheke then suggested that local tribal leaders debate whether to participate in a broader pan-tribal organisation opposing colonial rule, or to go for an alternative option which upheld 'the separate dignity and independence' of individual tribes. Most of the attempts by Maori in the early to mid-1850s to develop new political forms failed to gain momentum. They also tended to be concealed – at least from European gaze – by all the sound and fury of the wars that a succession of Maori communities fought with the Crown in the following decade.

War was the most visible and dramatic of these reactions, but it was not waged at the expense of other expressions of dissatisfaction with colonial rule and the desire for greater autonomy from government interference. One of the most significant of these – in terms of scale, influence and longevity – was the King Movement (also known as Kingitanga). The Anglican missionary John Morgan, who had followed closely the rise of Kingitanga, later reported on the reasons for the formation of this Maori political body: 'The origin of the King movement was, first, a land league to prevent the sale of land by aboriginal owners to the Government, or the private sale of such land to individuals of the European or Pakeha race; secondly, a desire to stop the rapid advance of European colonisation; thirdly, a desire to introduce a code of laws suited to their own requirements; fourthly, and chiefly, a desire to establish first in the Waikato, and afterwards gradually in all Maori districts, an independent sovereignty over all Maori and European residents in such districts.'

The reason Morgan gave for the inception of this organisation was that many Maori 'saw with fear the rapid advance of European colonisation and the earnest desire of the Pakeha to obtain possession of their lands. They also noticed what they considered the confined bounds to which some tribes who had sold land were reduced.'

However, it was not just a case of one tribe battling alone for its political sovereignty. A pan-tribal approach was believed necessary to give the King Movement even a semblance of the political strength that the Crown exercised in the colony. Those Maori who affiliated themselves with Kingitanga also aired their anxiety that 'as their own numbers were being so rapidly diminished by death, that unless European colonization could be arrested the white settlers would in a few years greatly outnumber them, and that then the Treaty of Waitangi would be set aside, and their lands seized by the English Government'.

This was the state of things in the 1850s. The outbreak of war in the following decade only intensified this feeling among some Maori (and it should be stressed there was great antipathy towards the idea of a Maori king among many tribes) that their cherished sovereignty was being sapped by the encroachments of the Crown. So ingrained had this sensation of declining power become that it became in itself an object worthy of fighting for – a fact that the colony's governments of the 1860s were not oblivious to.

In 1860 there had been a gathering of chiefs at Kohimarama in Auckland, convened by the Governor, where ideas about the role of Maori sovereignty and the authority of the Crown were debated. Further north, the early stages of what would become known as the Kotahitanga (unity) movement were underway in and around Kaikohe, as Maori there sought their own alternative to the King Movement. These and other reactions to the advent of British colonisation (including the establishment of fusion faiths such as Pai

Marire and Nakahi) were all indications that the process of Maori assimilation into the ways of the European was not only slowing but was mutating into new forms, spurred on by the desire to maintain autonomy or even independence from the Crown.

Representation in Parliament was the obvious solution to at least some of the concerns that were leading to separatist Maori bodies emerging; but as long as so few Maori met the threshold of entitlement to vote, this looked unachievable in the foreseeable future. Still, a seam of altruism continued to be tapped by some politicians who were keen that Maori not be shunted completely to the periphery of the colony's political life. Cynics later argued that the principle of power-sharing was becoming increasingly necessary 'if only to pacify Maori', although the idea of Maori representation in Parliament in the late 1860s was hardly in itself a significant force for pacification.

Yet by the mid-1860s the possibility that Maori might occupy some position in the House of Representatives was beginning to filter through the colony's Maori communities. For most it was a possibility that seemed remote and lacked allure. In 1864 James FitzGerald, Member of the House of Representatives, sought the opinion of around half a dozen chiefs on the issue of Maori representation and received letters claiming support for the initiative.

This one, from Poihipi Tukairangi, is typical: 'Friend Mr. FitzGerald, this is our word to you and your companions, that you may open the doors of the Parliament to us, the great discussion house of New Zealand, for we are members of some of the tribes of this island. Let us be ushered in, so that you may hear some of the growling of the native dogs without mouths . . . [which are currently] not allowed to have a voice in public affairs, so that eye may come in contact with eye and tooth with tooth of both Maori and European.' A few letters (many suspiciously almost identical in some phrasing) were hardly a resounding mandate with which to press ahead with the idea of Maori seats, but they were used by the Minister to further his case.

FitzGerald argued in 1865 that the status quo with respect to Maori representation was unjustified on philosophical grounds.

James Edward FitzGerald,
who served briefly as Native
Minister in 1865.

REF: 1/1-001316-F. ALEXANDER TURNBULL
LIBRARY, WELLINGTON, NEW ZEALAND. HTTP://
BETA.NATLIB.GOVT.NZ/RECORDS/22763847

'Two rules are deeply fixed in my mind,' he wrote to a colleague.
'1. To expect men to respect law who don't enjoy it is absurd.
2. To try and govern a folk by our courts and at the same time to say
that our courts shall take no cognisance of their property is amazing
folly. Two-thirds of the Northern Island is held under a tenure which
is ignored by our law. Is it possible to govern any people by a law
which does not recognise their estate in land?'

However, FitzGerald remained cautious about the precise means by
which Maori would appear in the House of Representatives. Instead
of devising an alternative himself, he guided the Native Commission
Act through Parliament in 1865. The resulting commission – made
up of a maximum of thirty-five Maori and five Europeans – was
charged with reporting to the Governor on options for Maori to be
temporarily enfranchised until such time as their land was converted
into individual title. The commission was also to recommend which
Maori ought to be made eligible to participate in elections.

99

The interruption of a general election and the subsequent change of government meant that the commission never met to report on options for Maori enfranchisement. Moreover, the goodwill shown by a few politicians towards the idea of Maori representation in Parliament in this period was continually overshadowed by an opinion from the Imperial Crown Law Office in 1859 which all but ruled out the possibility of Maori being eligible to vote unless they possessed individual title to land. The opinion had been sought by the New Zealand Parliament in 1858 at the behest of some members who felt that there needed to be a way for Maori to have their voice heard in the colony's legislature.

One of the more unusual suggestions to emerge around this time came from an Auckland member, George Graham, who proposed that Maori be granted universal male franchise (without any of the property restrictions that applied to European voters), but with the purpose of electing five European members whose task it would be to represent specifically Maori interests in the House. It was a form of proxy representation, but one which found little favour among other politicians.

It was Donald McLean (now a Member of the House of Representatives for the Napier electorate) who put his mind to this problem of a lack of Maori representation in Parliament and stitched together what he thought would serve as a makeshift solution in the short term. As far as McLean and many of his colleagues were concerned, the option of continuing to exclude Maori from Parliament – especially given the growing signs of Maori dissatisfaction with their absence from any role in governing the country – was no option at all. McLean was passionate on this issue, telling Parliament that Maori were 'a people paying taxes, and owners of three-fourths of the territory of the North Island', and on these bases alone 'they should feel that the Legislature itself was not closed against them'. The fact that the country's increasingly diminutive Maori population was paying £45,000 in tax a year was reason in itself for a formal Maori presence in Parliament.

The mid-eighteenth century slogan from the American colonies – 'no taxation without representation' – echoed loudly in this argument. Privately FitzGerald acknowledged that his views on Maori representation might lead some of his colleagues to look on him 'as a dreamer and a theorist', but this was no reason in his view to change his opinion. It was certainly a departure from the way in which almost all the world's other colonial legislatures tackled the issue of indigenous representation at this time.

The fact that Maori land was still mainly communally held should not be an obstacle to participation in elections, McLean believed – a point acknowledged in the preamble to his Bill: 'owing to the peculiar nature of the tenure of Maori land . . . the Native Aboriginal inhabitants of . . . New Zealand have heretofore with few exceptions been unable to become registered as electors or to vote at the election'. The solution 'for the better protection of the interests of Her Majesty's subjects of the native race' was for 'special representation' of Maori in the House of Representatives and the colony's Provincial Councils.

The Act allowed for Maori males aged twenty-one and over (including 'half-castes') to vote for a Maori member of the House of Representatives. Significantly, this right was conferred without the property provisions, which continued to apply to Europeans for the next twelve years. The definition of Maori, however, was jumbled in the legislation. Only full-blooded Maori could stand for election, whereas both full-blooded Maori and 'half-castes' were eligible to vote. Further potential confusion was added by the tendency to assign those with less Maori blood to the general roll. Exactly what constituted a Maori was thus made more intricate for the purpose of electing candidates to Maori seats.

The country was divided into four Maori electorates, each of which would elect one member (with the only provisos being that the elected member be male and not have a serious criminal record). The final section of the legislation made the interim nature of the Maori seats plain, with the Act continuing in force for just five years after its passage, whereafter the Maori seats would be removed.

Ostensibly the motives of McLean and his colleagues seemed noble, but the haste with which they advanced the principle of Maori representation in Parliament from idea to actuality seems unusual, at

Sir Francis Dillon Bell,
politician, fluent Maori
speaker, and advisor to
Governor Browne.
REF: 1/1-013504-G. ALEXANDER
TURNBULL LIBRARY, WELLINGTON,
NEW ZEALAND. HTTP://BETA.NATLIB.
GOVT.NZ/RECORDS/23036360

least outwardly. After all, another politician, Dillon Bell, pointed out in the debate on the Maori Representation Bill that there was little urgency for its passage because 'the Maoris would find it impossible to take part in debates'. It also appears, on the surface, that the five-year limit for the Maori population to have sufficient rights in privately owned property to put them on a par with the colony's European voters was ambitious to an unrealistic extent. Certainly, Maori showed sustained reluctance in this period for converting their land holdings to individual title, and a mere five years was unlikely to produce a profound change in that thinking.

The fact that the Native Rights Act (passed just two years before the Maori Representation Act) specified that Maori would be 'taken and deemed to be a natural-born subject of Her Majesty to all intents and purposes whatsoever', made the rush to establish Maori seats in Parliament even more inexplicable, regardless of the high degree of goodwill among some of the advocates of Maori representation in Parliament. One member of the House, Harry Atkinson, was open in his view that special representation for Maori through legislation was entirely unnecessary. It was just a matter of the passage of time – until Maori land titles had shifted from the collective to individual – that stood in the way of Maori having the same franchise as Europeans.

Another feature of the Maori Representation Act that requires a second, closer look is the number of Maori seats it brought into being. At the time that the Act passed into law, Maori would have been entitled to over twenty seats in the House of Representatives if these seats were allocated on the basis of the respective populations of Maori and Europeans in the country. When looked at from this angle, the introduction of Maori seats could be seen as a means of allowing Maori to have a presence in the House without ever being in a position to wield any influence in proportion to their numbers in the country.

In short, the Act served variously to pacify some Maori (whose cooperation with, rather than antagonism towards, the Government was undoubtedly beneficial to the country), to assist in the further assimilation of Maori, to safeguard the interests of settlers as the acquisition of Maori land continued, to undermine the strength of any separatist or independence movements, and to assuage Colonial Office concerns about the way in which the New Zealand Government had engaged in the confiscation of Maori land after 1865.

Regardless of motives, McLean maintained the line in public about the higher purpose of his initiative. With one eye firmly fixed on how posterity would record his accomplishment, he told Parliament that 'it would be a proud thing to have recorded, by the future historian of New Zealand, that the Anglo-Saxon race in this Colony had extended to its aboriginal inhabitants the highest privilege which it could confer, namely a participation in the Legislature'. Or perhaps that should have been second highest – the highest privilege being reserved for *representative* participation. The Native Department at this time treated the idea of Maori being elected to Parliament in special Maori seats as 'a matter of public relations and goodwill [rather] than a serious attempt at democratic representation', and seemed unconcerned that a Maori presence in Parliament would have any material effect on the workings of the legislature. This acknowledgement was possibly the principal factor that ensured the survival and continuation of the Maori seats long after it was envisaged by the drafters of the Act that the seats would be abolished.

Whether the seats were there to safeguard Maori interests or to serve those of Europeans is a matter open to interpretation. However, the reaction of many Maori communities to the legislation creating Maori seats was not one of unreserved enthusiasm. In 1868 the Government initiated a series of reports about the 'social and political state of the natives in various districts', which offered a first-hand account of sentiment in these settlements in the immediate wake of the creation of Maori seats. One magistrate wrote frustratedly that although Maori in his region had had the benefits of representation in Parliament explained to them in detail, the response was 'great apathy'. A magistrate in Russell noted similarly that Maori were 'utterly indifferent' to the prospects for representation.

One reason proposed for this lack of interest was that there were no immediate benefits from having a member in the House; to which was added the observation by a magistrate at Maketu that if each tribe had their own representative, there might be more interest. But as they stood, the Maori electorates were pan-tribal constructs which (to some extent ironically) eroded further traditional tribal-based authority in favour of new forms of Maori power, and excited 'the usual tribal jealousy'. As another observer put it, Maori 'do not understand how a Native of one tribe can represent another tribe'. A degree of pessimism about Maori politicians struggling with their English was also raised as a potential concern, and contributed to muted interest generally in the usefulness of the Maori seats.

In their early years of existence, more lustre was removed from the Maori seats by the fact that many of the elected members 'lacked the political acumen or the verbal skills to influence the outcome of legislation pertaining to the Maori race'. It was not until the turn of the twentieth century that a new generation of articulate and educated Maori entered the House of Representatives.

However, despite the flat reception that the Act received in many Maori communities, in 1872 the legislation was amended to extend the temporary five-year timeframe for the existence of the seats for a further five years. In 1876 the seats were made a permanent fixture, until such time as the General Assembly saw fit to remove them. There were occasional mumblings of dissent from some politicians in the early years of the twentieth century about the existence of the seats – including a suggestion from Sir James Carroll that the seats be abolished altogether – but the arguments in favour of removing the seats were overcome by those in favour of their retention, and the Maori seats consequently survived the crucial early decades of their existence and became an established part of New Zealand parliaments. While some politicians insisted that the franchise was being granted to 'a people utterly unable to appreciate it . . . and who were totally incapable of legislating either for themselves or others', over time the Maori members showed that they were a crucial voice for Maori in Parliament.

Given that Pakeha representation in the government of the country was just over a decade old, the inclusion of four Maori seats in the House of Representatives was a comparatively early initiative in the nation's constitutional history. And for all the convoluted motives behind the legislation, the fact that a Maori voice could be heard in the main legislative organ of the state was a crucial innovation which looked back to the commitments made in the Treaty of Waitangi and forward to the continued role of Maori in the running of the country.

In extending the initial five-year duration of the Maori seats that the Act prescribed, the Government tacitly acknowledged that the assimilationist project was not going to succeed to its fullest extent – that a distinct Maori voice would remain in the country's body politic. The belief that Maori and settlers constituted 'one harmonious union . . . and were rapidly and invisibly forming but one people' was increasingly looking like little more than wishful thinking – especially as the wars between these two peoples continued to scar the country during the 1860s.

The Maori Representation Act may have been, as Premier Edward Stafford suggested, a device to 'elevate the condition of the Maoris and to induce them to live in harmony with European institutions', but to the same extent it guaranteed a Maori perspective in Parliament, one which continued to be heard a century and a half later. There were still discrepancies in the legislation, including the fact that until 1937 there was no secret ballot, with voters in the Maori electorates going to polling stations in elections and showing support by a show of hands. However, the principle of a reserved place for Maori in Parliament persisted and gradually became an accepted and even lauded (although never universally so) part of the nation's democratic system.

9

WOMEN GET THE VOTE, 1893

Some classes are born to political power, some achieve it, and some have it thrust upon them. The last has been the lot of most, though not all, women in the three colonies and Commonwealth, where their sex may now vote to elect Members of Parliament.

—William Pember Reeves, *State Experiments in Australia and New Zealand*, vol. 1, 1902, p103.

We the mothers of the present, need to impress upon our children's mind how the women of the past wrestled and fought, suffered and wept, prayed and believed, agonised and won for them the freedom they enjoy today.

—Kate Sheppard, in P. R. Fogarty, 'The Shrieking Sisterhood', 1988, p. 9.

ALCOHOL, WOMEN'S RIGHTS AND politics. These three seemingly disparate areas of concern became attached to each other in New Zealand in a much more concerted way from the 1870s. In the case of the various temperance movements that either sprang up or experienced rejuvenation during this decade, women played an increasingly dominant role and were actively recruited, partly for their perceived status in society as being 'pure and holy/ Like the heroines of old', as one melodramatic recruitment appeal by a temperance society put it in 1877.

The previous year one of the country's principal temperance publications, *The Liberator*, argued for the prominent role of women in the fight against alcohol. 'There is another sphere for which women are more highly fitted than men, in which honour would rebound to themselves, and incalculable benefit for those for whom they might labour. We refer to the great work of temperance reform.' Women were sought in this field of activity because they were presumed (mainly by men) to be more effective at 'moral suasion'. In return, women were granted significant roles in the temperance movements that proliferated during the 1870s and 1880s, including the right to vote in society elections, stand for committees and even hold leadership positions. It may not yet have been full equality, but these anti-alcohol organisations afforded New Zealand women rights that were generally denied to them in most other institutions of society.

It might seem as though the temperance movements were little more than social clubs or glorified lobby groups – churning out tracts on abstinence, holding meetings and engaging in a fair amount of singing – but their commitment was to action as well as words. In Christchurch in December 1878, for example, a speaker at a temperance meeting told his audience that 'there was one nasty drinking shop in that borough which the ladies intended to shut up after the style of their "brave American sisters". The statement was received with loud cheers.' This was hardly some cosy tea-group meeting in a church hall. There is a strain of strong moral indignation that comes through such statements. Throughout the country, women were taking part in similar organisations committed to curtailing the evils of alcohol.

However, women were still not equal with their male counterparts, especially at the highest echelons of the various temperance movements. The strictures of gender, which were bound so tightly in Victorian society, were only just starting to be loosened, and men still dominated every aspect of public life, regardless of whatever cause was involved.

It may have been because of the stubborn insistence of men that they take the controlling positions in the various temperance movements that from the 1880s efforts were made by some women to form their own temperance organisations. One of the sources of inspiration for this was the Women's Christian Temperance Union (WCTU), which had been founded in the United States in 1873. The WCTU 'linked the religious and the secular through concerted and far-reaching reform strategies based on applied Christianity', and in the 1880s sent emissaries to New Zealand where there was a receptive audience for its message. One of the most influential of these was Mary Clement Leavitt, who 'left a far deeper and more lasting impression than any who preceded her'.

It seemed that New Zealand could not get enough of the American prohibitionist, as one newspaper noted in May 1885: 'The thronged appearance of the Baptist Church, Oxford Terrace, last night showed very conclusively that the interest taken by the public in the addresses of Mrs Mary Clement Leavitt is by no means abating.' In inaugurating the New Zealand branch of the WCTU, Leavitt ended up making 'one of the biggest contributions that have yet been made to rid New Zealand of the blight of the liquor traffic . . . the year 1885 marked the beginning of the women's march to victory under the banner of the W.C.T.U.' By the following year the New Zealand WCTU had fifteen branches throughout the country, with a total membership of 528 women.

The banner-waving, hymn-singing, crusading spirit of the WCTU was all undoubtedly uplifting for its members, but what helped propel the work of the WCTU during its fledgling period in New Zealand was its cooperation with (rather than independence from) other temperance groups in the country. In 1886 the New Zealand Alliance was formed – a body that united a diverse set of temperance movements 'for the purpose of securing, first of all, such an alteration of the law as would furnish the people with the power, by direct vote, to determine whether the liquor traffic should or should not exist, and then, when such power was secured, to induce the people to use their power of voting to bring the liquor traffic to an end'.

Moral improvement by earnest appeals to the public could only go so far, though. What the New Zealand Alliance perceived as vital was the role of legislation in changing the way society saw the evils of alcohol. A manifesto was assembled, with its objects being: 'The abolition and prohibition of the liquor traffic in New Zealand by the direct vote of the people; . . .To obtain from Parliament such legislation as will give to the people absolute power over the liquor traffic; To secure the return to Parliament of such candidates, irrespective of party, as will support these objects; To educate the people to exercise to their fullest extent such powers of Prohibition as the law at present allows, and to demand the completion of these powers as aforesaid; To promote all these objects by public meetings, lectures, the circulation of literature, and the organization of all persons favourable to such objects.'

Yet despite the fact that a significant proportion of the New Zealand Alliance's membership was comprised of women (some of whom were in leadership positions), many were still to be found 'at their old post in the kitchen, and we find that the Annual Public Tea at which two hundred people sat down was provided by the W.C.T.U. All along, the Union has assisted its big brother the Alliance by providing teas at local and general meetings, suppers at socials, as well as lunches at Area Councils.'

The WCTU still operated with some autonomy, partly because it was an all-woman organisation and partly because of the social circumstances in the colony at the time. The Victorian values of the era throughout the Western world were centred on family, decency, thrift, piety and sobriety, and yet in New Zealand, society appeared to face a threat to these values, particularly from the consequences of the abuse of alcohol by men. If male culture was undermining social values, then it followed that women needed to rectify the situation. And women were best placed to achieve this; as one historian put it: 'immediate steps had to be taken to ensure that respectability and morality were made the keystones of society and women were seen as the most effective agents to enact this policy'.

The reason for this faith in women was that they had always been seen in New Zealand as 'morally superior to men . . . Man's strength was physical, woman's moral, and both were equally essential for the development of the country's character.' And going against the later stereotype of the conservatism of the churches in the nineteenth

Kate Sheppard, a leading campaigner
for women to have the right to vote.
REF: PUBL-0089-1914-001. ALEXANDER TURNBULL
LIBRARY, WELLINGTON, NEW ZEALAND. HTTP://BETA.
NATLIB.GOVT.NZ/RECORDS/23087309

century, most of the Protestant denominations in New Zealand were
firm advocates of female suffrage and actively supported the WCTU
in its campaigns leading up to 1893.

By the late 1870s, harnessing the moral values held by the colony's
women and converting them into hard political currency was
increasingly coming to be seen by the WCTU (and indeed by other
temperance organisations) as the best way to get legislation passed
that would dent the prevalence of alcohol in society. In 1887 one
small step towards this goal was taken when the WCTU appointed
Kate Sheppard as Franchise Superintendent for New Zealand.

Sheppard appreciated from the outset that such a monumental
change to the way the country chose its governments could not
be made without the backing of politicians. Her preference was
to work in conjunction with supporters from within the House of

111

Representatives rather than batter politicians from the outside with petitions and protests. However, Sheppard did not vest all her faith with those members who were sympathetic to female suffrage. She also plunged her energies into making the WCTU's message of the right of women to have the vote a nation-wide cause.

The initial campaign led to Premier John Ballance supporting a reform to the electoral laws in 1892 in favour of allowing women to vote (although still prohibiting them from standing for Parliament). Despite being personally opposed to this half-measure, Sheppard wisely supported Ballance's initiative, seeing it as an important step in the right direction. And to keep the momentum going, Sheppard began organising petitions in order to appeal to the instinct for popular support that was central to politicians' careers. At first, these were unsuccessful, despite an 1892 petition getting 20,000 signatures. However, the 1893 'monster petition', as it was known, reached the target set by Sheppard of 30,000 names – by far the biggest petition in the country's history to that time.

With great pomp and ceremony, the petition was presented to Sir John Hall, one of the firmest supporters in Parliament of the suffragette cause. Hall brought the scrolled document into the debating chamber and unfurled it down the centre aisle 'until it hit the end wall with a thud'. Yet despite the growing popular support for women's franchise, the Bill was defeated. Accusations were made by the suffragette lobby that the Bill's defeat was due to politicians being influenced by 'traffickers in strong drink', before suggesting that 'If the choice has to be made between the rights of women and the selfish interests of the Liquor party, we have no fear of the ultimate result.'

Despite the petitions and the campaigning by the WCTU, there was still uncertainty in some quarters about the value of giving women the vote. There were doubts, for example, about the social effects of female suffrage, and questions were raised over whether women even desired the vote. For their part, campaigners for women's suffrage were hardly revolutionary in their outlook. 'No one asserts that the suffrage is to be the panacea for all women's ills,' wrote one anonymous suffragette in 1887, 'but that it would lead to

Premier Richard John Seddon,
who initially opposed but
eventually supported women's
right to vote.
REF: 1/2-029365-F. ALEXANDER TURNBULL
LIBRARY, WELLINGTON, NEW ZEALAND. HTTP://
BETA.NATLIB.GOVT.NZ/RECORDS/23087295

greater independence, raise her in popular estimation, and give her a
chance at least of a hearing in her own behalf is undeniable.'

One of the leading opponents of the Bill was Richard John Seddon,
who became Premier in April 1893 following Ballance's death. When
it came to the subject of voting rights for women, Seddon had made
his views plain seven years earlier. 'I say,' he pronounced, 'if you
give too much power you unsex women . . . if we had a number of
good sensible ladies in the House . . . they would wonder why it was
we wasted so much time in trying to give them power they do not
want.'

However, on succeeding Ballance, Seddon felt 'duty bound' to
support the proposed legislation of his predecessor giving women
the vote, even though his personal views on the issue had not shifted
(as was revealed by his expressed dismay when the legislation was
finally passed in the Legislative Council). Indeed, Seddon's previous
ambivalence about women's franchise was such that Sheppard
considered making a direct appeal to him to elicit his support. Hall
advised against the suggestion, however. In May 1893 he wrote

to Sheppard, revealing the Premier's private position on the issue in an extraordinarily candid letter: 'He [Seddon] really wants to defeat women's suffrage, and he is very cunning. There is no way of knowing which way he might turn or twist anything you say to him. Everything depends on whether the Legislative Council will recede from the position they took up last year. If they do not they will give Mr Seddon a weapon with which he will kill the franchise.'

Seddon, for his part, seemed to be coming around to the idea of women's franchise. But Sheppard's fear was that with an election looming in November 1893, the majority in the House favouring the necessary change in law would be reduced. Work on the 'monster petition' quickened from this time as Sheppard saw it as one of the best means of leveraging support from those politicians who were still undecided on the issue.

On 28 June 1893 the Electoral Bill was introduced into the House, and after its second reading was discussed in committee. One member attempted to introduce an amendment to the Bill, calling for a referendum on women's suffrage to be held at the same time as the 1893 general election, but the proposal was resoundingly defeated.

Opponents of the Bill suspected that they were in a minority, so they clung to the hope that the Legislative Council would reject it. One of the most vocal critics in the House of Representatives of women's franchise, Henry Fish, was reasonably confident (outwardly at least) that the measure would not advance much further: 'Only the old members but also the new members will rise to the occasion, and will give this measure the happy despatch which it deserves.'

When it came to the vote on the final reading of the Bill in the House of Representatives, the atmosphere was tense. The public gallery was full, and among the members, 'all sorts of rumours were flying round . . . No one seemed to know how the division would go.' One journalist noted that 'intense expectation was depicted on every countenance', but once the vote had been counted, there was 'quite a sensation'. The elation was palpable.

Numbers in the House of Representatives may have been weighed in favour of the Bill, but the Legislative Council was more evenly divided. One of its members, the freshly knighted Sir Patrick Buckley, gave voice to a sentiment that was probably still quite common around the country at the time: 'I hold, and hold with very great earnestness, that woman's proper place is not in the work of politics – that her proper place is in the domestic circle. I have too much respect for her to drag her into politics and place her on the husting.' However, such feigned 'respect' for women ultimately failed to convince a majority of the Legislative Council to reject the Bill.

A week before the Bill's passage into law, a petition was submitted to the colony's Governor, Lord Glasgow, by opponents of the proposed legislation. The petition's organisers urged the Governor not to give his assent to the Electoral Bill on the basis that it somehow ignored the rights of others in the colony, that the majority of the settlers of both sexes were allegedly opposed to the measure, and that voters had been given no opportunity to express their opinion on the subject. A newspaper noted that this petition was being 'numerously signed', but it was a case of too little too late, and the supposedly significant opposition to the Bill failed to materialise.

All that remained was for the Governor to assent to the legislation for it to become law. However, some opponents to the idea of women voting and even standing for Parliament were still unwilling to accept that the battle had been lost. On 7 September Glasgow received a telegram from an Arthur McDonald in a last-ditch effort to have the Bill quashed. 'Unbounded indignation here at the woman's franchise clause Electoral Bill,' the telegram began, before getting to the nub of the argument. 'We sincerely hope you will refuse assent . . . The country is now taken unawares.'

The following day the Governor received a more serious protest signed by eighteen members of the Legislative Council, similarly urging Glasgow to withhold his assent, claiming that the timing of the passage of the Electoral Bill constituted a 'political and social revolution', which had 'not been submitted to the electors for their decision on the subject'. Specifically, they alleged that the Bill could have serious financial implications and that the majority of both sexes in the colony were opposed to it (although for this claim there was no supporting evidence provided). The opposing councillors recommended to Glasgow that the matter be given directly to

Supplement to the New Zealand Times.   December 2, 1893.

OUR CARTOONS NO. X.

THE RESULT OF THE DOSE; LIBERALS, 54; CONSERVATIVES, 14!!
IT DID HIM GOOD!!!

A cartoon from 1893, with Young New Zealand reluctantly being fed a dose of 'Women's Vote'.

REF: A-225-020. ALEXANDER TURNBULL LIBRARY, WELLINGTON, NEW ZEALAND. HTTP://BETA.NATLIB.GOVT.NZ/ RECORDS/23122935

the voters for a decision. Not wishing for the suffrage campaign to be jeopardised at the last moment, Sheppard also wrote to the Governor, addressing the objections raised by some of the Legislative Councillors.

Ultimately such arguments were the domain of the Legislative Council, rather than providing the basis of appeals to the Governor to obstruct the accepted conventions of the legislative process. Glasgow therefore dismissed the final faltering bursts of opposition and on 19 September 1893 signed the new Electoral Act into law.

The right for women to vote in general elections was included in the legislation in the most perfunctory way: '"person" includes women'.

It was not a total victory for women, though. Section 9 of the Act made it clear that 'No woman, although duly registered as an elector, shall be capable of being nominated as a candidate, or of being elected a member of the House of Representatives, or of being appointed to the Legislative Council; and every nomination-paper of a woman as a candidate shall be absolutely void and of no effect, and shall be rejected by the Returning Officer without question.' It would be another twenty-six years before women could stand for Parliament, and it was not until 1933 – forty years after the passage of the Electoral Act – that the first woman (Elizabeth McCombs) was elected to the House of Representatives.

It would be naive to assume that the passage of the Act somehow removed the patronising way in which women were often portrayed. Almost a decade after New Zealand women won the right to vote in general elections, William Pember Reeves, who had been a minister in the Liberal Government in the 1890s, described the change in the law in what even for the time must have seemed a slightly patriarchal manner: 'So, one fine morning of September 1893, the women of New Zealand woke up and found themselves enfranchised. The privilege was theirs – given freely and spontaneously, in the easiest and most unexpected manner in the world, by male politicians.'

And as if this was not enough condescension, Reeves dished out some more, explaining to his readers that prior to the campaign for voting rights, 'women knew nothing of public life . . . They were as unprepared for the exercise of their novel right as any newly enfranchised class could be.' Finally, according to Reeves, every effort was made by male politicians and officials in 1893 to 'smooth the way' to enable women to vote. Clearly, the image of the helpless woman requiring male assistance was still firmly lodged in some minds, even if it went against how events actually played out.

What made this development so significant on the international stage was that it was not part of some global trend at the time. It was a pioneering internal initiative, in which New Zealand women made the nation a world leader in this final major advance in Western democracy. By 1900 women had gained the franchise in fewer than 1 per cent of the world's countries, and twenty years after New Zealand women got the right to vote, just seventeen other nations had introduced similar rights for their female populations. No wonder one newspaper described the passage of the Bill as 'the most important Parliamentary event in the history of New Zealand'. Moreover, New Zealand was the only British colony at this time in which universal suffrage for women included the indigenous female population as well as that of the settlers, although as the Maori women's vote would be confined to the four Maori electorates, their influence would be minimised – as it was for their male counterparts.

The legislation served as a platform from which the embryonic feminist movement grew. It ushered in the New Woman – a concept that Anna Stout (a founding member of the WCTU and wife of former Premier Robert Stout) explained just two years after the Electoral Act had come into effect: 'New Women wish to have the right to be educated physically, mentally and morally, so as to be able to live their own lives and support themselves without the degrading necessity of accepting a home at some man's pleasure without love or sympathy, or mutual desires and aims.'

It was a radical departure from how some of the colony's more traditional residents probably viewed marriage. And it did not stop there. Stout continued with what at the time was a strident position: 'We realise our responsibilities, and expect and demand that men will do the same, or we decline to enter the marriage bonds with them. We believe in marriage but not marriage where one is to be allowed freedom and liberty, and the other to bow perhaps to an inferior mind. Equality is necessary to perfect harmony.' Such ideals and the measures that followed in the ensuing century to advance the rights of women in society could all be traced back directly to the right to vote that New Zealand women won in 1893.

10

RECOVERY OF THE MAORI RACE

FEW FATES IN a nation's history can be as horrendous as the prospect of an entire ethnic group disappearing. When a group goes from being a majority in a country to almost disappearing within the span of one lifetime, the calamity is magnified. Such rapid decline – whether by design or circumstance or some combination of the two – constitutes a national crisis. Yet judging by the reactions of some Europeans at the time, the descent of Maori towards disappearance at the close of the nineteenth century was hardly treated as a catastrophe.

The reversal of the trend towards oblivion, which in demographic terms occurred at the very last moment, proved to be revolutionary for the country. An entire people was rescued, and the social and cultural landscape of the country thereafter was profoundly different as a result.

But how did it reach the point where a whole people, who were a majority in New Zealand at the start of the 1850s, almost disappeared by the 1890s? And how did this population manage to recover just as it was teetering on the precipice of extinction? The answer to the first part of the question involves a variety of explanations that are interconnected to a greater or lesser extent with each other. However, it is useful first to establish the 'starting point' of the decline, and trace some of the salient peaks along the way.

The time at which the Maori population was at its highest is subject to speculation, but it would be reasonable to assume that at the close of the eighteenth century, numbers were somewhere around 150,000 or even more. John Nicholas, who visited the country in 1814 and 1815, estimated the number of Maori to be 150,000, while the Reverend William Yate put the figure for the North Island alone at 160,000 in 1835 (as for the South Island, he conceded that 'we have hitherto had no means of ascertaining; but it is believed that the population there is very small, and thinly scattered over an immense tract of country'). The same year, the Reverend William Williams testified that the country's indigenous population was 200,000, although one observer suggested that this estimation was on the conservative side.

What all these figures reveal is that there was great uncertainty about the approximate number of Maori in the country, to the extent that even an average of the estimates would not necessarily make the resulting figure any more probable. However, by the second half of the 1830s, there was a sense in the country that the peak of the Maori population had already passed. In June 1837 Busby wrote to his superiors in Sydney, referring to the 'rapid disappearance' of Maori. The Resident was one of the first Europeans to acknowledge that this decline was the result of several factors: 'The introduction of firearms is alleged as one cause, but there seems good reason to doubt whether their wars were less sanguinary before firearms were introduced. The use of intoxicating liquors and tobacco are less questionable evils and, though their direct influence cannot, I think, be stated as at all remarkable, they are, in all probability, the original causes of diseases with which their immediate connection is not apparent. Venereal diseases are another means of undermining the constitution of the multitudes who, in one shape or other, are subjected to them.'

Even those Maori who were living under the guidance of missionaries were being 'swept off in a ratio which promises, at no very distant period, to leave the country destitute of a single aboriginal inhabitant', Busby continued. The consequence of all this death was a growing sense of fatalism. According to Busby, some Maori had reached the conclusion that 'the God of the English is removing the aboriginal inhabitants to make room for them; and

120

it appears to me that this impression has produced amongst them a very general recklessness and indifference to life'.

Prior to the 1870s the stages in the decline of the Maori population were more readily apparent. The conflicts of the 1820s and early 1830s – known collectively as the Musket Wars – produced a death toll of perhaps between 20,000 and 60,000 Maori. To this was added the ravages of diseases, for which Maori society had developed no natural resistance. In the 1830s, for example, about half of the Maori population of the South Island was wiped out by measles.

By the 1840s Maori probably numbered about 120,000, which represented a drop from the previous total, attributable mainly to disease and war. But while the Maori economy recovered and prospered in the following decade, the population did not. The reorganisation of some communities along more commercial lines, the accelerating rate of land loss and the ongoing effects of disease all conspired to bring about a further decrease in the Maori population.

If there was any doubt that the Maori population was still waning, the 1858 Census results cleared that up. The number of Maori was listed as 56,049 (although the figure was possibly lower than the actual number due to problems with enumeration). In reporting this figure to the Secretary of State for Colonies in 1868, the Governor, Sir George Bowen, quoted the former Premier William Fox on the reasons for this plummeting population: 'The one great cause of this has been, and is, their utter disregard of all those social and sanitary conditions which are essential to the continuing vitality of the human race. The result is, the constitution of the Maori is absolutely decayed, and they do not produce children to replace the current generation of adults. A people that has no children must die out.' Any faint chance that this decline could be arrested was dashed with the onset of the wars of the 1860s, which engulfed so much of the North Island and consigned around 2250 Maori to an early death (a figure which includes 250 so-called 'friendly Maori').

Thereafter the demographic rot set in. Although still beset with problems of accuracy in the collection and collation of data, the 1881 Census showed a total Maori population of 43,973. By the time of the next Census, in 1886, this figure had dropped by almost 5.8 per cent to 41,432.

Well into the twentieth century the decline of the Maori population towards its supposed terminal phase was attributed in varying degrees to a form of mental malaise that allegedly afflicted the population as a consequence of living through the wars in the 1860s. 'The effect upon the life and mind of the Maori people of this ten years' struggle . . . was profound,' wrote Ivan Sutherland, one of the preeminent European scholars on Maori society, in 1935. 'The disastrous consequences of the war were not only a matter of those killed, nor only one of material loss. Its psychological effects were even more important and far reaching . . . They had suffered not only outward, but what was more serious, inner defeat as well. The *mana* Maori was destroyed . . . In a fatalistic mood, and in terms of their old magico-religious beliefs the people now felt they could never regain physical, intellectual or spiritual vigour . . . This mental attitude had a profound effect on the Maori . . . Through subtle interrelations of mind and body in a people of strongly imaginative and suggestive temperament it led to physical deterioration and affected birthrate and numbers.'

The suggestion that this atmosphere of doom contributed to such sudden drops in population has little evidentiary foundation to support it, however. The more obvious explanations all seemed to have their roots in one issue in particular: the loss of land at the hands of the Crown and its agencies – a point acknowledged by one politician when speaking on the matter in 1885: 'I believe we could not find a more ingenious method of destroying the whole Maori race than by these Courts. The Natives come from the villages of the interior, and have to hang about for months in our centres of population . . . They are brought into contact with the lowest classes of society, and are exposed to temptation and the result is a great number contract diseases and die . . . Some little time ago I was taking a ride through the interior and I was perfectly astonished at hearing that a subject of conversation at each hapu I visited was the number of natives dying in consequence of attendance at the Native Land Court at Wanganui.'

The ongoing cause of Maori depopulation was comparatively easily diagnosed. Yet the attitude of some Europeans towards the dwindling number of Maori in New Zealand was often nothing short of callous. The notion of a 'dying race' took hold and soon became received wisdom. As early as 1854 one visitor to the country observed that 'the Maories, as such, are disappearing. Those whom their own depopulating wars have left surviving, are dying very rapidly away. The number of the children is small; they do not replace their fathers . . . Whether the decree is irrevocable; whether the finger of time can go back upon the dial, and the past can be so far recovered as to give this race yet a chance of prolonged existence, is a question which the experience of the next few years will enable us to answer.'

The answer, when it came, was in the form of a succession of self-fulfilling prophecies. Writer after writer predicted the end of the Maori race – some with a clinical sense of scientific detachment and others with a barely veiled sense of relish. In 1881 Alfred Newman, a doctor and part-time ethnologist, prepared a paper entitled 'the Causes Leading to the Extinction of Maori', and assessed that on balance 'the disappearance of the race is scarcely subject for much regret. They [Maori] are dying out in a quick, easy way, and are being supplanted by a superior race.'

But rather than rush to rescue this beleaguered people, a handful of Europeans assumed the stance of spectators looking on at an anthropological curiosity. The naturalist Walter Buller wrote in 1884 how the 'Maori race was dying out very rapidly', and estimated that in another twenty years there would be only a 'remnant' left. Rather than offer any remedy, though, Buller proposed that the balm of European compassion instead be applied. He recommended that the Government in particular, and European New Zealanders generally, 'smooth down their [the Maori] pillow. Then history will have nothing to reproach us with.'

The turning point in this decline came in the last decade of the nineteenth century, when the statistics were at their grimmest. In the 1891 Census the Maori population was calculated to have dropped to 41,303 people, which was troubling enough, but the 1896 figure

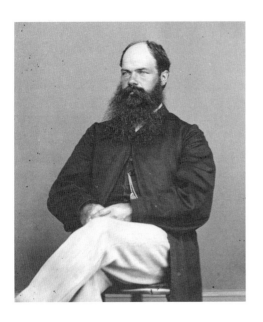

Walter Lawry Buller, who in 1884 predicted the imminent demise of Maori.
REF: 1/4-004505-G. ALEXANDER TURNBULL LIBRARY, WELLINGTON, NEW ZEALAND. HTTP:// BETA.NATLIB.GOVT.NZ/RECORDS/22845639

was even more bleak. According to the official count, the number of Maori living in the country had sunk to a mere 39,805. Surely there was now no hope of a recovery.

However, one demographer has noted that there was a 'slow increase' in the Maori population between 1891 and 1901 of around 0.6 per cent. It was barely discernible in the official figures, but from the benefit of hindsight, it represents the period when the Maori population hauled itself from the brink of extinction. Yet the signs of a recovery, though admittedly barely noticeable at this time, were not enough to reverse the tide of pessimism that seemed to swamp just about every analysis of the issue in this period.

Henry Hill, who described himself as an 'educationalist', wrote a paper in 1902 in which he surveyed and summarised the works of others in the field of Maori demographics. Entitled 'The Maoris To-day and To-morrow', his review of the existing literature on the topic concluded that 'the interest in the native race to-day is mainly centred in the question of their probable continuance as a people and a nation . . . the question has more than once been discussed as to whether the Maori race is doomed to disappear before the advancing strides of civilised Saxondom'. Given Hill's commitment to accuracy, it is surprising that he failed to register the significance of the Census figures. Instead, they were dismissed as an aberration to what all informed Saxons knew was a fatal depletion in the number of Maori. The race was clearly dying. All that remained was to undertake a demographic autopsy on its causes and consequences.

Maori women came in for special attention for their alleged role in the falling population. One government official reported that 'Unfortunately, the [Maori] women, not being trained to a satisfactory condition of domestic economy, gradually tire of the restraint of keeping a home clean, neat, and in pakeha style, and eventually find it so irksome as to warrant falling back into the free-and-easy style of living pursued by their forefathers.' It was the sort of view that relied on dredging up earlier stereotypes about Maori and then attributing low birth rates to them. Hill was fully supportive of such a position. 'There is hardly a more pitiful sight,' he wrote, 'than the Maori woman, ambitionless, homeless though not houseless, indifferent to opinion, to responsibility, to home. To gossip, to smoke, and while away the time in frivolous conversation . . . and apparently without the ambition to have her surroundings improved.'

'The Maori has lost heart and abandoned hope,' was the verdict of the Reverend Philip Walsh in 1907. His fatalistic conclusion was that the Maori race was 'sick unto death, and is already potentially dead', and made references to how Maori purportedly anticipated 'with a fatal resignation . . . the final extinction of their race'.

Even attempts at assimilation by Maori were deemed a failure by Walsh, as they had 'largely contributed to the decay of the Maori, and that which under other conditions might have been a blessing has only proved a curse. This is nowhere more apparent than in the case of their housing . . . The Maori's attempt to live like the *pakeha* is generally a failure.'

Maori housing was indeed often substandard in this period, and examples of it were not hard to find. One doctor came across a sleeping house of about sixteen square metres which contained 'twenty individuals of both sexes and all ages' squeezed into every corner, giving as much breathing space 'as would be afforded by a comfortable full-sized coffin'. In some Maori settlements, wells were dug near toilet facilities, turning what ought to be drinking water into 'nothing more than an imperfectly filtered disease producing liquid'.

Epidemics such as measles continued to afflict some Maori communities, as did tuberculosis. The housing conditions were sometimes atrocious, although in many settlements the link between poor housing and sanitation and the onset of disease was not immediately apparent to the occupants. However, instead of any consideration of the consequences of massive land loss or the impact of disease in the preceding decades, the blame for Maori depopulation was being placed firmly at the feet of Maori themselves. The demise they awaited was one apparently of their own creation.

The statistics were at last beginning to tell a different story. Like a thin ray of light piercing the gloom, the 1901 Census revealed that the Maori population had grown from a low of 39,805 five years earlier to 43,101. Not only was this a significant turnaround in a downward trend that had been evident for almost a century, it would prove to be the start of a sustained reversal. A decade later, the number of Maori had risen to 49,350, establishing a pattern of population growth that was to last for the rest of the century and into the following one.

There was no single factor that enabled this recovery to occur, however. Rather, it was a concoction of several developments which arrested the decline in the Maori population within a relatively short space of time.

The creation of the Department of Public Health was one of the initiatives which had a direct bearing on the health of Maori communities. Fears of a plague epidemic had led to the creation of the department, but its orbit of activity quickly expanded into more general areas of public health, including Maori health. One of the crucial innovations that were introduced by the department was for the health issues affecting Maori communities to be addressed wherever possible by Maori themselves. A 1901 report by the country's Chief Health Officer revealed how this worked in practice. Maori in some communities 'were invited to *korero*, at which sanitation was the chief topic'. The response to these meetings was

126

Dr Maui Pomare, who was instrumental in guiding the recovery of the Maori population.
REF: 1/1-014581-G. ALEXANDER TURNBULL LIBRARY, WELLINGTON, NEW ZEALAND. HTTP:// BETA.NATLIB.GOVT.NZ/RECORDS/23176239

so positive that the department decided 'to continue the work of physical salvation amongst the natives'.

Another crucial development was the appointment of Dr Maui Pomare, a Maori medical doctor, as Health Commissioner for Maori throughout the country. His duties would include visiting Maori settlements, assessing their general health and making recommendations regarding sanitation and water supply. His visits were 'received with open arms and enthusiasm'. Being Maori, he was able to talk to his compatriots and 'enter into their thoughts and minds', and to 'view objects from the native point of view'.

The appointment of a Maori Health Commissioner was not a cure in itself. According to the department, changes in attitudes in Maori society were still needed. Poor clothing, an unwillingness for cultural reasons to burn anything with blood on it, and generally unhygienic practices continued to retard efforts to improve the health of some Maori communities. From the 'old crone coughing up millions of bacilli, which she distributes impartially over all parts of the whare', to 'indolence and laziness' which was 'undoubtedly productive of much poverty and consequent sickness', there was still much to overcome if the population was to be saved. Reforms in housing and sanitation were seen as the next stage in improving the health conditions in Maori communities.

Under the 1900 Public Health Act, the Government could declare a Maori settlement a 'special district'. Each district would have a Health Committee of between six and twelve people elected by the residents of the settlement (or failing that, by the Governor) to devise and enforce sanitary rules for the settlement. The emphasis was on the prevention of disease rather than on the cure, which, given the comparatively limited extent of medical knowledge at the turn of the twentieth century, represented an important advance for these communities.

The work of the Native Health Officers continued to be a crucial factor in the recovery of the Maori population in this period. As examples of their efficacy, during visits between 1900 and 1903 to a number of Maori settlements they variously ordered the burning of rubbish and of dwellings that were too filthy to be cleaned, shifted some houses to drier sites, instructed communities on hygiene, investigated outbreaks of disease, and organised for the treatment of the sick.

The creation and growth of a Maori nurse scheme in the first decade of the twentieth century also made a substantial contribution to the eventual growth of the population. The resulting Native Health Nurse service suffered from a constant shortage of supply to meet the demand of Maori communities – something which itself was an indicator of the success of the scheme. European as well as Maori nurses worked for the scheme, and although there was sometimes a degree of suspicion about these arrivals in some Maori communities (occasionally compounded by the need for interpreters), a high degree of trust evolved over time as the benefits of nurses visiting Maori settlements became apparent.

The extent of the success of Maori health schemes quickly filtered through to the Government, and between 1901 and 1910 annual government expenditure on Maori health almost doubled as officials and politicians appreciated the need for health measures in many

Maori communities, and as reports from those in the field revealed the value of such approaches to remedying Maori health problems.

Still, the image of a revival in the Maori population was a faint one. In 1907 a Commission on Native Land and Native Land Tenure reported that 'There are many of the tribes and *hapu* in what we might term a decadent state. They have lost the habits of industry of their ancestors, and they have not acquired the habits of the European in this respect, and they are looking to the future with no hope. The race in many parts of the colony has declined, and seems vital in only a few parts. What is to become of the Maori people? Is the race to pass away entirely?' The authors of the report condescended to agree that Maori were worth saving, but that 'the burden and duty of preserving the race rests with the people of New Zealand', after which Maori would be turned into 'active, energetic, thrifty, industrious citizens'.

Although such patronising attitudes towards Maori were slow to recede, the Maori population continued to flourish during the twentieth century. By 1956, the total number of Maori in the country had increased to 135,015; and fifty years later 643,977 New Zealanders were of Maori descent.

One of the ways of assessing the significance of a turning point is to imagine what the country would have been like if it had not taken place. In this case, the very real prospect that the Maori population might have died out by the 1930s is suggestive of the possibility of a radically different and indisputably impoverished social and cultural terrain in New Zealand. But the demise did not end in disappearance, and Maori survived.

In many ways the reasons for that survival were down to Maori themselves. Maori politicians such as James Carroll, Peter Buck, Maui Pomare and Apirana Ngata pushed hard for health projects for Maori settlements. Maori nurses and health officers coordinated assistance where it was most needed, and the communities themselves remained receptive to health reforms. These factors in combination were a prescription for the revival of the Maori population and were fundamentally important in ensuring that there would never be a relapse to the precarious state of the 1880s and 1890s.

11

THE FIRST WORLD WAR, 1914–1918

NEW ZEALAND ENTERED THE second decade of the twentieth century still very much at heart a British colony. Admittedly since 1840 there had been some loosening of the ties that bound the country to Britain. Some developments, such as the 1852 Constitution Act, produced tangible changes. Others, such as the achievement of dominion status in 1907, were more symbolic.

So when what looked like merely another imperial skirmish was announced in August 1914 there was an almost euphoric patriotic response from New Zealand; as one newspaper editorial bullishly suggested: 'The war spirit of a nation is something to marvel at – it is like no other spirit on the face of the earth . . . announce to him [a New Zealander] that his country has declared war, and at once he is like a primeval savage, with the desire to rend and tear his enemies . . . In New Zealand at the present time, as in all other parts of the British Empire, the war spirit is upon us . . . Britain is in trouble, and we are sons of Britain. The Mother Country has been goaded on to war by her most powerful enemy, and we, the daughter Dominions of the Old Land, must stand by her in her hour of trial . . . We, in the Southern Hemisphere, are proud to be Britishers, and are even ready to give the British nation reason to be proud to own us.'

Parades were held, patriotic speeches delivered, bands played and there was a generally jubilant sense of anticipation of what – by all previous experience – was expected to be a brief and relatively painless

Politicians and a crowd outside Parliament Buildings, upon the declaration of war with Germany, August 1914.
REF: 1/2-048457-G. ALEXANDER TURNBULL LIBRARY, WELLINGTON, NEW ZEALAND. HTTP://BETA.NATLIB.GOVT.NZ/ RECORDS/22834581

war. Even as late as the end of September 1914, troops were still being told that they would be 'home by Christmas', although within a matter of weeks it would become obvious that this war would be a much more intractable conflict than anyone had anticipated.

The contribution New Zealand made to the war was enormous and ranks as one of the biggest commitments of troops per head of population of any country involved in the conflict. When the war began around 1,150,000 people lived in New Zealand. Of this number, 120,000 enlisted to fight, of whom 103,000 served overseas, with another 3370 men serving in forces in other parts of the Empire, mainly Australia. In addition 2600 Maori and 346 Pacific Islands troops were also part of the New Zealand forces.

To put these figures into some sort of proportion, roughly one in every four adult New Zealand males fought in the war. Women contributed 550 nurses who served with the New Zealand Expeditionary Force; and other New Zealanders enlisted in Britain.

131

Judging by the tenor of newspaper reports of the time, there was a great rush to enlist, but in fact most of the troop contributions that New Zealand made were done with the aid of conscription. Two years after the war had broken out, close to 70 per cent of men in New Zealand who were eligible for military service had yet to volunteer.

The Government was increasingly anxious about this reticence and responded by introducing conscription. There was still one source of fighting men that remained untapped at this time: Maori. Realising this, the Government removed the prohibition on 'native peoples' fighting in a war among Europeans. There had been a Native Contingent, but in 1916 this was displaced by the Pioneer Maori Battalion. Although instigated through state regulation, subsequent Maori participation in the fighting was later dressed up in the predictable propaganda prose of the period to give the impression that this was something that Maori had themselves sought. One writer claimed shortly after the war that it was 'easy for the modern Maori to appreciate the importance of united action in defence of the congeries of great families called the British Empire. He was quick to perceive the truth of the motto that unity is strength, and to realise that his duty as a citizen of the Empire was to come into alignment with his white brothers and cousins against the common danger.'

Maori were now stereotyped not as the savage enemies of the white race, as had been the case intermittently throughout the previous century, but as brave warriors, coming to the aid of their European compatriots and acting as the best of the Empire's indigenous populations: 'Not merely were the native New Zealanders superior to all the coloured Troops – a distinguished General said that the famous Ghurkas [sic] were but children as compared with the Maoris – but they proved superior to many of the white troops in directions which suited the genius of the race. They were as grim and thorough as any Highland regiment in attack work with the bayonet, and they proved themselves equal to the tremendous nerve-test of sustained shellfire, the greatest test of all. They were the only native troops who hung out the whole of the bitter trench work in

France in 1916–18. They were fully the equal of their forefathers in fortitude and endurance as in dash and energy.'

Until 1915 the war was portrayed in the press as a series of victories being notched up by the Allies against an irrational and often barbaric Germany. The belief in a short conflict (despite the evidence of its rampant escalation) continued to be held by most people in New Zealand, and the view that the war was a chance for heroism and adventure still provided the impetus for men to enlist. All that romanticised, jingoistic enthusiasm for the war altered drastically in April 1915 on the beaches of Gallipoli, in an event which was a turning point on which popular perceptions of the entire conflict turned.

The idea for an assault on the Gallipoli Peninsula had first been raised in November 1914 but at the time was considered too risky. However, as the area assumed greater strategic importance in the subsequent weeks, in January 1915 the British War Council approved a naval attack on Gallipoli.

The plan was to commence with a naval bombardment, followed by a large-scale troop deployment of soldiers under the banner of the Mediterranean Expeditionary Force, which was put under the command of General Sir Ian Hamilton. His strategic aim was to capture the peninsula and thereby establish control over the Dardanelles Strait, which lay on its southern coast. With this foothold secured, British commanders envisaged a quick campaign to seize Constantinople.

The Australian and New Zealand Army Corps (from where the name ANZAC derived) was a part of the Expeditionary Force and was placed under the immediate command of Lieutenant-General William Birdwood. However, Hamilton was anxious about the plan to attack Gallipoli, in particular about the lack of forethought from high command. He wrote of these concerns at the time: '(1). No detail thought out, much less worked out or practised, as to form or manner of landing; (2). Absence of 29th Division; (3). Lack of gear (naval and military) for any landing on a large scale or maintenance thereafter; (4). Unsettled weather; my ground is not solid enough to support me were I to put it to K[itchener] that I had broken away from his explicit instructions.' As if these deficiencies were not bad enough, there was no indication of how successful or otherwise the earlier Allied bombardment of the location had been. As it turned out, it had been plainly inadequate – another miscalculation that was to have fatal consequences.

The build-up to the infantry assault reached catastrophic proportions at the final stage, with some troops landed in the wrong areas and many losing contact with their commanders in the confusion on the beach. Meanwhile, the Turks, who were well secured in the cliffs that rose from the shore, unleashed their barrage, putting the landing troops in a highly precarious position. 'All the time,' one private wrote as he and his comrades mounted bayonets and prepared their equipment on 25 April, 'the machine gun on the cliff above us had been pouring out a hail of bullets into the landing parties.'

As more troops were thrust onto the beach the casualty toll continued to mount. Hamilton described the carnage at daybreak: 'the landing of the lads from the South was in full swing; the shrapnel was bursting over the water; the patter of musketry came creeping out to sea; we are in for it now; the machine guns muttered as through chattering teeth – up to our necks in it now. But would we be out of it? No; not one of us,' he wrote in his journal, following this with an embittered observation that the failure of this campaign was ultimately the result of a military hierarchy and decision-making process that was the product of 'five hundred years stuffed full of dullness and routine'. There would be plenty of time after the event for criticising the high command. At this point all efforts were focusing on keeping a foothold on the beach, and as that began to look as though it was slipping away, the possibility of a retreat was considered.

However, the Dardanelles Committee (as the War Council had been renamed) was in no mood to sanction a retreat, especially from what it regarded as an inferior force. It responded by sending reinforcements in the following days and weeks. This ended up only prolonging what was now obviously an unwinnable campaign. The fighting dragged on until early in the morning of 20 December 1915,

THE FIRST WORLD WAR, 1914–1918

The landing at Anzac Cove, 25 April 1915.
REF: D-017-010. ALEXANDER TURNBULL LIBRARY, WELLINGTON, NEW ZEALAND. HTTP://BETA.NATLIB.GOVT.NZ/
RECORDS/22774419

when the order was given to the ANZACs to evacuate Gallipoli. By this time New Zealand had suffered around 8000 casualties.

Gallipoli wiped away any notions of the First World War being a grand adventure. After April 1915 it was seen for what it was: bloody, injurious, deadly and often futile in any strategic sense. Yet the mass waste of human lives in fighting did not end there for New Zealanders. In the lexicon of wartime locations of horror, Gallipoli was soon followed by Passchendaele, both of which became bywords for the unprecedented murderous character of this conflict.

Again it was poorly conceived strategy that proved to be so costly, as one soldier caught in the fighting recorded: 'Our commander has since told us that no troops in the world could possibly have taken the ridge under similar circumstances. Some "terrible blunder" has been made. Someone is responsible for that barbed wire not having been broken up by our artillery. Someone is responsible for the opening of our barrage in the midst of us instead of 150 yards ahead of us. Someone else is responsible for those machine gun emplacements being left practically intact, but the papers will all report another glorious success, and no one except those who actually took part in it will know any different.' With comrades being killed all around him in a landscape disfigured by shell craters and countless miles of muddy, stinking trenches, such stark cynicism was easily understandable.

Meanwhile, the New Zealand public was to a large degree being kept in the dark about events in places like Passchendaele. Indeed, while New Zealanders were being ripped apart by enemy shelling, or drowning in a morass of mud, blood and faeces in the trenches, the domestic newspapers reported on the 'consolidation of captured ground', 'a successful attack', 'a slight improvement in the line', 'unknowable valour and sacrifice' and other such phrases designed to allay any suggestion that what was unfolding at Passchendaele was a military catastrophe. No mention was made of the conditions on the front lines, the futile advances that were lost often shortly after they were made, or the trainloads of the dead, dying and injured being freighted back to London daily. By October 1917 the death toll had reached its highest point yet, and still there was no sign of anything even resembling a victory.

That month the 3rd Battalions of the Otago and Auckland Regiments were ordered to capture Gravenstafel Ridge – a small rise less than two kilometres from the town of Passchendaele itself. On 12 October, as part of that operation, an attack was launched on Bellevue Spur, which resulted in the deadliest day of battle in the country's history. The shells, bullets, poison gas and aerial bombardment that the New Zealanders faced that day inflicted 3296 casualties, with more than 1800 killed.

The numbers were so great that for modern historians the temptation is to let them fade into anonymous statistics. Yet each fatality left its own legacy of grief for those left behind. It was the silent mourning of parents, wives and siblings that remained long after the weekly tally of those killed was revised upwards. In some cases the bodies were unidentifiable; and even those whose names were known frequently ended up being interred in that ubiquitous 'foreign field'. Even in the dying days of the war, newspapers still printed what were euphemistically referred to as rolls of honour – a list of the latest New Zealanders killed in action making their final parade across newsprint.

As news of the horrors of the war filtered back to New Zealand (despite the best efforts of censors), some people in the country felt more than just a slight moral twinge about the rectitude of fighting in such a hugely destructive conflict. Objecting to fighting for reasons of conscience was not new. The 1909 Defence Act made provision for people to be exempt from military service on the basis of religious conviction, and five months before the outbreak of the war, a Department of Defence report noted that consideration was being given to extend this exemption to those who objected to military service on 'conscientious' grounds. However, at that time the total number of objectors was just sixty-nine men, which the Department acknowledged was 'not considerable'.

Yet four and a half years later, at the end of the war, 400 New Zealanders had been imprisoned for refusing to serve in the armed forces, and penalties had been imposed on a further 2600 conscientious objectors, which included being prohibited from voting for ten years and being excluded from employment in government departments. Despite these impositions, along with having to live for the rest of their lives with the stigma of having refused to fight for king and country, the anti-war sentiment spread, and it manifested itself again years later in the form of a growing peace movement in the country, particularly from the 1960s.

When the war finally ground to a halt on 11 November 1918 – as much out of the utter physical and financial exhaustion of the combatants as anything else – it was left to each country to assemble its inventory of loss. New Zealand had suffered on a massive scale, with casualties in proportion to its huge commitment of personnel. A total of 18,500 New Zealanders died either in the fighting or directly because of it, with a further 50,000 wounded. Expressed another way, New Zealand lost 3.28 per cent of its entire male population in the conflict.

And those who returned could not simply put the experience of the war behind them. For many (and the exact number cannot be known) the shock of what they had endured remained with them for the rest of their lives, affecting their own mental health and their relationships with family and friends. Unfortunately the rigidities of the country's social system, with its lingering emphasis on a 'stiff upper lip', ensured that the demons that afflicted so many veterans remained locked up tightly in their minds.

The experience of the First World War was a major turning point for the country in several ways, some more apparent than others. The most immediate impact was in the enormous loss of life, on a scale that left no community in the country unaffected. Just about every town erected a memorial to local men (and occasionally women) who were killed in the conflict. The unprecedented scale of death inflicted a trauma on the nation and a weariness about war that would have been barely conceivable four years before.

In a more subtle way, the legacy of the war opened up a small space between Britain and New Zealand. It was barely noticeable at the time and only widened very gradually, but it did give cause for the country to reflect (and later question) the nature of its close connection with Britain. In this context, the war helped in that longer process of New Zealand beginning to see its role increasingly as a South Pacific nation and less as an appendage of Britain. Now Maori were portrayed for the first time as part of modern New Zealand – or at least able to make a serious contribution to the Dominion – rather than as some legacy from the colonial past.

The First World War – unlike any previous conflict that New Zealand had been involved in – awakened in thousands of people an abhorrence of fighting that was so intense that they were prepared to be classified as conscientious objectors. This was a still numerically small but nonetheless vocal body of New Zealanders who were open in their opposition to all war – something that would have been unthinkable on this scale just a generation earlier. At the same time there was a profound reverence for the sacrifice so many more thousands of New Zealanders had made in the war. The need to commemorate this traumatic and large-scale loss of life resulted in what became known as Anzac Day.

As the first anniversary of the devastating events at Gallipoli neared, a popular movement rose in New Zealand which sought to commemorate the losses at that engagement and to show support for the troops still fighting in the war. A memorial service for fallen New Zealand and Australian soldiers was organised for 25 April 1916. In Sydney a memorial service was attended by 60,000 people. Although a national returned services association had not yet been formed in New Zealand, there was enthusiasm across the country for some sort of recognition for the troops who had been fighting in the Great War. Ironically, it was a civilian delegation that approached the Government and convinced it to make 25 April 1916 a general half-day holiday. In Auckland special church services were held, and there was a procession of Gallipoli veterans up Queen Street. Following that they gathered in the Town Hall, where a dinner was provided. Speeches made by the city's mayor and by the Governor-General, the Earl of Liverpool.

The Governor-General told the audience of the King's sentiments about the ANZAC contribution to the war effort: 'I know from private letters which he has written to me how deeply touched His Majesty has been at all the gallant deeds which were wrought in that small area on Gallipoli. Probably – and I dare say it has struck some of you – I should almost have preferred to have known this day as Gallipoli Day, because there are others with you who shared in the glory and in the triumph of what happened on the Peninsula.' He suggested to the crowd that there was now a need to form a 'permanent association of men who fought at Gallipoli in order that annual reunions might be possible'. This was the start of the New Zealand Returned Services' Association (RSA), which was formed in Wellington just three days later.

For their part, the returned servicemen were clear on how they wanted to commemorate Anzac Day: 'the boys don't want to be split up among twenty or thirty different churches on Anzac Day, and it is certain they don't want to go to a meeting to hear people who haven't been there [to war] spout and pass resolutions'. Instead, returned servicemen preferred a public service conducted by an army chaplain.

In the final year of the war, the Reverend H. Steel Craik spoke at the Anzac Day service at the Auckland Town Hall and offered

Anzac Day commemoration at Petone, 25 April 1916.
REF: APG-0590-1/2-G. ALEXANDER TURNBULL LIBRARY, WELLINGTON, NEW ZEALAND. HTTP://BETA.NATLIB.GOVT.
NZ/RECORDS/23153785

a prediction of how the war would be perceived in the future. He believed that Anzac Day would become one of the most potent symbols in the national life of New Zealand. 'The Dominion had "come of age"', he told those in attendance. It had 'reached maturity, had plunged its hands into great doings'. New Zealand was therefore justified in claiming its nationhood, he concluded. So amid the terrible trauma inflicted on the country, which was to last years after the fighting was finished, a new and more vital sense of national identity was born. The counterpoint to the mass loss of life was New Zealand's rejuvenated sense of self and a growing determination that from that point on, the country would take a greater role in deciding on its own future.

Legislation followed public sentiment, and on 7 October 1921 the Minister of Internal Affairs, W. Downie Stewart, introduced the Anzac Day Amendment Bill into Parliament. He explained that the proposed legislation was a response to what one Legislative Councillor had described as the 'universal sacrifice' of New Zealand troops. This sentiment has remained for all Anzac Days since.

At the close of the Second World War, New Zealand writer John Mulgan looked back on the events of the Great War and expressed how it occupied a unique role in the country's perception of its past. Even though the world had been caught in a greater conflagration in the first half of the 1940s, the shock at the sudden loss of innocence that the First World War created left a profound imprint on the nation's consciousness: 'We had never, in fact, outgrown the shadow of that earlier war, which our fathers had fought. It brooded over our thoughts and emotions. Old wars take on a dignity and a grandeur. As children we had heard men's stories coming home, had stood silent in parades of remembrance, knew the names of old battles and heroes as part of our lives. We felt the tragic waste and splendour of this first Great War.'

12

THE SAVAGE GOVERNMENT ELECTED, 1935

T HE ARRIVAL OF a severe economic crisis in New Zealand in the early 1930s forced an entire generation to reassess its ideas about the role of the state in national life. Just after the peak of the Depression had passed (but while its effects were still being felt), policies developed by the Labour Party suggested that the state could play a more direct part in the welfare of its citizens. The election of the first Labour Government in 1935 saw many of these ideas put into practice. One of the lasting results was what was known as the Welfare State, the principles of which have remained largely intact since the 1930s.

News of the stock market crash in the United States in October 1929 probably meant very little to New Zealanders at the time. The accompanying warnings of economic hard times would have been better understood, and therefore more cause for concern, but as 1929 ticked over into 1930 the New Zealand economy still seemed to be in good health. Any trepidation about the country's immediate economic future was hardly at alarmist levels. But it should have been. Fears about a more serious impending economic crisis were being aired in the United States and elsewhere, and when the American economy began to implode, the effects were quickly felt beyond its borders. This new and frighteningly large-scale economic collapse was transmitted swiftly throughout the world, and New Zealanders soon discovered that geographic isolation and social provincialism offered no immunity from its ravaging effects.

When the Depression finally reached New Zealand's shores, the impact was dire. By 1933 unemployment reached approximately 80,000, which constituted about 12 per cent of the workforce, although this concealed a much higher rate because women and Maori were excluded from calculations (joblessness among Maori men, for example, was closer to 40 per cent) and because under-employment did not register in the count.

Two years from the onset of the Depression, exports fell by 45 per cent, with staple products such as wool dropping in value by 60 per cent. The flow-on effects of this were drastic. By 1933 the national income had plummeted by 40 per cent from its 1929 level, and there was an ensuing decline in wages as the state, as well as private employers, did all they could to cut costs. The conventional wisdom of the period was that the only way out of such a financial crisis was ever greater efforts at thrift. In practice, however, this had the opposite effect, producing a spiral of reduced spending and reduced income.

The effects of the Depression on people were in many cases even more pronounced than the statistics might suggest. As the economic crisis worsened, people throughout the country started to feel a profound lack of security. The fear of losing one's job, one's house, one's family, was widespread. Those without jobs worried where their next meal might come from. Those with jobs felt besieged by the crisis and awaited news that they too would be made unemployed. Shop-owners waited with escalating anxiety for customers who never came; and people with assets watched as their value eroded.

Who was responsible for all this? Certainly not the unemployed, whom the writer James Thorn depicted at the time as 'the victims of a faulty industrial system'. According to Thorn, 'they should not be penalized by destitution and starvation. Only the ignorant and the malicious therefore will object to the demand that work must be found for the workers at satisfactory rates of wages and conditions, and that failing this, they and their wives and children shall be afforded maintenance.' Thorn, and many others like him, saw the Government as having the primary duty to remedy the worst effects of the Depression.

The Government, however, would not be budged. It followed the orthodox economic policy of the day and invested its energy in balancing the budget. So as tax revenue fell dramatically, the Government responded by cutting wages, dismissing staff, lowering pensions, and postponing or cancelling public works. On top of all that it raised taxes to compensate for falling income. The result of this constrictive approach to the flow of money was disastrous. Unemployment spiralled upwards, tax revenue continued to diminish and businesses throughout the country were driven bankrupt.

Although the worst of the Depression had passed by the end of 1935 the sense of gloom lingered, and it was in that environment that the Labour Party entered the election campaign. On paper at least its challenges were formidable. There had never been a Labour government before in the country, and the policies the party was proposing – centred on the government offering a helping hand to those in greatest need and, more generally, of spending the country's way out of the economic slump – would have seemed counter-intuitive to those people who viewed the national economy in the same way as they saw their own household economy. Surely you don't fix an economic problem by spending your way out of it? Surely greater thrift is what is needed most of all? The problem was that greater thrift had been tried and shown not only not to work but even to exacerbate the effects of the Depression. And given the desperation being experienced by so many New Zealanders at the time, Labour's promise of a radically new approach to tackling the country's economic woes appeared to an increasing number of voters as a prospect at least worth a go. After all, there was little left to lose if it did not work.

The general election took place on Wednesday, 27 November 1935, and produced a high voter turnout. Among Labour circles there was a thickening air of expectation, followed by elation when the provisional results were announced, as one party official recalled: 'We were in the old Pacific Building on the corner of Wellesley Street and Queen Street. The Labour Party had rooms on the top floor, and thousands of people gathered down in the square there, and then later at the *Auckland Star* office [in Fort Street], which were

144

publishing the results as they came through and putting them up on the window in large lettering so that people down below could see what was happening. Now that was an astounding spectacle. All along Fort Street was just one solid, hard mass of people, cramming themselves together to see the results, and cheering as Labour was winning. That was fantastic.'

The press assessed that there were two factors above all others that contributed to the win. The first of these was the personality of the Labour leader, Michael Joseph Savage. He might have been 'more tender with his opponents than some of his followers wished him to be', but he had 'sensed the true feeling of an electorate which is not to be won altogether by demagogic methods'. Rather, Savage and his colleagues had displayed 'boundless enthusiasm, untiring hope and effort', for which the electorate rewarded them.

A pleasant demeanour was not enough on its own to win the election, however. Labour's policies were crucial to its victory. It had promised 'more generous relief for the distressed . . . [and] a more direct attack on poverty', which appealed to those voters who saw the necessity for the 'immediate relief of hardship' as easily outweighing traditional orthodox arguments about economic management.

When the final count of the general election was confirmed, Labour had won fifty-three seats, while the governing coalition was reduced to just nineteen. It was a landslide, but with it was carried a great weight of public expectation that substantial economic and even social change would be imminent.

The high-water mark in the first Labour Government's welfare policy was the 1938 Social Security Act. The Bill was introduced into Parliament on 12 August of that year, and in the ensuing debate the ambitious thinking behind some of Labour's proposed measures was made clear. Walter Nash, who was the minister in charge of the legislation, described the Bill as 'the best step forward ever taken in this or any other country – small in itself, but magnificent in its conception to give everyone by right what they ought to have received years ago'. He concluded his speech to Parliament by proclaiming that 'It needs no gift of prophecy to say that the Act now being written into the statute-book of the Dominion is not only to be a

Michael Joseph Savage, Prime Minister from 1935 to 1940 and one of the architects of the welfare state.

REF: 1/2-043438-F. ALEXANDER TURNBULL LIBRARY, WELLINGTON, NEW ZEALAND. HTTP://BETA.NATLIB.GOVT.NZ/ RECORDS/23007170

Social Security Act, but is also to be the first Social Security Act, on any proper definition of that term, ever written in any statute-book in the world . . . If it brings the benefits I believe it will bring, then once more this country will be "God's Own Country".'

The claims to originality did not actually stand close scrutiny. Three years earlier the United States passed its own Social Security Act, which at the very least provided a general ideological blueprint for Labour's version (although it did not offer full social security in the manner the New Zealand Act did). The other factor against claims of the 1938 Act's uniqueness was that many of its provisions were not innovations as much as adaptations. In some cases it was more an extension of existing measures than a radical departure from what had gone on before.

However, it was still indisputably a major legislative accomplishment, which transformed drastically the role of the state in the lives of thousands of New Zealanders. More universality was applied to benefits, along with a less restrictive approach to entitlement. And instead of a contributory scheme – which had been a popular option by some proponents of welfare reform – the Savage Government made the state fully responsible for funding the welfare regime.

The near-elimination of poverty was at the ideological core of the Act – an audacious goal that was, in the words of the legislation itself, 'designed to safeguard the People of New Zealand from Disabilities arising from Age, Sickness, Widowhood, Orphanhood, Unemployment, or other Exceptional Conditions; . . . to provide a System whereby Medical and Hospital Treatment will be made available to Persons requiring such Treatment; and, further, to provide such other Benefits as may be necessary to maintain and promote the Health and General Welfare of the Community'. In providing comprehensive state-backed coverage for the main causes of poverty, expectations were high for a revolution in the living standards of New Zealanders.

Savage even went so far as to claim a divine basis to the scheme. Initially he explained that he wanted to 'bring about security for everyone . . . I should think it was the inalienable right of every person,' he suggested, 'to be secured against distress in any form.' It may not have made economic sense, he acknowledged, but it was 'common-sense'. Then, going several steps further, the Prime Minister ventured to say 'that it is applied Christianity'. Reference to Christianity also appeared in the report of the Select Committee on the Bill, where it was claimed that it was 'quite clear . . . that public opinion in the Dominion requires that the normal Christian attitude of helping those in need, whatever the cause of their need, should be carried on into community life'. Invoking Christianity to buttress the philosophy of the Bill gives some impression of how seriously and how sincerely its backers believed in their 'mission'.

Another important principle that appeared in the Social Security Act, and which separated it from much existing welfare legislation, was universality, particularly in the provision of pensions and medical care. What was known as the Superannuation Benefit would be paid to all people who had reached retirement age, provided they met residency requirements. Age, widows', sickness, unemployment, invalids' and orphans' benefits would be means tested, but miners' benefits would not be; and eventually the newly created Family Allowance (later the Family Benefit) would also be made universal.

Universal superannuation was an important plank of the legislation. Prior to the passage of the Act, many New Zealanders had to rely on contributory schemes, many of which were inadequate for their recipients on retirement. Some of these schemes contained exclusion clauses (for widows, for example), while others accepted only 'approved' applicants. Universal superannuation would bypass these deficiencies.

Such was the scale and reach of the Social Security Act that it attracted international attention. In November 1938 the *Manchester Guardian* described the legislation as 'moderate Socialism', of a sort that England could learn from. 'New Zealand pursues an ideal of environmental equality,' the paper stated. 'It is an ideal every just man hopes to see achieved even though we live among the hard and disappointed peoples of Europe.' In contrast, New Zealand was depicted as 'an enlightened and prosperous country in the middle of a great social adventure'.

The various benefits devised by the Labour Government still didn't go far enough, however, in addressing one of the most fundamental problems afflicting thousands of New Zealand families: inadequate housing. This had been a concern prior to the 1930s, but there is no doubt that the conditions brought about by the Depression had made matters much worse. Surveys of housing in various parts of the country were carried out in the 1930s and revealed a filthy underside to life in the country's main areas of settlement. A survey of houses in parts of Dunedin in 1937, for example, revealed that 63 per cent were classified as being 'satisfactory', 32 per cent were considered 'unsatisfactory but repairable', and the remaining 5 per cent were assessed as being in such poor condition that they were suitable only for demolition. Admittedly, not all New Zealand cities were as bad as Dunedin, but all had their areas of dramatically substandard housing. In 1936 in Auckland, for example, the city's Medical Officer of Health found 'several' houses that he believed should be condemned because of their unsanitary nature.

In September 1937 the *New Zealand Herald* published an article which alerted readers all over the country to the appalling state of some housing in New Zealand's largest city: 'Great numbers of dwellings in the poorer areas are overcrowded to a degree that the worst slums of the old world cannot surpass. While the slum tenements in London and Glasgow are of fairly substantial brick, their Auckland equivalents are usually decrepit, insanitary old wooden places which cannot be trusted even to keep out the weather . . . Inspectors have found appalling numbers of families crowded into single rooms which have to serve for sleeping, eating and cooking. Even damp and ill-lighted basements are used in this way.' This was not the way New Zealanders liked to see their country, but it was a fact of modern life in their cities in the 1930s. Cases such as this were becoming distressingly common as increasing numbers of people lacked the means to afford accommodation that met even the most basic standards.

Labour's plan to tackle both inadequate and insufficient housing was an all-embracing one. Betraying its socialist origins, Labour put the blame for the existing situation at the feet of those who made profits from housing. The party's rationale was that if the private profit motive could be removed from house construction, the buildings themselves would be more affordable. In addition, the state could ensure that land was supplied in sufficient quantity to enable the mass provision of housing. Standardised production techniques would achieve economies of scale. Thus sawmilling, cement and other branches of the building industry were nationalised, private landlords would be barred from any role in the provision of state accommodation, and a government department would be established to manage the supply of housing, guaranteeing weekly wages for builders and even appropriating private land if it was deemed suitable for state housing.

For roughly nine months after Labour's election win, various government departments undertook planning involving politicians, builders, architects, suppliers and other related groups to coordinate putting the state housing plan into action. In theory, the landslide election win that Labour had achieved in 1935 signalled that the public would support its state housing measures, but such a far-reaching and radical alteration to the provision of housing meant that public goodwill had to be maintained.

This fitted in with the utopian vision that some people in the Labour Party had long nurtured for state housing. Instead of producing rows of cheap, cramped accommodation, the Savage Government wanted to create houses well above the average standard that New Zealanders were accustomed to. Not only would this raise the opinion of state houses in the minds of some New Zealanders (thus hopefully convincing doubters that the scheme was worthy), but it would mean that the poorest in society would not be forced to accept tawdry housing from the state. The first state houses were therefore built with the best materials and constructed to a standard that would make them outlast conventional New Zealand homes of the period.

Of course, state housing was hardly a New Zealand innovation, but its significance was in not only the scale of the policy (by February 1939, just two years after state-house building began, the foundations had been laid for the 5000th state house) but the fact that unlike experiments in state housing elsewhere in the world at this time, New Zealand did not opt for building large blocks of apartments to house the masses. On the contrary, state houses built under the Savage administration were designed to be almost indistinguishable from privately owned houses.

One of the reasons for state housing appearing 'in disguise' was that the Labour Government appreciated the risk of a stigma being placed on residents who lived in them. More importantly, it realised (with great foresight) that cramming people into apartments was the route to what would eventually mature into urban slums; and it was urban slums that had led to the formation of Labour's state housing policy in the first place.

Overall, the early state houses were relatively traditional in style, but with a layout that suited the latest appliances. In an additional effort to avoid the possible standardised appearance of state houses, a variety of plans were devised, which was also a departure from the sort of uniform planned housing that was being made for workers in other countries in the 1930s. Labour's goal was to provide

State houses being built in Wellington, June 1938.
REF: 1/4-048806-G. ALEXANDER TURNBULL LIBRARY, WELLINGTON, NEW ZEALAND. HTTP://BETA.NATLIB.GOVT.NZ/
RECORDS/23111595

accommodation for New Zealanders who might otherwise be forced into substandard living arrangements, with the purpose of allowing these people to 'fulfil their rightful destiny'.

As the policy went from the planning stage to building, the Housing Minister, Walter Nash, revealed the likely cost of the initial phase of the scheme. For the first twelve months £3,500,000 would be made available to the Ministry of Housing for the construction of houses for the state and for loans to local authorities for the same purpose. Nash explained that the aims of the policy were 'The provision of high-grade, reasonably-priced residences grouped in accordance with the best town planning principles . . . The utilisation of the unemployed artisans and labourers in their construction, and as far as possible, that all materials be sourced from within the country'. This did not necessarily mean that the homes that were eventually constructed would be the cheapest; but creating employment in all areas related to the design and construction of state houses was a crucial dimension to the scheme.

The country's first state house was formally opened on 18 September 1937 by the Prime Minister and several of his Cabinet colleagues at 12 Fife Lane, Miramar, Wellington. Hundreds of people jammed the street to watch the spectacle of Savage helping to unload furniture and carry it into the house. The rhetoric flowed thick and fast. These would be 'smiling homes', in the Prime Minister's words: 'homes worth living in – homes for the Native race; homes for their pakeha brethren'. The numerically largest and most long-lasting housing project in the country's history was underway.

The Minister of Public Works, Bob Semple, had an equally utopian view of state housing, but instead of seeing the policy achieving a new type of society, his view was more nostalgic. At the opening of the first state house he announced to the assembled crowd that 'we are endeavouring to develop the saying that an Englishman's home is his castle into a living reality'. A little England or a futuristic New Zealand? From its outset, state housing was a policy that could apparently accommodate a number of ideological positions.

The first Labour Government's extensive welfare measures affected the country unevenly, and it would be simplistic to see them as a panacea for the economic crisis that the country experienced in the 1930s. By the outbreak of the Second World War in 1939 the worst of the Depression had receded and exports were rising in quantity and value, contributing to a recovery that would almost certainly have happened with or without Labour's reforms.

However, the timing of the war was significant for the ultimate fate of the Social Security Act and for the principle of state housing. Not only did the war disrupt the equilibrium of the economic recovery, but by the time it ended in 1945, and as tens of thousands of troops returned home, the so-called 'welfare state' was regarded as a normal part of the country's society and economy. The sense that the Savage Government's reforms were radical, or even socialist, was largely lost in the years after the Act's passage, as popular attention swung to the greater crisis that the war represented. Consequently, the creation of the welfare state became a turning point for the country that endured and, despite intermittent adjustments, became an accepted feature of life in New Zealand.

In later years there was a tendency to diminish the uniqueness of the first Labour Government's social security measures. In 1946 one critic claimed that the underlying principle of the Social Security Act was simply one of fairness; while a 1972 Royal Commission report asserted that the Act 'did not introduce sweeping theoretical change'. Yet at the time that the Savage Government's welfare measures were introduced, they were popularly seen as a radical departure from anything that had gone before in terms of state involvement in the welfare of the population. Within the Government's first term, not only state policy but also public expectations of the role of government were revolutionised.

13

THE ANZUS PACT, 1951

FTER THE TERROR EXPERIENCED by New Zealand troops and the deprivations endured by the rest of the country's residents during the Second World War, most New Zealanders wanted, and expected, life to return to normal at the end of the war. To some extent, returning to the values and circumstances of the pre-war era was the best recipe for the country to revert to normality. However, international relations had been thrown into a state of confusion during the war, and at its conclusion a drastically altered balance of global power was swiftly emerging from the rubble of the conflict.

The complex and often intertwined roots of the new relationship between the ANZUS countries – Australia, New Zealand and the United States – extended back to the period after the Japanese bombing of Pearl Harbor in November 1941, when the vulnerability of America's interest in the Pacific region was exposed. But what focused the regional security needs even more acutely in the minds of Australians and New Zealanders was the fall of Singapore to the Japanese in February 1942. Churchill described Singapore's capitulation, in somewhat melodramatic terms, as 'the worst disaster and largest capitulation of British history', and it certainly came as a profound shock to countries in the Pacific, which had taken for granted the ability of the Royal Navy to defend the interests of the Empire. Plainly, it could not. As one observer noted three years later, 'in 1942, even the most unimaginative citizen of this Dominion learnt that the vast distances of the Pacific were no longer the protection he had fondly hoped. He knew little of the great ocean and had scant realization of . . . [its] strategic importance.'

The immediate result of the fall of Singapore was the formation of the Pacific War Council in Washington. While Britain was strongly represented in the Council, it was nonetheless evident that a change in attitudes towards regional defence had taken place in Australia and New Zealand. An important aspect of this change was that these two Commonwealth countries now took more direct responsibility for voicing their concerns for the security arrangements in the Pacific, and were no longer content to rely on Britain to speak on their behalf with the Americans.

One of the fruits of this more assertive stance was the Canberra Pact, which was signed between Australia and New Zealand in January 1944. Although not a military alliance, it was an indication that the two countries wished to work more closely in dealing with regional issues, and that they wanted their position heard amid the din of the larger nations. At the same time that the Canberra Pact was being finalised, plans for a network of American airbases across the Pacific were being devised in Washington. Following the Japanese attack on Pearl Harbor, Australia had proposed to American officials the possibility of establishing a more secure air route between the United States, Australia and New Zealand. It was an idea that foreshadowed a closer post-war defence relationship between the countries.

The American interest in such proposals came, in part, from an acknowledgement that Britain, Australia and New Zealand between them had sovereignty or control over several Pacific islands which could be of potential strategic importance. Rather than the United States attempting to violate the sovereignty of these territories, thereby incurring the ire of the Commonwealth countries, it made more sense to achieve American strategic goals through cooperation with these nations. Just how far United States interest in the Pacific had burgeoned by the end of the war can be gauged by its 1945 strategy for the region, in which consideration was given to either gaining control or 'full title' to several Pacific island groupings. This sort of blinkered ambition broadened over subsequent months to take into account the possible wishes of the nations in the region.

However, Australia and New Zealand were still dubious about the extent of American intentions in the region, while Britain feared that if the United States went ahead in establishing bases in the Pacific this would give the Soviets encouragement to seek equivalents in the Atlantic. In the meantime, the global strategic situation was gradually settling, and the South Pacific in particular was becoming less of a priority for the United States from the second half of 1946. Roosevelt's idealistic vision of a chain of bases extending through the Pacific serving as an international police force subsided into much more moderate expectations. And as American attention moved to the containment of Soviet expansionism in Asia, New Zealand and Australia (and, by proxy, Britain) lost much of their bargaining power when it came to securing an American commitment in the South Pacific. This, in turn, would have an effect on subsequent negotiations for a regional security agreement.

The idea of collective security held an appeal for small countries such as New Zealand. Even in the 1930s New Zealand was advancing such concepts in the League of Nations, as Britain's policy of appeasing Nazi Germany proved increasingly ineffectual. What New Zealand wanted, in the words of one of its senior foreign affairs officials, Sir Carl Berendsen, was to 'have an eye and an ear and a voice . . . wherever world events are being settled'.

At the conclusion of the war the threat posed by Japan had been neutralised, but in its place the fear of Soviet-backed communist expansion throughout South-east Asia became one of the principal sources of apprehension that shaped New Zealand foreign policy. One of the responses to this was the Colombo Plan of 1950, which was the product of the Commonwealth Conference of Foreign Ministers held in Sri Lanka that year. The 'plan' was ostensibly a comprehensive scheme of foreign aid that would be provided to South-east Asian nations in order to strengthen their economies and make them less vulnerable to communist influences. Unlike other aid programmes, it was primarily a strategic political measure rather than a humanitarian one. It 'proved to be something of a progressive force which prepared the ground for a much closer relationship with (and within) the Southeast Asian region'. Communism was seen

New Zealand diplomat Sir
Carl Berendsen.
REF: 1/2-043579-F. ALEXANDER
TURNBULL LIBRARY, WELLINGTON, NEW
ZEALAND. HTTP://BETA.NATLIB.GOVT.NZ/
RECORDS/22852335

as both an ideological and a territorial threat, so measures were constantly being considered to counter it.

Although the Colombo Plan was a Commonwealth initiative that was overseen by Britain during this period, one expert assessed that 'there was a new note of reality in . . . [New Zealand's] consideration of the Pacific', leading the country to acknowledge that it was 'in a new sense within the American political sphere'. The focus of tension of the world was shifting uncomfortably close to New Zealand at this time. Asia, rather than Europe, was where the superpowers were looking to confront each other, and this fact made regional security much more than a mere exercise in diplomatic niceties.

Ironically it was a particular relationship in the region – that between the United States and Japan – that threatened to halt the advance of a regional security agreement. The memory of Japanese aggression in the Pacific was still very fresh in the minds of New Zealanders and Australians, and although the United States had also

157

suffered from Japanese actions in the Second World War, it was now looking to the shape of the post-war world, in which communism was the far bigger threat. The conclusion of the Sino-Soviet Treaty of Friendship, Alliance and Mutual Assistance in February 1950 confirmed this changing trend in the balance of power in the Asia–Pacific region and gave extra incentive for the United States to secure a peace treaty with Japan. It would help 'break the vicious cycle of war, victory, peace and war', according to the American President's negotiator, John Foster Dulles.

The treaty with Japan, concluded in September 1951, momentarily put relations between the United States on the one hand, and Australia and New Zealand on the other, slightly off balance. One of the immediate achievements of the ANZUS Pact would be to make the Japanese peace settlement palatable to the Pacific Dominions. It was no coincidence, then, that the ANZUS Pact was signed the same month as the peace treaty with Japan. It was the 'price exacted by Australia for assent' to the peace treaty with Japan, according to one Australian diplomat. The United States was clearly eager to ensure its diplomacy in the region ended up (as much as possible) being all things to all people.

As the parties went into negotiations on the ANZUS Pact in 1951 the motives of the signatories were therefore varied. The United States was primarily concerned with establishing a strong Japan that was capable of repelling Soviet expansionism, while New Zealand and Australia were keen on a regional defence zone because of fears that had originally stemmed from (ironically) a fear of Japan.

From the outset New Zealand acknowledged that its own military forces were so small that there was never a chance that it could be in a position on its own to defend itself from any outside aggression. Yet due to the way in which the global political situation was unfolding, in the late 1940s there were a number of potential options for New Zealand to consider when looking for strategic relationships. First there was Britain, which although militarily weak was still linked to New Zealand by strong cultural and diplomatic ties. Through Britain, the Commonwealth also offered some possibilities for collective defence arrangements.

Then there was the United Nations, which had been founded in 1945 and was still in its formative stages, but which promised 'to take effective collective measures for the prevention and removal of threats to the peace, and for the suppression of acts of aggression or other breaches of the peace, and to bring about by peaceful means, and in conformity with the principles of justice and international law, adjustment or settlement of international disputes or situations which might lead to a breach of the peace'. In the immediate post-war period, the United Nations seemed to offer as good an opportunity as any for collective security, especially as it appeared that there was no imminent threat to peace in the region.

However, the geopolitical landscape was altering at this time. Countries were gradually being classified as belonging to one of three groupings: they were either communist, anti-communist or non-aligned. Within each category, of course, such simplistic branding was exposed as faulty (the differences between the Chinese and Soviet brands of communism were an example), but as a working model by which the superpowers of the day viewed the world, it was a useful system. New Zealand was, through a combination of its values, system of government, history, culture and diplomatic links, firmly positioned in the anti-communist camp, so membership of a defence pact with the leader of the anti-communist bloc seemed a logical, almost inevitable next step for the country. For some people, on the other hand, the United Nations still seemed at least equal in terms of preference to an alliance with the United States.

One of the possible reasons for hesitating to rush into an alliance with any single power was New Zealand's wartime experience, in which it had been obliged to commit troops to theatres of war in the northern hemisphere, even while the threat to New Zealand's own borders from the advancing Japanese forces continued to grow. If there was to be any agreement with another nation or international organisation, New Zealand was determined that it would focus on its own direct sphere of interest rather than serving the strategic requirements of another country.

At the turn of the 1950s, however, the perceived threat of communism was becoming acute and was forcing New Zealand to

159

Crowd at Aotea Quay, Wellington, as K-Force troops leave New Zealand, December 1950.
Ref: PA1-Q-311-0124. Alexander Turnbull Library, Wellington, New Zealand. http://beta.natlib.govt. nz/records/23019434

re-evaluate its stance on relying solely on the United Nations for its collective security needs. The Berlin Blockade, the communist victory in China, the Soviets' acquisition of nuclear weapons and the start of the Korean War were, considered collectively, as much of an alert as it was possible to have of the advancing menace of communism. At least that was how these developments were portrayed in the West. An agreement with the United States would offer New Zealand and Australia a means of enhancing the security of the Pacific by contributing to the West's effort at the containment of communism – an effort led by a virile United States rather than a militarily redundant Britain.

For its part, the United States would get closer cooperation with two friendly Pacific states which were sizeable enough to make a useful contribution to any American actions in the region, should the need arise. And although New Zealand diplomats were 'pessimistic' about the prospects of an American war with Korea, on 29 June

1950 – only days after the fighting had started – New Zealand offered two frigates in support of the United States and followed this up with troop commitments.

Two years earlier, the New Zealand diplomat Frank Corner had produced an assessment of New Zealand's security position and requirements. He explored the idea of the country becoming neutral because of its physical isolation – a stance which would reduce the likelihood of hostilities from communist nations while not generating any threat from non-communist states. However, such a stance, while theoretically a good idea, was out of keeping with New Zealand's long-established relations with Britain and other Commonwealth countries in particular. An alliance with the United States, together with New Zealand's closest partner – Australia – increasingly came into view as the best option for the country.

'It would seem,' Corner wrote, 'to be in our long-term interest to establish as soon as possible the most intimate relationship with the United States in order that she may develop the habit of thinking of New Zealand as a close associate and ally. It is not fanciful to suggest that the grand aim of New Zealand external policy and diplomacy might be to secure in some form an American guarantee of the security of New Zealand.' ANZUS became the fulfilment of this policy goal.

However, the security guarantees in the ANZUS Pact were not quite as firm as those that the United States agreed to with its European allies. In the North Atlantic Treaty Organisation (NATO), which came into being in April 1949, an armed attack against one or more members would be considered an attack against all; in such circumstances, each member would render assistance to the attacked party 'including the use of armed forces to restore and maintain the security of the area'. By contrast, the ANZUS agreement simply recognised 'that an armed attack in the Pacific Area on any of the Parties would be dangerous to its own peace and safety and declares that it would act to meet the common danger in accordance with its constitutional process'.

It was not the sort of firm assurance of protection that other Western allies had received from the United States at this time. Indeed, from the perspective of the United States Defence Department, American military resources were already stretched dangerously thin across various parts of the world; so the ANZUS Pact amounted to a general statement of intentions in the event of an attack on Australia or New Zealand, 'but nothing more'. Percy Spender, the Australian Minister for External Affairs, looked on this aspect more optimistically, asserting that 'there is no doubt . . . that this warm-hearted nation [the United States] would immediately and effectively come to our aid in the event of an act of aggression against Australia', but he still felt that a guarantee to this effect – along the lines of that in operation among NATO countries – would be helpful.

There was also a sense of vagueness in the Pact as to what precisely constituted the Pacific region. Later events in Borneo and Malaya were examples of the three parties agreeing that certain territories were within their field of interest. The Pacific, in this context, became as much a political as a geographical concept, whose boundaries could expand or contract on a case-by-case basis.

In addition to the limited scope of military backing initially offered, the US Army Chief of Staff, J. Lawton Collins, clarified with considerable cynicism the role that New Zealand and Australia would play at a command level within ANZUS: 'we are not much interested in joint planning for the Pacific. Our interest is to get some Australian and New Zealand troops into the Middle East. If they engage in joint planning for the Pacific their prestige will become involved and they will feel they will have to do something in the Pacific. The whole point of this [ANZUS] has been to protect them in the Pacific in order that they could do something in the Middle East.'

Both the US State Department and the Joint Chiefs of Staff wanted to keep defence contacts with New Zealand and Australia 'as superficial as possible'. Of course this reasoning was not disclosed by the United States to its allies in the Pact, and overall New Zealand and Australia were 'happy and contented' with their role in ANZUS. And to ensure the two countries did not feel starved of intelligence, the American Secretary of State, Dean Acheson, made sure to provide enough material to the other two partners in the pact to 'give them indigestion', as he inelegantly put it. New Zealand

John Foster and Mrs Dulles, Robert Scotten (American Ambassador to
New Zealand) and Sir Keith Holyoake, February 1951.
REF: 114/264/05-G. ALEXANDER TURNBULL LIBRARY, WELLINGTON, NEW ZEALAND. HTTP://BETA.NATLIB.GOVT.NZ/
RECORDS/22315575

and particularly Australia may have wished for a greater role in the
formation of United States policy in the Pacific, but the relative scale
of the partners meant that American dominance in the relationship
was an inevitability from the outset.

The ANZUS Pact may have gone down the route of a largely
token agreement among friends had it not been for the deepening
crisis in Indochina, which forced the United States to collaborate
much more closely and sincerely with Australia and New Zealand.
The fear of encroaching communism proved to be the lifeblood of
the agreement and kept the alliance members securely bonded to
each other until the 1980s.

In 1945 Japan had been an enemy of New Zealand, and the Soviet Union an ally. Five years later, the relationships had reversed, with Japan emerging as a friend in the Asia–Pacific region and the Soviet Union (and its satellites) now a clear threat. As far as the United States was concerned, its intention was 'to keep the Pacific as an American lake', as President Eisenhower later expressed it. To achieve this objective, it was drawn to its natural allies in the region. New Zealand and Australia alone among Commonwealth countries had been pushing for a 'tough' peace settlement with Japan, but Dulles was adamant that there would be no repressive peace, seeing Japan more as a potential ally than a defeated enemy. The Japan issue – which had preoccupied much Australian and New Zealand thinking as the countries entered negotiations for the ANZUS agreement – was therefore relegated by the United States as a matter beyond discussion.

While there was no direct attack on the parties to the Pact in the whole Cold War era, there were certainly advantages of membership of ANZUS. Richard Casey, the Australian Minister of External Affairs at the time of the first ANZUS Council meeting held at Honolulu, expressed the benefits of cooperation that the Pact brought for New Zealand and Australia. He described the 'intimate consultative relationship' established by the Pact, and stated how there was a 'meeting of the minds on the problems of the Pacific seen in their world setting'. New Zealand was now in the closest form of diplomatic relationship possible with one of the world's two superpowers.

The fact that there were just three members in this alliance was also important to New Zealand. It fostered an intimate relationship without the additional complications of a pact with a wider membership, and it avoided some of the potential commitments that would have arisen if Asian countries had been included. To a considerable extent, limiting ANZUS to just three members went against American instincts, especially as Dulles and others in the United States administration favoured the inclusion of other countries, particularly the Philippines. It was New Zealand, more than Australia, who opposed an extended membership of the

Alliance, succeeding in limiting the involvement of ANZUS to just three countries. New Zealand also sensed that if the membership of ANZUS was limited to the United States and the two Commonwealth countries, Britain would be less perturbed by the existence of the pact. Australia, in contrast, was more ambivalent about the role of Britain in the Pacific region (an attitude that extended back to wartime relations between the two nations), and was therefore much more willing to act independently of its former colonial power.

ANZUS was important as much for what it did not say as for its formal provisions, particularly in relation to the role of Britain. The fact that a nation that just a decade earlier had been one of the major powers in the region was now not even included in a treaty signed by its most important ally and two members of the Commonwealth indicates how far Britain's strategic role had sunk in the post-war period. It also illustrated how prepared New Zealand was to accept this reality and to choose its strategic allies accordingly. The response of the British Government at the time – that ANZUS membership 'would not have been unwelcome to us if we had been included in the proposed pact' – was hardly the sort of statement expected of a great power, which Britain had ceased to be by this time. Put simply, Britain lacked the military power to contribute to the defence of Commonwealth nations in the South Pacific, even though it wished otherwise.

Although there was rhetoric in the New Zealand Parliament about the country having betrayed Britain, and 'hanging on to the coattails of Uncle Sam', the new strategic shape of relations in the Asia–Pacific region made this sort of agreement crucial to New Zealand's security. It signified the point after which the nation turned to the United States and not Britain for its sense of military protection. It may have been a 'painful process', but as New Zealand matured as a nation, old ties were gradually weakened in favour of new ones, and practicality dominated over sentimentality.

14

MAORI URBAN MIGRATION

While much has been accomplished by the country during
the present century in improving the living conditions of
the Maori people, western civilisation has also brought
them the problem of having to face an unknown social
and economic future. The Maori youth is uncertain of his
ability to adjust himself to the new social habits of modern
times. He is uncertain of the reception he will receive in the
new environment of the modern community in which he
is being sought to enter . . . Knowing so little of the social
habits of modern life, they have found it difficult to enter
into the closely knit society of the European.
—Tipi Tainui Ropiha, *Te Ao Hou: The New World*,
    no. 19, 1957, p. 10.

The iwi will need to work hard to reclaim the minds that
have been colonised . . . an iwi is not an iwi without all the
people. Those legions of us who live in the cities also look
forward to representation. Will our iwi come to town to
reclaim us all, or shall we borrow a strategy from age-old
tradition, or start anew, and form our own?
—Ross Himona, *Te Putatara*, 1989, p. 1.

IT WAS NOT JUST in the international realm that post-
war life altered for New Zealand. Domestically, there was
a plethora of social changes taking place, and none of these

was as comprehensive as the mass migration of Maori from rural parts of the country to its towns and cities. The statistics of this exodus from rural New Zealand reveal its startling scale when laid out bare. In 1926 fewer than one in ten Maori lived in urbanised parts of the country. By the mid-1990s – easily within one lifetime – around eight in ten Maori had made their homes in New Zealand's urban environment. And what added to the conspicuousness of this migration was that the percentages related to a rapidly growing Maori population. At the beginning of the 1920s the number of Maori in the country was around 53,000. Seventy years later, this figure had expanded tenfold to approximately 560,000.

The causes of this great population shift between roughly 1945 and 1975 were manifold, as were its consequences, but the immediate catalyst was the onset of the Second World War. As tens of thousands of the country's men were shipped off to fight overseas, an urgent demand was created for labour in the domestic economy. It was a demand that acted like a gravitational force on many rural communities, including those with predominantly Maori populations. For the first time, Maori (and particularly Maori women) were drawn into urban areas.

The declaration of war in 1939 led to the formation of the Maori Battalion, which extracted thousands of Maori – also primarily from rural New Zealand – and deployed them in the northern hemisphere. For many of them it was their first experience not only of urban living but of being an ethnic minority in a community. They were also experiencing the freedom of living away from the traditional structures that applied in their home communities. These were all experiences that made the prospect of living in an urban part of New Zealand much more enticing than it may have been before the war.

The earliest stages of this migration can be traced back to the pre-war years, but it was the alignment of a series of factors after the war that caused the earlier drift to the cities to accelerate with unprecedented velocity. The various benefits of the country's urban areas were obvious: better housing; better educational options for children; forms of entertainment and social life that simply did not exist in rural areas; and above all the prospect of jobs, which in the

1950s and 1960s seemed to be available in abundance. It was like a modern-day Industrial Revolution in miniature, only without the overcrowded urban slums (not yet, anyway).

But what about the deep cultural and psychological bonds of ancestral land – were they really that easily forsaken? On the surface, the answer was evidently 'yes'. Of course the connections with what was commonly referred to as 'back home' remained solid, at least for the first generation of migrants. However, the fact that every year thousands of Maori chose to put some geographical space between themselves and the land where their whanau and hapu resided indicates that the forces at play that led to Maori urban migration were potent.

While the appeal of the cities was obvious, Maori were at the same time effectively being squeezed out of many of their rural territories, in some cases as a consequence of the recovery of their population. In true Malthusian fashion, the number of Maori steadily increased in the post-war decades, while the already diminished supply of available land remained constant. As a result, Maori land in several regions around the country was struggling to sustain, let alone provide employment for, a population that was bursting at the seams. The cities were thus a vent for the additional numbers of Maori being pressured out of uneconomic rural areas.

As Maori urban migration began to gather pace, the state took on a much more active role in the process, perceiving it as one that was beneficial both to Maori and to the country as a whole. In 1948 the Secretary of Labour and Director of Employment, Herbert Bockett, insisted that the role of the Government was to seek out 'practical measures for ensuring the ultimate absorption of the Maori Race into full employment', which included, for example, providing temporary accommodation for Maori arriving in the major cities. Even though the Government was not keen on bringing 'large numbers of Maoris to the main cities for employment', policies had to accommodate that fact that this was occurring regardless. A Labour Department survey in 1948 showed that there were few vacancies for young Maori outside Auckland and Wellington, and that the training of Maori would be necessary so that they could 'take . . . [their] place in

A new suburb in an industrial part of Auckland in the early 1960s.
Ref: WA-58009-G. Alexander Turnbull Library, Wellington, New Zealand. http://beta.natlib.govt.nz/
records/23163134

the economic and social structure of New Zealand'. However, it was
the invisible hand of the free market, rather than the guiding hand
of the state, which was the main driving force for Maori integration
into the European urban economy.

The governments of the 1940s and 1950s therefore directed their
attention to housing the influx of Maori to the cities, particularly
in Auckland, where the demand was the most pressing. Military
hostels left over from the war were converted into accommodation
for single males, and limited assistance was also made available for
boarding and renting. There was some resistance among landlords
to letting properties to Maori because of fears of overcrowding, as
other relatives arrived from the country and needed a place to stay.

Attitudes towards Maori in the cities were evidently slow to
change. At the close of the 1950s, a full fifteen years after the

169

mass migration to the cities had got underway, some prejudices still appeared to be firmly lodged. Auckland was identified as the part of the country where the need for housing for Maori was at its most acute. But because of the demand, it was observed that 'pakeha landlords with homes to let are inclined to give preference to pakehas and to refuse accommodation to Maoris. Many of these landlords feel that the Maori is not as capable as the pakeha in looking after rented premises, basing their opinions on the many dilapidated Maoris homes they see in some localities. This tendency to discriminate against coloured people and to generalise unduly on questions of Maori behaviour is a contradiction of the proud claim of New Zealanders that Maori and pakeha are equal.'

According to a journalist in 1959, discrimination was a key element affecting Maori moving to Auckland at the time: 'The prejudices against Maoris are more apparent in Auckland than elsewhere. Early in the process of migration of the Maori from the country to the town there was a determination by many pakehas to discourage the movement. They insisted that the Maori was better off in the country where he could pursue his communal habits and cultural interests than he would be in the city. But this attitude was really prompted by the feeling that the Maori, with different social and cultural standards, would become a problem in a closely-settled and essentially European community.'

Attitudes were changing, but slowly. Anecdotally 'there were fewer objections to the presence of Maoris in the city', and there was a generally greater level of acceptance of Maori in urban areas. In the workplace, Maori had 'proved that they are capable of undertaking types of work for which they were thought to be unsuited 12 years ago', while on the home front, 'many Maoris have shown that they are just as competent as the pakeha in home management, indicating to the earlier critics that generalisations about Maori behaviour are unjustified, if not dangerous'.

Into the 1960s Maori continued to be over-represented in semi-skilled or unskilled occupations, with only a small portion employed in 'white collar' sectors such as nursing, teaching and clerical work. Non-Maori were almost five times as likely to appear in professional and technical occupations as Maori. But regardless of the type of jobs being taken up by Maori, the 1960 Hunn Report confirmed that this search for employment had caused an 'irreversible migration' in Maori society.

Exactly how Maori would be assimilated to become 'brown Europeans' was at the forefront of the minds of those officials and politicians whose responsibility it was to respond to this urban migration. One proposed solution that achieved decidedly mixed results was the indelicately named policy of 'pepper-potting'. This was a programme run by the Department of Maori Affairs in which Maori housing was deliberately spread across Pakeha suburbs in the belief that some of the values of the surrounding neighbours would rub off on those Maori residents.

In hindsight, the pepper-potting policy achieved very little, with many Maori preferring to live among their own extended whanau, and some enduring discrimination from their non-Maori neighbours. However, in the 1950s, at the height of the policy, it was viewed as a triumph in assimilation. 'Not only has it stimulated self-reliance among the Maori occupants,' one observer wrote, 'but also it has impressed on pakeha neighbours that their pre-conceived ideas about Maori attitudes have not always been correct.' And the proof of the value of the policy was judged at the time by the extent of assimilation it seemed to achieve: 'Most of the Maori families settled in this way have been those who have shown that they are able to measure up to the required living standards in a predominantly pakeha community.'

Yet a more reliable view suggests that far from achieving the material standards of Europeans, Maori who migrated to the cities in the 1950s did not experience the assimilationist utopia that policy-makers and politicians had hoped for. In 1953 one social anthropologist observed how the 'movement from pas to individual farms, to towns and to cities, and the high rate of increase of those Maoris who live amongst pakehas contribute to bringing Maori and pakeha closer and closer together', but that in the course of this closer relationship, 'new problems' emerged: 'The most obvious and urgent of these problems arise in the cities. The acute housing shortage has forced the majority of Maoris to congregate in the poorer parts of most towns, where over-crowding and inadequate sanitary arrangements endanger their health and standards of living.'

For many in the first wave of Maori migrants, increasing incomes gradually allowed them to move to better residential areas, but in their place the next influx of rural Maori workers arrived – by the 1950s in ever-growing numbers – often to end up in accommodation just as crammed as in the previous decade. Thus Maori were regarded in the 1950s by some Pakeha as having 'been only partially successful in adapting themselves to pakeha conventions of urban life and industry'.

Housing affordability for the migrants was the main barrier to improved living conditions, a fact accentuated by the relative youth of the migrant population. In the mid-1950s, for example, almost half the Maori living in Auckland were aged between fifteen and thirty-five, meaning that comparatively few would have been in employment long enough to have accumulated sufficient savings for a deposit on a house. Poor housing led in some cases to poor health and did not offer the sort of environment that was conducive to improving children's education. The main requirement of people once they had reached working age was exactly that: to work.

Other changes were also anticipated. A demographer writing in 1961 explored the possibility of 'emergent' characteristics appearing among the migrant population – characteristics that would 'evolve' and 'become mature' in a way that would not occur in the rural homelands of these migrants. Given the likelihood of such developments, some sort of support would be needed for this developing group. Probably the most significant initiative devised to meet the needs of recently urbanised Maori – combining a visionary outlook with practical methods – was the Maori Women's Welfare League.

The League came into existence after a gestation of fifteen months starting in June 1950, during which time there was a flurry of meetings and planning. The guiding aim of the organisation was to promote improvements in Maori society, principally through the work of Maori women. Although it drew on the structure and success of

A teacher points out details on a mural with a Maori theme to a class at Wellington Technical College, 1956.

REF: EP/1956/0254-F. ALEXANDER TURNBULL LIBRARY, WELLINGTON, NEW ZEALAND. HTTP://BETA.NATLIB. GOVT.NZ/RECORDS/22900173

earlier women's groups such as the Women's Christian Temperance Union, the League was no pale imitator. Its aim was to 'promote fellowship and understanding between Maori and European women and to cooperate with other women's organisations, Departments of State, and local bodies for the furtherance of these objects.' Evidently it was an ambition that held some appeal. By September 1951, 187 branches administered by fourteen district councils were in operation throughout the country, and at its inaugural conference that year eighty-seven delegates were present, representing 2500 members. 'It seemed to shoot into prominence without any warning. It was suddenly laid before us, tailored to fit the occasion, apparently ready-made, for us to step into,' is how one member recalled this formative period.

Very quickly the League began to draw attention to some of the problems facing urban Maori in particular, including drunkenness, poorly kept homes and the dangers of some forms of city entertainment; as well as advocating for better opportunities for apprenticeship programmes for Maori youth, more parenting programmes for Maori mothers, and for more Maori to be appointed to teachers' training colleges. The philosophy behind these goals was to 'encourage the Maori individual to take his [sic] place in our European society, not with feelings of inferiority and reluctance, but with confidence, realising that as well as being Maori he is also a New Zealander, and as such has rights and claims on the community similar to those of the Pakeha'. With the varied needs of recently urbanised Maori requiring some sort of response by Maori themselves, the League played a vital role and continued to grow, with its membership reaching a peak of 4000 in 1956 and its many tentacles reaching out to most Maori families in New Zealand's cities in this era.

Not all the expected benefits of Maori assimilation into the urban European environment came to fruition as had been expected. Indeed, one of the most anti-social developments in society – gangs – was partly a product of the mass migration of Maori to the cities in the post-war period. The traditional structures that nurtured a particular form of community in rural areas were not fully transported as part of the Maori drift to the cities after the Second World War. Consequently new forms of social organisation and social leadership were experimented with. Most of these were positive, in the sense that they fostered success within the community.

However, gangs offered alternative forms of community organisation, cohesion and leadership. They were the dysfunctional side of the Maori urban migration; but the extent to which they were a 'Maori' phenomenon is debatable. Although the membership of some of the largest gangs was predominantly made up of Maori, the bric-a-brac of gang membership – leather jackets, gang patches, modified motorcycles, alcohol and drug abuse, and criminality – were all part of a gang archetype that had its origins in the United States. The dislocation of urban migration might have made some Maori more vulnerable to the temptations of gang lifestyles, but this is not the same as claiming that the gangs were specifically an urban Maori trait.

Predictably, the mass movement of the majority of the country's indigenous population within the space of fifty years had a huge range of consequences, many of which bore their own series of effects that spread out (and continue to do so) in a myriad of ways. There is little question that the impact of rapid urbanisation on Maori culture and language was severe. The normal transmission mechanisms by which the language and the nuances of culture were passed from one generation to the next were largely broken down in the post-war decades. As the Waitangi Tribunal reported, 'The new generation of parents was convinced that their children had to speak English to get ahead, and thus a whole generation grew up who either knew no Maori or knew so little that they were . . . unable to use it effectively and with dignity. The total domination of English-language mass media also acted as an incessant barrage that blasted the Maori tongue almost into oblivion.'

The statistics bore this out. In 1913, 90 per cent of Maori children spoke Maori. By 1950 this figure had dropped to 55 per cent, and after a generation of urbanisation, in 1975, just 5 per cent of Maori children were fluent in Te Reo (the Maori language). Yet some academics have gone so far as to argue that urban migration was responsible, to some extent, for maintaining traditional Maori culture, albeit in a new setting. There may be some element of truth in this; but the language loss is indisputable and its later revitalisation became a particular focus of Maori society from the final decades of the twentieth century.

For some, the cultural changes brought about by the mass migration of Maori to urban areas did not go far enough. Writing in 1961, one American academic claimed that 'Although culture contact has increased markedly since World War II, Maori adolescents are currently handicapped in implementing their academic and vocational aspirations because their elders still cling to traditional nonachievement values.' In this view of Maori, a lot of work lay ahead to remove those aspects of traditional culture that supposedly were an obstacle to advancement. Over time, 'back home' – the rural settlements from where the Maori migrants originated – increasingly became regarded as socially fairly static places where traditional culture was preserved. Maori from the cities could return home to immerse themselves in this culture, but they would then return to the radically different cultural setting of the urban environment. Even toward the end of the 1960s there were hardly any urban marae in New Zealand.

These aspects of city life ensured that many Maori remained in touch with the rural areas they came from. But distance, increasing work demands and the responsibilities of young families had the effect of gradually weaning many Maori from their home areas – a task that was completed in some cases for the second and third generation of city-dwelling Maori. Apart from major events such as tangi the visits 'back home' became fewer over time and for some eventually ceased altogether.

'Back home' was also changing in another noticeable way. The fact that it was mainly younger people moving to the cities meant that rural Maori communities were aging, and the populations of many of these communities were dwindling over time. If such locations were indeed the repositories of Maori language and culture, then their depopulation was an ominous sign for the future.

On the plus side of the ledger, Maori culture did not simply dissolve as a result of being immersed in a more voluminous European one. The formation of Maori social clubs in the cities (some extending back to before the Second World War) gradually evolved in some cases into urban marae, which in turn acquired tacit recognition as urban iwi. These were not of the sort that replaced traditional iwi affiliation, but were complementary to it.

Although it was inevitable that, over the generations, the connections that urban Maori had to their iwi would weaken, the rapidity with which even the most basic buildings blocks of iwi identity were swept away was alarming. By 1991, just over 27 per cent of Maori acknowledged no iwi affiliation. And if a person had no link to any iwi, what effect did this have on their claim to being Maori? The whole issue of what constituted a Maori was opened up for debate as one of the consequences of the sudden spurt of urbanisation of preceding decades.

One Maori Member of Parliament, Peter Tapsell, went so far as to argue in 1993 that 'Many Maoris were clinging to tribalism in desperation during a time of great change, even though tribal groupings were of more relevance to the past century than this one.' Such views were born out of the tension between two diverse ways of looking at Maori identity, and revealed that four decades after the period of mass migration had begun, important issues about Maori identity in the urban setting were yet to be settled.

Aspects of Maori culture were altered dramatically as a result of the post-war urban migration – something that was inevitable and even predictable. However, what has garnered much less attention is the effect that this migration had on the country's culture overall. Maori urbanisation changed the culture of the destination as much as that of the migrants. Maori culture was more evident in the centres of Pakeha settlement in the post-war years than arguably at any other time since the 1850s. Maori words found their way into popular spoken English in the country; contemporary Maori art, literature, music and dance became part of the national artistic expression; and, perhaps more intangibly, both cultures came to learn more about each other than would otherwise have been possible.

15

BRITAIN JOINS THE EUROPEAN ECONOMIC COMMUNITY

ONE WAY OF LOOKING at the history of New Zealand from the 1850s onward is as a progression of events contributing towards the increasing independence of the nation from Britain. The 1852 Constitution Act was one of the earliest signs of this, but the achieving of Dominion status in 1907, membership of the League of Nations in 1919, the adoption of the Statute of Westminster in 1947 and the ANZUS Pact in 1951 are all milestones in this advance towards full political autonomy. This, then, is the constitutional portrayal of New Zealand's evolution as a nation state. However, from an economic perspective the country's heavy dependence on exports has meant that its relations with other nations have often become closer over time, even when it has appeared that the country is moving towards greater political independence.

From the mid-nineteenth century, in particular, New Zealand developed strong trading links with Britain – links which remained, and were increasingly taken for granted at times, until the 1970s. This economic relationship saw New Zealand serve as a supplier of primary produce – wool, dairy products (mainly cheese and butter), meat and timber. And what made this relationship so significant from New Zealand's point of view was the extent to which exporting (particularly to one prime market) dominated the economy.

Even as early as the 1850s, exports featured as a critical part of the nation's economy. Per head of population, Britain earned around £5 per annum from exports, the United States £3 and France £2, whereas New Zealand earned £10 per capita in exports every year. In 1857 the value of the country's exports reached £360,000 – an increase of 20 per cent on the previous year – and by 1873 this had grown to £543,500.

From the 1820s to the 1870s Australia was the single biggest market for most of the goods produced in New Zealand, followed by Britain. Australia's high consumption of New Zealand goods during these decades is attributable to two factors: the proximity of the two colonies to each other; and the fact that perishables such as butter and meat could not last the long voyage to Britain. The prospect of Britain as a potential market for New Zealand beef and lamb was a tempting one, but apart from the minuscule exports

The *Invercargill*, sister ship to the *Dunedin*, was the second refrigerated ship to take frozen meat to Europe from New Zealand.
Ref: G-538. Alexander Turnbull Library, Wellington, New Zealand. http://beta.natlib.govt.nz/records/23140401

of cured or canned meat, the distance from Britain meant that such a market was out of reach. What was needed was an advance in technology to allow New Zealand meat to be exported to the northern hemisphere.

This crucial development finally occurred with the introduction of refrigerated shipping. On 15 February 1882 the first shipment of frozen meat left Dunedin, bound for London. Its cargo included rabbit skins, butter, wheat and, most importantly, 5000 frozen sheep carcases. From this point on, the floodgates opened to Britain as a market for New Zealand meat, and the country's farms expanded accordingly to meet what seemed like near-limitless demand.

The introduction of refrigerated shipping coincided with a rapid growth in the number of sheep being farmed in New Zealand. From around 760,000 sheep in the country in 1855, on the eve of export of the first frozen carcases, the number had increased to a staggering thirteen million. And beef production, while it never reached the same levels, also experienced a boom in the second half of the nineteenth century. As the British demand for beef and lamb appeared insatiable, farming in New Zealand burgeoned.

The effect of this strongly pulsating artery of trade spread well beyond simply a sanguine balance of payments. New Zealand evolved in the twentieth century to become one of the only developed Western nations that was overwhelmingly dependent on primary production. Indeed so heavy was this dependence on agricultural exports – mainly to Britain – that it arguably prevented the country's economy expanding into other sectors.

To give some sense of the degree of the reliance on Britain as an export market, at the turn of the twentieth century New Zealand's annual exports to Britain were valued at around eight million pounds, while exports to all other countries combined just topped two million pounds. And although refrigerated meat had been the crucial breakthrough in the transportation of primary products, dairy products were approaching similar values. In 1909 mutton was still the largest category of commodity that New Zealand shipped to the Mother Country, earning the colony around three and a half million pounds that year. Dairy exports to Britain exceeded two and a half million pounds in 1909, with the value of cheese exports doubling over the previous two years.

The risks of this overdependence were acknowledged even in the early years of the twentieth century, when economic recessions in Britain had a direct bearing on New Zealand's economic performance. But with no good alternative market, and with the trading links with Britain apparently set in stone, there was little option but to wait for the inevitable improvement in British fortunes to have a flow-on effect on the value of New Zealand exports.

The longevity of the dependence that New Zealand had built up on exporting its meat and dairy products to Britain tended to mask for many New Zealanders developments that were taking place closer to Britain, particularly in Europe after the Second World War. From the second half of the 1940s Western Europe – a newly configured part of the Continent in which recent enemies were bound together by a common fear of the Soviet presence in Eastern Europe – underwent two decades of sustained economic growth, with West Germany's so-called economic miracle leading this recovery after the war.

Britain's proximity to an increasingly prosperous Western Europe produced an ambivalence in its foreign policy. The connections it had forged with its former colonies were still firm in the immediate aftermath of the war, but as Britain's role as a global power was eclipsed by the United States, old loyalties began to become a bit more diffuse – something discussed earlier in chapter thirteen about Britain's response to New Zealand's commitment to the ANZUS Pact.

And while much of Western Europe experienced a dramatic post-war economic recovery, Britain's economy struggled, well into the 1950s, to deal with the overbearing financial burden that the war had imposed on it. As a consequence, Britain's habitual orientation to its former colonial dependencies for its trade relationships was under pressure as Western Europe loomed increasingly large in Britain's economic relations.

It was on the back of a resurgent economy in Western Europe that, in March 1957, six Western European nations signed the Treaty of Rome, which brought into being the European Economic Community (EEC). One of its driving purposes was to construct an economic union between member states, as stated in its second article: 'The Community shall have as its task, by establishing a common market and progressively approximating the economic policies of Member States, to promote throughout the Community a harmonious development of economic activities, a continuous and balanced expansion, an increase in stability, an accelerated raising of the standard of living and closer relations between the States belonging to it.' This would require member states to eliminate customs duties, establish shared tariffs towards countries outside the Community, devise a common agricultural policy and encourage common laws among member states to assist in the functioning of a common market.

None of this worried New Zealand inordinately at the time, and nor did it need to. New Zealand's combined exports to the member countries of the EEC (or Common Market as it came to be known) in the 1950s amounted to just 15 per cent of its exports to Britain. As long as Britain was not a part of this Common Market there was little risk to New Zealand's export sector. Still, the country was exposed to a greater degree than most other nations to international markets. Per head of population, New Zealand earned more in the 1950s from exporting than any of the nations it traded with. This fact, coupled with the country's diminutive size, meant that, crudely speaking, New Zealand needed other countries in an economic sense more than they needed New Zealand.

In 1960, 53 per cent of New Zealand exports went to Britain, compared with 22 per cent of Australian and 12 per cent of Canadian exports. New Zealand's dependence on Britain was exacerbated by the fact that the bulk of its exports were made up of dairy products and meats for which there were few alternative markets. Dairy production was a heavily protected industry in other countries, and New Zealand's disproportionate output of sheepmeat was directed squarely at British tastes. In several other parts of the world, sheepmeat was regarded by consumers as 'greasy and unappetizing'.

Britain also seemed locked into trading patterns that potentially made it vulnerable to developments in the global economy, and

A flock of Border Leicester ewes and lambs in a sheep pen.
Ref: 1/1-009500-G. Alexander Turnbull Library, Wellington, New Zealand. http://beta.natlib.govt.nz/
records/22850328

the impact of these export patterns was already starting to have a
noticeable effect. British exports were spread far too thinly over a
range of often remote markets – something that was obvious when
British trade was put alongside that of other leading industrial
economies. The fact that some of Britain's markets were very remote
was another historical inheritance that Britain was living with; by
contrast in the 1950s France, Germany and Italy were already well
advanced in establishing regional trading blocs in which the members
were all in close proximity to each other.

Germany lobbied Britain hard to join the Common Market,
in part because the two countries were already important trading
partners to each other and in part because Britain had been pursuing
a separate European Free Trade Association, which it established
in the 1960s as an alternative trading bloc for those countries that
were hesitant to join the EEC. Its founding members were Austria,

Denmark, Norway, Portugal, Sweden and Britain (with Finland joining a year later). If this substitute organisation gained the ascendancy, then Germany's trade with some of the Scandinavian countries in particular might be disadvantaged in some way.

The political and economic intricacies produced a bottleneck in all efforts to get Britain to join the EEC at several periods during the 1960s. But so important was Britain's membership of the Common Market that had the country not eventually made some moves to join then the entire project 'might break up or fade away', as one British diplomat observed. There was therefore mounting pressure during the 1960s for Britain to be more assertive in its desire to become a part of the EEC.

What was so reassuring to New Zealand at this time was that Britain appeared resolute in its refusal to join the Common Market. There were a number of reasons that led to the British developing such a stubborn position against membership. The first of these was its role as the head of the Commonwealth. There was a feeling in some British Government circles that membership of the Common Market would somehow constitute a betrayal of the principles of the Commonwealth. As one observer wrote, membership would result in 'the replacement of discrimination in favour of Commonwealth goods by discrimination against them. Commonwealth preferences would have been eliminated and replaced by reverse preferences'.

Also a matter of principle was the strong British suspicion that membership of the EEC would represent an incursion into Britain's sovereignty. This became an enduring concern for the British in their relations with their European neighbours in the post-war period. The particular issue that Britain was resolute on was its right to act independently of other Common Market members when dealing with countries outside Europe.

The issue of national sovereignty was brought into focus by the Treaty of Rome's apparent requirement for signatories to surrender some of their functions as nation states to supranational European institutions. To the British the Common Market looked less like a union of states and more like the start of a federal system in which an increasing number of decisions regarding the external relations of member nations would be decided by a representative body rather than by each member.

Devotion to what looked like an increasingly idealised notion of national sovereignty became harder to justify as members of the EEC enjoyed a golden age of economic growth in the 1960s. Britain, of its own choice, was left outside. It was able to peer in at the success of member nations, but as long as it refused to join it had to contend with its comparative drop in economic growth. Ultimately, idealism waned in such circumstances, and in 1961 pragmatism drove the British Prime Minister, Harold Macmillan, to begin negotiations for Britain to join the Common Market. Although the decision seemed to bode ill for some of Britain's Commonwealth trading partners, particularly New Zealand, Britain had no credible alternative. To stay out of the EEC would only endanger its own economy.

However, after months of high-level negotiations between Britain, France and Brussels, the French President, Charles de Gaulle, announced at a press conference on 14 January 1963 that his country would veto any British application to become a member of the EEC. It was a gesture that caught the British off guard and left Britain out of the fold of the Common Market for another decade, shattering Macmillan's ambitions for his country. De Gaulle's opposition to Britain was built on the hesitancy of Britain to entertain de Gaulle's notion of Europe becoming a third superpower – somehow wedged between the Soviet Union and the United States. Britain's close ties with Washington made this an untenable proposition.

With the EEC looking as though it had turned its back on Britain, there was a sense of relief in New Zealand – so much so that during the 1960s toasts were drunk to General de Gaulle, the saviour of the nation, at annual conferences of the New Zealand Association of Economists.

De Gaulle's resignation in 1969, for domestic reasons, represented the removal of the biggest obstacle on the path of Britain's accession to the EEC. Britain formally became a member of the European Economic Community on 1 January 1973, and was joined by Denmark and Ireland, expanding the Common Market from six members to nine.

There was no doubt that the emergence of a European trading bloc in the post-war years, and Britain's sometimes stumbling entry into its orbit, signalled a tougher time for New Zealand in terms of its important access to the British market. And as Britain's political and military power dwindled in this period, it proved to be no longer in a position to advocate for New Zealand to the extent that it might have been able to do in the pre-war era.

Yet even as Britain began its final advance into Europe at the start of the 1970s, a few faint rays of optimism managed to illuminate New Zealand's view of events. In 1970 the New Zealand political scientist Keith Jackson explored the possible benefits of Britain's move into Europe, arguing that the 'threat' of British entry to the EEC had probably done us some good as a nation. 'It has, for example, given an impetus to the reassessment of our economic structure and to the slowly evolving sense of independence or consciousness of ourselves as a South Pacific nation.' However, Jackson then went on to acknowledge that, in the short term at least, 'the potential problems posed by Britain's entry still loom as large as ever'. In 1970 Britain's move into the EEC was being portrayed in New Zealand (admittedly with some melodrama) as a 'fight for life'. According to one Cabinet minister it was a matter of national 'survival'.

The period of optimism highlighted by Jackson was short-lived; and New Zealand's view of itself as 'Britain's other farm' was under threat by the end of the decade. The position facing the country was stark, as the Government explained: 'If Britain joins the European Economic Community and the great volume of trade in and out of New Zealand is to be preserved, the enlarged Community must take over the complementary role which Britain has played for so long. If it does not, Europe will undermine our economic and community life, [and] cause the disintegration of the most efficient dairy industry in the world . . . for New Zealand, the loss will be catastrophic – amounting to economic disaster – with its attendant social consequences.' This was not some fear emanating from the political or academic wilderness, but a government publication expressing official anxiety. And nor were there any apparent alternatives. 'There are no other markets anywhere in the world which will take the vast quantities and types of agricultural products which New Zealand produces for Britain.'

In the early 1970s New Zealand did manage to squeeze some concessions from Britain, however. New Zealand was a special case in the context of Britain's negotiations for entry to the Common Market on two bases: 'the degree of dependence on the British market that New Zealand's export trade has developed', and 'the efficiency of the New Zealand farming industry', as the country's deputy Prime Minister Jack Marshall argued. The 'special case' argument became the sole thread which New Zealand clung to in the early 1970s in the hope that it would not be altogether shut out of what was still the nation's single most important export market.

In May 1961 Macmillan had promised the House of Commons that 'satisfactory arrangements . . . in respect of the interests of our fellow members of the Commonwealth . . . are a prerequisite of any closer association with the European Economic Community'. It was a sentiment echoed by one of his successors, Edward Heath, the following year. However, Britain's eventual entry into the Common Market 'exposed the fragility of Commonwealth cohesion, the dominance of national interests, [and] the absence of trust on all sides', according to one analyst.

Yet New Zealand was made a special case, at the behest of Britain. The old ties of the Commonwealth (and the Empire before that), together with the heavy contributions New Zealand had made to Britain in two world wars, proved that they were not so easily unbound. Of course, the fact that New Zealand could provide British consumers with lower-cost products had some influence too.

Britain was thus wedged into an awkward position because of its commitment to New Zealand. 'How much easier for Britain and the Common Market negotiators if the Commonwealth would just go away,' was the acerbic observation of *The Economist* at the height of the negotiations.

The Luxembourg Agreement was the solution to this impasse. It allowed for New Zealand butter, cheese and sheepmeat effectively to be partially exempted from Common Market restrictions for a limited period, to give the New Zealand economy time to be weaned

A cartoon showing Jack Marshall off to Europe to negotiate New Zealand's case for access to the EEC.

Ref: H-705-023. Alexander Turnbull Library, Wellington, New Zealand. http://beta.natlib.govt.nz/records/23233553

off its dependence on the British market. Still, Britain's membership of the Common Market did indeed prove to be 'traumatic' for New Zealand, with agricultural exports to the EEC falling from 68 per cent to 32 per cent between 1965 and 1977.

To some extent, the Common Market was initially common in name only, but by the mid-1980s there was the political commitment to move towards a single market, with protectionist barriers erected even higher for imports from countries outside the EEC. What made the situation even worse for New Zealand was that as the Community enlarged, new members such as Spain and Portugal would add dramatically to its horticultural capacity, thus removing the need for imports of apples and pears, in particular, from countries such as New Zealand.

However, as the protectionism of the Common Market tightened in this period, New Zealand was already well adjusted to the need for diversification in its markets and so was prepared for increased efforts at excluding its exports to EEC members. Britain's decision to join the Common Market undoubtedly forced New Zealand to look for alternative markets for its primary produce, and following on from that it encouraged the primary sector to diversify the range of goods it produced. Just how far Britain had fallen away as a significant export market is revealed in the fact that by 2007 the value of New Zealand's exports to Britain amounted to a mere 4.5 per cent of the country's total exports.

Britain's entry into the EEC in the early 1970s had far-reaching consequences for the Commonwealth and was a major turning point for New Zealand. Up until that time, the relationship of the Commonwealth members with Britain seemed unshakable – a constant that transcended the political turbulence of the day. The Commonwealth's pedigree extended back to the days of the British Empire, and New Zealand saw itself, with justification, as one of the most devoted members of that long relationship.

The possibility that the country which headed the Commonwealth would veer off in a new strategic direction, partially at the expense of New Zealand, would have been inconceivable even as late as the 1940s. However, the economic dependence of New Zealand on

Britain had already begun to weaken. By the time that it became inevitable that Britain would join the Common Market – in the 1960s – New Zealand had already begun to diversify its export markets. Part of this was a natural evolution in the New Zealand economy, but certainly part of it was prompted by the apprehension that the single largest market for New Zealand produce would soon be severely restricted in how much it could purchase from the country.

New Zealand was forced to confront what was seen by many informed observers at the time as a crisis, and it responded by acknowledging the need for the economy to undergo a fundamental restructuring. New Zealand was free from dependence on one primary market for its exports, but to the same extent it was now exposed to a much less certain international trading environment. The fact that the country managed to extricate itself from the predicted 'catastrophe' before it even struck – and indeed that it prospered in subsequent decades – revealed how successfully the New Zealand economy was able to navigate this turning point.

16

THE MAORI RENAISSANCE

AS THE MAORI POPULATION continued to recover and become more urbanised in the decades following the Second World War, concerns among some Maori about the fate of their language and culture became more acute. A long-standing argument has been that assimilationist policies did have a positive impact on Maori health, particularly in the early part of the century. But there was a growing acknowledgement that elements of traditional Maori culture were draining away. By the 1970s, however, a generation of mainly young, educated, urban Maori began to wrestle with this threat. In various ways in the subsequent two decades, they sought to preserve those traces of their culture that had survived the forces of assimilation, and to breathe life back into those that had been subsumed by the strident advances of European New Zealand.

The first that the New Zealand public saw of this resurgent Maori identity was the provocatively named protest group Nga Tamatoa (the Young Warriors), which was established by Maori students at the University of Auckland, and which by 1972 had branches in Wellington, Huntly, Napier and Christchurch. Imitating protest movements in other countries, Nga Tamatoa focused on the existing challenges facing urban Maori more than on historical grievances, as one of its leaders explained: 'we were the first generation that really lost it all . . . the loss of land that we all had; the cultural links that we were all by that stage losing. We were so aware of what we had lost, and in the losing of it was that rage that we didn't want to lose it . . . We had become assimilated pseudo-Pakeha. And what now?'

A group of young Maori on the steps of Parliament, 1972.
Ref: EP/1972/5388/11A-F. Alexander Turnbull Library, Wellington, New Zealand. http://beta.natlib.
govt.nz/records/23069211

The answer to that question was to protest. The first instance of this occurred at the Treaty of Waitangi commemoration in February 1971, when Nga Tamatoa were involved in a flag-burning incident, and attempts were made to disrupt a speech being delivered at Waitangi by the Finance Minister, Robert Muldoon. This protest was the prickly start to what would later be referred to as the Maori Renaissance – a rebirth of Maori identity for the modern age which would involve various struggles over the next two decades in order for Maori culture and identity to be preserved and rejuvenated.

Just how widespread Maori concerns were about threats to their culture and landholdings became apparent during the 1975 Hikoi, or Land March. Thousands of people joined the march, which finished outside Parliament in Wellington. It was a sign to New Zealanders that the Maori desire to protect those things that they regarded as important, even sacred, had awoken after lying dormant for decades.

It was in the 1980s, however, that the biggest strides in the Maori Renaissance were made. In October 1984, the Hui Taumata – one of two 'summit' conferences organised by the recently elected Labour Government – was convened by the Minister of Maori Affairs, Koro Wetere. It was a gathering of Maori leaders that its organisers hoped would herald a period of vigorous and substantial progress for Maori. The overriding emphasis of the Hui Taumata was on the need for Maori to be the authors of their own subsequent development.

The planned resurgence of Maori in New Zealand was going to be hindered, however, by their relatively grim situation at that time. The communiqué issued by the Economic Summit in 1984 concluded gloomily that 'the position of Maori is of major concern. The gap between Maori and Pakeha is widening. Racial tension has been growing and many Maori young people have been alienated from the wider community. Maori people and their resources continue to be under-utilised and under-developed.' It did not seem like the base from which a renaissance of any sort could be constructed, and the statistics bore this out.

By 1984 the Maori population had just passed 400,000, out of a total New Zealand population of 3.25 million. Maori life expectancy, however, was seven years less on average than for non-Maori; Maori infant mortality rates were at 18.4 per 1000 compared with 10.7 per 1000 for the rest of the population; and in the age group 25 to 64 years Maori unemployment was at least 70 per cent higher than for non-Maori.

And although Maori made up just 12 per cent of the population at this time, half of the people languishing in prisons were Maori, Maori admission rates to psychiatric care were substantially higher than for any other ethnic group in the country, and Maori youth suicides accounted for 27 per cent of all youth suicides in the country. On top of all of this, what made many Maori even more anxious was the falling rate of use of Te Reo, which needed urgent remedy.

The language issue, coupled with the will for political activism demonstrated in the previous decade and the desire for Maori to take the lead in their own cultural recovery, all converged in the 1980s and heralded the blooming of the Maori Renaissance. The emphasis on the language was a deliberate strategy. Nurturing Te Reo Maori for a new generation of speakers was identified as the cornerstone of Maori cultural development.

The groundwork for the recovery of the language had begun at the start of the 1980s, with the formation of the kohanga reo movement. Kohanga Reo were preschool 'language nests' in which students would be fully immersed in Te Reo. On the back of the success of the kohanga reo, kura kaupapa were eventually formed, where schooling would be undertaken in Maori. But it was in the kohanga reo, above all, where the advances in Te Reo were noticeable. By 1985 there were 416 kohanga in the country, and that figure peaked at 765 in 1996.

A small amount of funding had initially been provided for kohanga reo by the Department of Maori Affairs, but their subsequent expansion was funded and managed by Maori communities themselves. It was only later in the decade that the Government finally came to accept the value of this initiative and provided financial support for the continuation of kohanga reo.

In 1987 the Maori Language Act was passed, making Maori an official language of the country and establishing the Maori Language Commission. These initiatives had come about largely as a result of pressure applied to the Government by Maori communities. Meanwhile, other developments were also gathering pace. The pan-tribal urban Maori organisations from the late 1980s, equipped to meet the needs of urbanised Maori, emerged in some contexts as de facto tribal organisations, serving some of the both formal and informal functions that previously were the sole domain of traditional hapu and iwi bodies.

The mid-1980s was in some respects the high-water mark in the Maori Renaissance: the decline of Te Reo looked not only to have slowed but possibly even reversed through the work of the kohanga reo; Maori enterprises were beginning to be formed and to prosper; between 1984 and 1986 the seminal exhibition of Maori art, *Te Maori*, toured the United States and then New Zealand; and in

The Hikoi (Maori Land March) in Auckland, September 1975.
REF: PA7-15-17. ALEXANDER TURNBULL LIBRARY, WELLINGTON, NEW ZEALAND. HTTP://BETA.NATLIB.GOVT.NZ/
RECORDS/22898633

the contemporary arts scene, Maori writers such as Witi Ihimaera, Patricia Grace and Keri Hulme were coming to greater prominence in this period, as were Maori artists like Robyn Kahukiwa, Ralph Hotere, Kura Te Waru Rewiri, Shona Rapira-Davies and Cliff Whiting.

The corollary to all these social, organisational and cultural advances in the mid-1980s was a transformation in the way that the state dealt with breaches of the Treaty of Waitangi. By 1985 the Waitangi Tribunal had been operating for ten years, since the passage of the Treaty of Waitangi Act 1975, serving as an ongoing commission of inquiry into Crown breaches of the Treaty. Partly as a concession to its Maori constituents, and partly in an effort to expand the 'arena of catharsis' which the Tribunal seemed to offer, the Labour Government amended the Act in 1985 to extend the Tribunal's jurisdiction back to 1840. This represented a convenient marriage between the Government's preparedness to confront its Treaty obligations and the immutable urge of many Maori communities to seek redress for grievances that had existed like an abscess, scarring their development often for generations.

Faced with the prospect of finally bringing these grievances out into the open, the organisational apparatus of hapu and iwi throughout the country cranked into action. Numerous Maori communities now began to excavate the rich quarry of their own history, and by December 1987, 140 claims had been lodged with the Tribunal. For most of these claimant groups, the settlement of their grievances was still years away; but there was an immediate benefit in the claims process. As hapu and iwi started to investigate their past – particularly bringing into the public domain a previously untapped seam of oral history – a renewed sense of identity was galvanising many Maori individuals and communities.

In addition to the growing number of claims being researched and reported on by the Tribunal, new scholarship on the Treaty was now being fed into the public domain. Claudia Orange's *The Treaty of Waitangi*, published in 1987, and Sir Hugh Kawharu's edited collection of essays, *Waitangi: Maori and Pakeha Perspectives of the Treaty of Waitangi*, issued two years later, both made important contributions to the understanding of the Treaty's history, current role and implications for the country.

In the six years since 1984, the tangible importance of the Treaty for Maori society had expanded greatly; but what about the rest of the country? The view of non-Maori towards the Treaty was mixed, but in general terms it seemed to be one of disaffection, periodically accentuated by the odd scowling politician or ill-tempered commentator. Worse still, non-Maori antagonism over the Treaty sometimes shielded a deeper intolerance and prejudice aimed directly at Maori society.

To commemorate the inelegantly titled sesquicentenary of the signing of the Treaty, and to assuage the underlying trepidation many non-Maori felt over larger and more numerous Treaty claims,

1990 was designated by the Government as a year of national celebration. Predictably, perhaps, it turned out to be for the most part an exercise in political ornamentation, choreographed to cleanse the nation's conscience as much as to inform the public of the underlying issues relating to the history of the Treaty. The past was re-moulded in an image that was palatable to the electorate at large. There was a re-enactment of the first signing of the Treaty, a parade of dignitaries gave speeches, a plethora of publications was produced, a commemorative coin and stamp were issued, regional events were organised throughout the country, and the Queen visited in February to attend the commemoration.

While the general public was offered this theatre of the Treaty, the real advances for Maori in Treaty issues were taking place backstage in the Tribunal. Among the prominent grievances settled in the 1990s were the Ngai Tahu claim (1991), in which the tribe received a settlement valued at $170 million; the fisheries settlement – known as the Sealord Deal (1992) – to which the Government contributed $150 million; and the Tainui Raupatu claim (1995), valued at $170 million. Partly as a result of these settlements, the total value of Maori assets in 2001 had grown to $8.99 billion – almost double the value just four years earlier.

Furthermore, there were generic reports issued by the Tribunal during this time on matters relating to broadcasting, the Maori electoral option and radio spectrum management, among others. Moreover, the inclusion of Treaty principles in legislation, which had begun tentatively in the 1980s, was quickening. By the end of 1999, there were references to the Treaty in twenty-nine statutes, of which eleven contained some clauses requiring action in respect of the Treaty.

Although it would clearly be wrong to underestimate the importance of the major Treaty settlements of the 1990s, there were signs that Maori society had come to a fork in the road in this decade. One path led to further Treaty claims, negotiations with the Crown and the faint whiff of settlements many years later. The other path was the route towards greater economic development and independence. Those embarking on this latter course carried the hope of others with them. Increasingly, Maori were becoming disillusioned with the sluggishness of the Tribunal process and with the failure to see any direct benefits flowing from the meagre settlements when they were finally reached.

Maori economic development in the 1990s, on the other hand, surged ahead in almost spectacular fashion. By the end of the decade, Maori exports were worth around $650 million per annum, and there had been a net gain of 8591 jobs for Maori in the preceding nine years. Increases in Maori education and training rates were higher than for non-Maori, and indicators of potential economic innovation ranked Maori as being poised for even more rapid development in the near future.

The Maori Renaissance was not without a few bumps along the way. Between 1996 and 1997 the rate of reduction between Maori and non-Maori in a range of socio-economic indices, which had been evident since the beginning of the 1990s, had stalled in some cases and begun to widen again in others. In the twelve months from September 1996, Maori unemployment rose from 16 to 18 per cent, representing an estimated increase of 5500 unemployed Maori. The annual average household income for Maori throughout the decade rose at a slower rate than for non-Maori; and in the second half of the decade there was a slight increase in the number of Maori who were dependent on benefits as their primary source of income.

Unlike previous decades, however, these short-term setbacks were not sufficient, in themselves, to blight the preconditions for a Maori economic and social take-off. One of the underlying reasons for this was that the profile of Maori society had undergone a fundamental change in the 1990s. The foundations for a recovery had been dug deep and would not easily be shaken. Education had become one of the main tenets of this new phase of development. Between 1994 and 2000 Maori enrolments in tertiary education rose from 27,000 to 40,000, and by the end of the decade the highest rates of growth in Maori employment were in the highly skilled and then the skilled sectors. Maori were increasingly becoming managers, professionals and technicians, and their earnings were rising accordingly. All this appeared to be the fulfilment of Sir Apirana Ngata's hope that

Maori would one day live 'according to the material standards of the Pakeha and joining with him in the work of the country'.

Of course to achieve such aspirations, political influence was a prerequisite, and during the Maori Renaissance a specific form of Maori politicisation took place. This assumed two main forms in the 1990s: the revival of the protest movement, and a greater Maori presence in Parliament.

The introduction of the controversial Fiscal Envelope Treaty-settlement policy by the National Government, coupled with mounting general concerns over land and Treaty issues, manifested in a range of Maori protest activity in the 1990s that had not been seen since the mid-1970s. The Moutoa Gardens in Whanganui were occupied in 1995 by a branch of the local iwi, claiming ownership rights. Hui were organised around the country to give vent to anger over the Fiscal Envelope policy; the Takahue School in Northland was occupied by Maori protesters, as was the disused Tamaki Girls College in Auckland; and there was a series of attacks on supposed symbols of British colonialism, including various Victorian-era statues and the lone pine on Auckland's One Tree Hill.

Changes were also occurring for Maori in Parliament. From 1868, when the first four Maori were elected to Parliament – representing the Maori seats that were established by legislation the previous year – the Maori presence in the House of Representatives stagnated and eventually became less significant as the number of general seats rose. In 1996, following the introduction of the MMP (mixed member proportional) system of voting, there was an increase to five Maori seats in the House, followed by a further rise to seven in 2002. The growth in the number of Maori MPs – both in Maori and in general seats – led to new political arrangements flowering. In 1991 Mana Motuhake, which had battled since 1980 for the promotion of greater Maori autonomy, merged with the Alliance Party, and its first MP, Sandra Lee, was elected to Parliament in 1993. After the 2002 General Election there were a total of twenty Maori serving as MPs.

Bigger shake-ups were ahead. Following the 1996 General Election, the National and New Zealand First parties formed a coalition government. In a surprising result, New Zealand First had succeeded in seizing all the five Maori seats from Labour. It seemed to have become a de facto Maori party, making it an unfamiliar and uncomfortable bedfellow for the centre-right National Party. However, when this coalition collapsed in August 1998, New Zealand First unravelled. Out of the debris, two essentially new parties were strung together. One was a rump New Zealand First, and the other was an attempt ostensibly at a Maori and Polynesian party – Mauri Pacific – which was made up of the Maori ex-New Zealand First MPs in Parliament. Following a series of high-profile disclosures about the activities of some of the MPs in Mauri Pacific, the party cobbled together a minuscule 4008 list votes and 9321 candidate votes in the 1999 General Election and duly self-destructed soon afterwards.

At the heart of this shifting and sorting process in Maori parliamentary politics was a principle that far too few Maori politicians were inclined to accept: that Maori were just as pluralistic as any other people, and that the presumption that there could possibly be a 'one-size-fits-all' Maori political party appeared to be exactly that – presumptuous. Yet in 2004 the Maori Party came into being, attempting to represent as wide a range of Maori interests as possible, although its electoral results suggested that it fell well short of its ambition.

As a turning point, the Maori Renaissance lasted the best part of a quarter of a century and should be marked as a revolutionary episode in the country's history. Attitudes about the role of Maori in New Zealand society were altered not only among Maori themselves but for everyone else in the country as well. Treaty principles gained a foothold in the country's unwritten constitution, and Te Reo was restored to a prominence and given a value it had arguably last enjoyed back in the early nineteenth century.

Also over this period, the number of people in the country identifying as Maori had risen by around 210,000, giving a total Maori population in 2004 of approximately 610,000. The gap in life expectancy between Maori and non-Maori was roughly the same throughout this period. However, for both groups, life expectancy had grown by about four years in the two decades from

Maori language students at Thorndon School, Wellington, 1992.
REF: EP-ETHNOLOGY-MAORI LANGUAGE-01. ALEXANDER TURNBULL LIBRARY, WELLINGTON, NEW ZEALAND.
HTTP://BETA.NATLIB.GOVT.NZ/RECORDS/22843660

1984. The number of Maori leaving the education system with no qualifications had plummeted drastically during this time – another sign that a revolution was taking place in Maori society. Whereas in 1986 the figure had been close to 70 per cent, by 2003 it was below 40 per cent. Similarly, in the category of school and post-school qualification attainment, 24 per cent of Maori achieved a qualification in 2003 compared to just 9 per cent in 1986.

The most impressive educational achievements for Maori lay in the tertiary sector. Around 85,000 Maori were enrolled in the public tertiary sector in 2003, compared with just 27,000 a decade earlier. This increase was in large part attributable to the establishment of Te Wananga o Aotearoa, a tertiary education system with a strong Maori focus. The increase was complemented by the rise in the number of Maori industry trainees, from 10,600 in December 2000 to 16,400 by June 2004.

But the gulf between rates of unemployment for Maori and non-Maori had widened in this period. In March 2004 Maori unemployment was just over 9 per cent, while the non-Maori rate was almost a third of that figure. However, the type of employment Maori were acquiring mitigated these figures to some extent. Between 1992 and 2003, there was an almost 120 per cent growth in the number of Maori in highly skilled employment.

The one achievement that really illuminated the extent of the Maori Renaissance since 1984 was the revival of Te Reo. Largely through the energetic and resourceful efforts of both Te Taura Whiri i te Reo Maori – the Maori Language Commission – and the persistent and often enterprising endeavours of several Maori communities throughout the country, the almost terminal decline of the Maori language by 1984 had been not only halted but reversed. Moreover, gains in the language were spreading into mainstream New Zealand culture and society in a fashion that only the most optimistic would have conceived of two decades earlier.

Another conspicuous area of progress was Maori broadcasting, which by 2004 included several local Maori radio stations and a national Maori television station that in turn was helping to sustain a flourishing Maori media production sector. From its inception, maintaining and developing knowledge and use of Te Reo was an explicit outcome for the station. It augured well for the language's survival into the foreseeable future.

In the health field, Maori had a presence on all regional health boards; traditional Maori healing was gaining currency among Maori, non-Maori and even the health profession; and by 2004 there were 240 Maori health providers in the country, all of which operated under a specifically Maori kaupapa (approach) to provide more relevant health and disability services predominantly to a Maori clientele.

The trait that perhaps made the legacy of the Maori Renaissance so enduring was that this catalogue of often startling improvements was initiated by Maori communities. It was these communities that came up with plans, engineered policies, stitched together resources and pursued ideas with the sort of commitment and creativity that high-handed government departments could follow (sometimes with a dose of goodwill) but never really match. Perhaps this was the real key to the successful evolution of Maori society in the two decades after 1984: a sort of self-fertilising development, achieved as much in spite of government assistance as because of it. It was Maori communities and a reinvigorated Maori leadership that defined the kaupapa for this development and that led the charge from the front.

This, then, was where the epicentre of the Maori Renaissance was located. By 2004, at its closing stages, examples of Maori achievement had become as varied as they were numerous. In education, industry, government, the arts and a host of other fields, the presence of successful Maori was first anticipated, then expected, and then finally accepted as the norm. As Maori explored new tributaries of development, the profile and perception of Maori society began to evolve. With a higher proportion of Maori university graduates than ever before, greater recognition of Treaty issues, both in legislation and in the public arena, more Te Reo speakers than at any other time in living memory, and a stronger Maori political voice in the country overall, Maori society had undergone a revolution, leaving it in a healthier state in 2004 than it had been in for generations.

17

THE SPRINGBOK TOUR, 1981

> The member countries of the Commonwealth, embracing
> peoples of diverse races, colours, languages and faiths, have
> long recognised racial prejudice and discrimination as a
> dangerous sickness and an unmitigated evil and are pledged
> to use all their efforts to foster human dignity everywhere.
> At their London Meeting, Heads of Government
> reaffirmed that apartheid in sport, as in other fields, is an
> abomination and runs directly counter to the Declaration
> of Commonwealth Principles.
>
> —Commonwealth of Nations, *Gleneagles Agreement*, 1977

THE 1981 TOUR OF the country by the South African national rugby team, the Springboks, was one of those turning points in New Zealand's history which relied on the convergence of several social and political developments at one moment. The result was a significant adjustment in the way the nation saw itself, set against a background of civil unrest on an unprecedented scale.

The tour represented the collision of traditional New Zealand rugby culture with a strengthening culture of concern for social and human rights issues. In addition, it put up what many identified at the time as the values of the World War Two generation of New Zealanders against those of the so-called baby-boomers – that generation born between the late 1940s and early 1960s. Furthermore, some of the participants in the anti-tour protest movement saw glimpses of a chance to influence events in apartheid South Africa as well as fighting more immediately what they considered to be a 'racist' tour.

The advent of the tour, and the reactions to it, exposed two New Zealands: one was a liberal, mainly younger and vocal one, struggling for a change in social attitudes; the other was mainly slightly older, possessed of more conservative values, wanted the country to remain as it was and viewed the actions of the anti-tour protesters with a mixture of indignation and incomprehension.

This year was not the first occasion that the issue of racism and rugby in South Africa caused disquiet in New Zealand. In 1948 the New Zealand Rugby Football Union (NZRFU) capitulated (with little sign of any struggle) to the demands of their South African counterparts, who had insisted that only an All Black team that consisted solely of European players would be allowed to tour South Africa the following year. The All Blacks, it was announced with regret by the Rugby Union, could not be 'other than wholly European'. There was opposition to the position of the Rugby Union, but there was also support from members of the public, some of whom believed that the apartheid system in South Africa was in no way morally offensive at all. There was also consideration of the other issue at stake, which was the propriety of interfering in the internal policies of another nation – something that the *New Zealand Herald* suggested in 1948 was wholly inappropriate, particularly in the case of a fellow Commonwealth country.

In South Africa, if the press was anything to go by, offence was taken at even the thought that New Zealand might refuse to comply with the whites-only rule for visiting national rugby teams. Excluding Maori from the All Blacks was 'simply recognition of a social fact', as one South African newspaper put it. And after all, surely Maori would not find the tour enjoyable anyway, wrote another newspaper editor.

The official response from New Zealand to South African demands for a racially segregated All Blacks team was to wash its hands of all moral consideration of the matter. With what would become like a mantra in subsequent decades, the Government refused to mix sport and politics. This was not to say that there was official support for an All Blacks team that excluded Maori, but more importantly nor was there any expressed opposition. The tour consequently went ahead in 1949 without any Maori players.

Just over three decades later, plans were underway for a Springbok test series in New Zealand. The apartheid regime was still in full discrimination mode in South Africa, but rugby officials could never have anticipated the extent to which the proposed tour they were organising for 1981 would cause such a dramatic rupture in the image of New Zealand society and would lead to the biggest protests in the country's history. At the conclusion of the tour – which lasted from July until September – between 100,000 and 150,000 people were involved in protests, participating in one or more of the 200 demonstrations that were held in various locations throughout the country. An idea of the fervour with which some of those protests were pursued is suggested by the fact that around 1500 individuals were charged with offences arising from their anti-tour activities.

It is little wonder that such a volatile mass movement gave rise to the suggestion that the 1981 Springbok tour was the point in time when New Zealand 'lost its innocence'. In hindsight, such claims ignore the longer periods that are necessary to shape social change, but certainly in the immediate aftermath of the tour there was much soul-searching within the country. Was New Zealand really such an agitated and even violent society that large numbers of its citizens seemed to have such contempt for law and order – or were the protests simply more limited manifestations of righteous anger at the Rugby Union's willingness to embrace a team representing an openly racist regime?

Naturally, the answer varied depending on who was responding to the question. For many protesters, here was a ready-made moral cause that, although it related to actions in another country, was nevertheless something for which they developed a strong passion. The moral repugnance of apartheid, once it was made evident (thanks to a planned rugby tour which brought attention to the issue), found a ready audience willing to find out more and somehow vent their opposition to the apartheid regime. Maybe this was the issue that would breathe new life into the nation's social conscience?

The protest movement was about more than just marching, however. There were opportunities for planning, organising, printing leaflets and publicising marches through their network of family, friends and work colleagues. For a select few, the protest organisations they helped to establish specifically to fight the progress of the tour lasted long after 1981 and continued to serve as activist organisations for a variety of causes.

As planning for the imminent tour was finalised in the autumn of 1981, there was still no inkling of how virulent the atmosphere would become, and how ferocious the encounters between anti-tour groups and the police (and some pro-tour individuals) would be. Such extreme responses were not even conceived of by the vast majority of anti-tour protesters. Indeed, HART (Halt All Racist Tours – the largest anti-tour movement) made explicit its aim to have only non-violent protests; and no lesser a person than the country's Anglican archbishop, Sir Paul Reeves, added his voice of opposition to the tour on behalf of the country's churches. Peaceful opposition to the tour seemed to be almost a foregone conclusion.

Even within the Government there was nervousness about the tour proceeding. The Deputy Prime Minister, Brian Talboys, had written to the NZRFU urging it to withdraw its invitation to the Springboks and to cancel the tour on the basis that by hosting the South African team, New Zealand might give the impression that it somehow was not opposed to the apartheid regime. With such a diverse range of high-profile opponents to the tour, it could be easy to foresee on the eve of the arrival of the Springboks that there would be a relatively sedate, albeit numerically strong, show of opposition.

But given the scale of the opposition, apparently from such a broad cross-section of New Zealand society, why did the tour proceed? One of the main reasons was the position of the Prime Minister, Robert Muldoon, who eventually adopted the view that sport and politics should not mix, and from that point firmly and steadfastly repeated that line. Muldoon had initially done much to prevent the tour from going ahead, including a considerable amount of behind-the-scenes lobbying of the Rugby Union, and was anxious that there would be 'trouble' if the tour was not called off.

Sir Robert Muldoon, Prime Minister during the 1981 Springbok tour.
REF: EP/1983/4156-F. ALEXANDER TURNBULL LIBRARY, WELLINGTON, NEW ZEALAND. HTTP://BETA.NATLIB.GOVT.
NZ/RECORDS/23196315

It was not just the moral dimension of the tour that concerned
Muldoon. It took little imagination to anticipate the reaction of
the Commonwealth nations – particularly those in Africa – to any
South African tour of New Zealand going ahead. The response from
some nations was acrimonious, and there were threats of boycotts
and sanctions made against New Zealand if it did not prevent the
Springbok tour from proceeding – or, at the very least, make serious
efforts to prevent it.

Commonwealth opponents to the proposed tour protested that
sporting contacts with South Africa, particularly at such a high level,
constituted an open breach of the Gleneagles Agreement, which
New Zealand along with the rest of the Commonwealth countries
had signed four years earlier. The statement issued at the conclusion
of the Gleneagles meeting made the position of the signatories

abundantly clear on this matter. The heads of governments 'specially welcomed the belief, unanimously expressed at their Meeting, that in the light of their consultations and accord there were unlikely to be future sporting contacts of any significance between Commonwealth countries or their nationals and South Africa while that country continues to pursue the detestable policy of apartheid'.

By allowing the tour to go ahead, the very clear impression would be given that New Zealand was prepared to break ranks with its Commonwealth partners – and maybe even fracture the Commonwealth itself – all in the interests of some games of rugby. Yet it was not as though the New Zealand Government was unanimous in its support of the tour. Some members were opposed for moral reasons and others for the awkward diplomatic position it would place the country in.

However, almost all members of the National Government were united in their view that it was not the role of the Government to insist formally that the Rugby Union call off the tour. Instead, some politicians had met privately with rugby officials, encouraging them to see that the costs of the tour outweighed any potential benefits. The rugby administrators saw it differently: their main focus was on what promised to be a historic test series, and they were unrepentant about what they considered to be peripheral issues.

Only at the last moment, when it was clear that the Rugby Union had dug its heels firmly into the ground and was refusing to budge, did the Prime Minister announce that the tour was going ahead. He advised the nation of the news on 10 July 1981, just twelve days before the first match was due to be played at Gisborne.

Opponents of the tour, now beginning to be roused with moral indignation, began to coalesce and then to devise means of protesting against it. In the preceding months emerging protest groups had been considering courses of action, but Muldoon's announcement in mid-July that the Springboks were definitely coming hardened the resolve of those already committed to opposing the tour and added immensely to the numbers in these organisations.

With a decade of experience behind them, some Maori protest groups joined the anti-tour movement, offering valuable advice on aspects of organisation and tactics. For their part, the police and other authorities began to prepare responses to any protest activity. But neither side still had any real inkling of what scale or form the protests would assume. All anyone had to go on was previous experience, which would prove to be no measure for what was about to happen.

The first Springbok game, played in Gisborne on 22 July, attracted a rowdy but otherwise unremarkable protest, which had no bearing at all on the rugby being played. Clearly, some more innovative method was needed if the protests were going to have any more than a peripheral effect on the tour. However, the protesters learned some lessons from their early attempts at taking to the streets. Firstly, they became familiar with some of the basic operating procedures of the police; and, secondly, they quickly appreciated that more novel methods would have to be conceived of and implemented if they were to have any serious impact on the progression of the tour.

On 25 July the Springboks game against Waikato in Hamilton was called off after one of these new tactics – the pitch invasion – was used. Of more importance than the fact that the game was prematurely ended was the substantial international media coverage of the event, ensuring that the anti-tour movement was achieving the publicity for its cause that it had sought from the outset.

For the Springbok players, it was a terrifying episode, as one later recalled: 'That whole debacle with the Waikato game, that really was quite frightening, very intense. We didn't know if the tour was going to carry on then the [police] red squad came in – it was like war. The scary part was in the changing room standing on a bench looking out the back window. A whole bunch of demonstrators came out the back of the pavilion and overturned one of those big trailers, we realised they wanted to come in and have a go at us. There were a few policemen that held them out.'

Another variant in the arsenal of the protesters' tactics was the venue of their activities. Four days after the Waikato game was called off, the Springboks played Taranaki in New Plymouth. However, on that occasion, instead of simply repeating a pitch invasion, for which the police would have been prepared, a protest march was held in Wellington, as well as a small protest march in New Plymouth. And for the first time, the clash between protesters and police turned violent. However, if the protesters thought that the police would back off in the face of aggression, they were mistaken. This resulted in an escalation of tension, and for some opposed to the tour gave the impression that the police were 'the enemy'. As the tour went on, not only did the number of protesters balloon, so too did the antagonism between opponents and supporters of the tour. Throughout the country there were sporadic outbursts of violence as rugby fans vented their frustration at protesters. Feelings on both sides of the issue were becoming inflamed.

The final game on the tour was the third test at Eden Park in Auckland on 12 September. Throughout the country there was a palpable sense of expectation that this would be the climax of the protests against the tour. And given the mounting violence that had attended anti-tour activism up until this time, there was now an even greater apprehension of conflict.

The police shared this sense of impending trouble and, as in Wellington during the second test, lined some of the streets leading to Eden Park with containers and bins as a means of funnelling fans to the game and keeping them separated from protesters. This time, some portions of the protest movement were intent on provoking physical conflict, making the situation that much more volatile. The ground itself was almost choked with security, with rugby officials and the police adamant that they were not going to allow a pitch invasion to disrupt the game.

As the game got under way, outside Eden Park a group of protestors began to advance on police lines, hurling rocks, bricks, fence palings and anything else that could be thrown. The anti-protest units in the police, most famously the Blue and Red Squads, were armed with batons and protective gear and were committed to standing their ground and then forcing the protesters back. What followed was a series of street battles as both sides seemed to take turns at charging at each other and then retreating. It was a hellish scene, according to one journalist, with a small group of anti-tour activists crossing the line from protest to planned riot.

211

The cordon around Eden Park had held and the protesters were unable to penetrate it. However, the police had not anticipated one activist flying a Cessna aircraft over the park at dangerously low altitude, and dropping flour bombs and smoke bombs on the field. It was a violent and angry climax to the Springbok tour that had caught most people in the country and overseas off guard. Were these scenes of street battles really taking place in sedate New Zealand?

Maybe the notion of a national loss of innocence was not such a melodramatic way of seeing the 1981 Springbok tour after all. The unprecedented scale of protests and the violence that increasingly characterised encounters with the police as the tour went on may have been the result of many people being swept up in the excitement of the moment. However, when the tour was finally finished, and the South African team had returned home, New Zealand was left staring at a scene of social disorder that to some extent disfigured the country's previously cosy, friendly perception of itself.

And it was not as though the protests were over an issue directly affecting the country. Ostensibly, the focus of the anti-tour movement was on the apartheid regime in South Africa. However, the frenetic organisation, the euphoria of solidarity in a protest and the sense of a righteous cause proved to be a potent mix. It not only enabled the mass mobilisation of supporters but it also gave the cause a life of its own, to the point where by the time of the final test at Eden Park the momentum of the protesters was almost unstoppable, leading them to crash into the unyielding resolution of the police.

The international publicity for the anti-apartheid cause was certainly achieved by those protesting in New Zealand against the tour. Yet when it was all over, some protesters spoke of feeling desolate and even defeated: 'Politically, the Government had lost. It had been forced to use force or the threat of force against peaceful demonstration . . . But emotionally we knew we had lost.'

Ironically, the police, who had been at the receiving end of the angry protesters and who in turn had faced accusations of using excessive force, were confident when looking back at their role in

Anti-Springbok tour demonstrators overturn a car, Auckland, September 1981.
Ref: Ethics-Demonstrations-1981 Springbok tour-04. Alexander Turnbull Library, Wellington, New Zealand. http://beta.natlib.govt.nz/records/23168677

events: 'We had won, and we had done it without firing a shot – so to speak. We had shown the New Zealand public that the police could deal with mobs competently and without overreaction.' Yet the divisions opened up by the tour lasted long after the reflections on the protests themselves had passed.

For some, the Springbok tour and the protests that followed in its wake had 'come to represent all that was wrong with the country', including 'the arrogance of the political leadership, the pattern and effects of colonial dispossession, the maintenance of patriarchal power' – a power that allegedly endorsed 'apartheid as legitimate'. Others, though, saw the anti-tour activists as 'commies', radicals, Maori extremists, gangs, troublemakers and misguided liberals who were all bent on foisting their own values on everyone else, even by force if necessary.

213

After the immediate disruption of the tour had settled, life in New Zealand outwardly returned to its normal routines, as one anti-apartheid activist observed: 'Despite the mobilization of tens of thousands on the streets, and of thousands willing to confront the police, wearing helmets and carrying shields to protect themselves from the unprecedented scale of police violence, the movement evaporated as quickly as it had formed. Focused on a single issue and with a predetermined timeframe, the momentum was lost once the Springboks had left the country. Of course it was inevitable that the intensity of activity could not have been sustained without a tangible target, and that exhaustion would take its toll. But the reality was that most people simply retreated back into their old lives . . . and engaged in no further radical political activity.'

However, the return to normality did not mean that the events of 1981 were forgotten. The next time a Springbok team came to New Zealand was after apartheid had been dismantled in South Africa. Neither successive governments after 1981 nor the public generally had any appetite for a return to the eruptions of mayhem that had occurred in 1981, and it almost went without saying that a tour by any sports team from apartheid South Africa was out of the question from that time onward. A significant portion of New Zealanders had mobilised behind a cause and had flexed their muscle in a way that shocked the entire country.

214

18

THE HOMOSEXUAL LAW REFORM ACT, 1986

> No doubt society will continue to include, as it always
> has, those who feel threatened by or uncomfortable with
> those whom they perceive as different. And the bigots are
> always with us. Perhaps most threatening are the forces of
> reaction, and in particular the ultra-conservative Christian
> political parties, many of whose members display attitudes
> which are anything but Christian. We must take more care
> than usual as to where we place our votes.
>
> —Tony Millett, *Friends of LAGANZ*, 1996

NOT ALL THE TURNING points in New Zealand history
affected directly a large proportion of the country's
population. In the case of the passage of the Homosexual
Law Reform Act in 1986 the response by hundreds of thousands
of New Zealanders to the provisions of a piece of legislation that
would not have any immediate bearing on them indicated that
sharp divisions still existed in the area of what was considered
morally acceptable. This Act represented the point at which many
New Zealanders were confronted with advances in attitudes in the
area of public morality. And because only a small percentage of the
population was homosexual, it was always going to be a case of the
law shaping public opinion (even if gradually) on the issue, rather
than being a response to a popular demand for change.

To some extent, homosexual law reform shared similarities with the anti-Springbok tour movement, in that both represented a distinct departure from public values that had typified New Zealand for decades; both triggered reactions from hundreds of thousands of New Zealanders over an issue that they were not directly affected by; and both were based on a moral issue in which one sector of society was legally forced to be apart from the rest of that society by virtue of a feature of their birth.

Homosexuality had been illegal in New Zealand since British law was introduced into the country, although there were few periods, particularly in the twentieth century, when there was a systematic effort to enforce the law with rigour. This was partly due to the fact that the illegality of homosexuality forced almost all gay people in the country to conceal their sexuality and to pretend outwardly to live the lives of 'straight' people. The introduction of the Crimes Act in 1961 reinforced the illegality of what the legislation referred to as 'indecency of a male with a male', and 'sodomy with either sex'. Indeed, the notion of homosexuality being morally repugnant seemed as strong as ever – so much so that the relevant section of the Crimes Act was not debated in Parliament. So fixed was this view of public morality that there was no question of restrictions on homosexuality being relaxed in any way.

Typical of the popular attitude towards gay New Zealanders at this time was a piece that appeared in the *New Zealand Herald* in 1959 which asserted that in the case of homosexuality there was no room for a range of opinions: 'perversion remains perversion, and . . . the country will not condone it' was the verdict of the press, and few seemed to disagree, at least publicly.

In part because of the shared sense of moral repugnance with which the majority of New Zealanders appeared to view homosexuality in the 1950s and 1960s, its propriety was never a matter for debate. The presumption was that being gay was wrong, and that was all there was to it. Consequently there was little actual public debate on homosexuality, and it seldom attracted informed discussion.

However, by the early 1980s the law prohibiting homosexual acts between consenting adults was in general increasingly being

216

honoured more in the breach than in the observance by authorities. Convictions for homosexual acts that were carried out in private between consenting adults had practically ceased by the middle of the decade. There was no appetite among authorities to seek out and arrest gay people – although such apparent laxity was often based on homosexuals, for their part, going to extreme lengths to conceal their sexual orientation.

There was little premonition during this period of relative calm of the huge and sometimes agitated reaction by a large portion of New Zealanders when the Homosexual Law Reform Bill was introduced. The legislation was devised by Labour MP Fran Wilde, following a meeting she had with members of the Wellington Central gay community in July 1984 to discuss law reform options. Labour was elected to government in the middle of July, and the following month a survey of new MPs carried out by the gay newspaper *Pink Triangle* found that fifteen of twenty-three new MPs supported both decriminalisation and human rights legislation; and the number of supporters could have been higher if there was agreement on the age of consent.

Rumours that a bill seeking to reform the law as it applied to homosexuality began to circulate in Parliament from the beginning of 1985. On 6 March of that year the Gay Task Force released the findings of research it had been carrying out which revealed that sixty-five out of ninety-five MPs supported some form of homosexual law reform. Two days later Wilde introduced her Bill into Parliament.

The campaign to decriminalise homosexuality in New Zealand coincided with the worldwide rise of the AIDS pandemic. Gay men were initially the group most vulnerable to the virus – a fact that was employed by opponents and supporters of Wilde's Bill. In January 1985, for example, the Wellington Gay Task Force had called for reform of the law criminalising homosexuality as a measure that would help fight the disease, while on the other hand some opponents of the law reform referred to AIDS as a divine judgement on gay people. It was difficult to imagine views on the issue being any more polarised.

Poster for rally in support of the Homosexual Law Reform Bill, May 1985.

REF: EPH-C-GAY-1985-02. ALEXANDER TURNBULL LIBRARY, WELLINGTON, NEW ZEALAND. HTTP://BETA. NATLIB.GOVT.NZ/RECORDS/23049997

Wilde's Bill was divided into two sections. The first related to repealing those sections of the Crimes Act which criminalised consenting homosexual acts between adult males (lesbians had not been criminalised under the Crimes Act). The following part of the Bill (supplemented by later human rights legislation) aimed at removing any legal basis for discriminating against gay New Zealanders. The Bill opened up a debate on several fronts: some religious groups saw the issue as purely a moral one; health professionals viewed homosexual law reform in the context of dealing with the AIDS epidemic; while for others the proposed legislation was a human rights matter above all.

While most politicians did their best to avoid expressing too firm a commitment either in favour of against the Bill, a few saw the issue as one worth fighting for. Wilde found herself pitted against National MP Norman Jones, who was the most vociferous opponent of the Bill both inside Parliament and in rallies organised around the country aimed at preventing the Bill's passage into law.

Jones' strident denunciation of homosexuality undoubtedly inflamed opposition to the Bill. He saw before him a wave of homosexuality about to crash on the nation, 'perverting' the country in the process. 'Go back into the sewers where you come from . . . as far as I'm concerned you can stay in the gutter', was his response to an opponent who interjected at one of his speeches. And Jones was not content merely to shout the heckler down. The MP went on the offensive. 'Turn around and look at them,' Jones told his audience. 'Gaze upon them . . . you're looking into Hades . . . don't look too long . . . you might catch AIDS.' It was a breathtaking display of contempt by a politician for a group of fellow New Zealanders, but it found a ready audience, and Jones' brand of unsophisticated and hateful rhetoric ensured he spoke to full halls and churches wherever he appeared.

How could so many thousands of New Zealanders endorse such a view and applaud the comments that Jones and others of his ilk were delivering day after day as the Bill moved through its parliamentary stages? Part of the answer goes to the heart of the sort of social change the country was experiencing in this period, and of which in many ways the Homosexual Law Reform Bill became a focal point. The campaign against the Bill reflected a wider and more deeply rooted anxiety in some sectors of New Zealand society about moral decline and the discontinuities brought about by rapid social change. This explained the otherwise flawed logic of suggesting that the decriminalisation of homosexuality would put New Zealand families and New Zealand's youth under threat, that it would encourage paedophilia and that it would increase suicide rates.

Around 2000 submissions were received by the Select Committee hearing evidence on the Bill. Several churches made individual submissions, but there were also joint efforts. The main arguments against reforming the law as it stood are easily distilled. First, many (but by no means all) churches believed that homosexuality was the product of upbringing rather than biology – it was nurture, not nature, that made someone gay. It was 'a maladaption [sic], a faulty way in which a person adapts to life', in the words of one submission. 'There is no concrete evidence that anyone has ever been born a homosexual . . . We rule out genetics entirely.'

This argument was advanced so strongly because it gave the impression that being homosexual was a matter of personal choice and that it was a moral failing that could be 'rectified'. One group of churches took this line of reasoning as far as to compare the responsibility for being gay with the responsibility of a criminal for a theft.

On top of this novel argument were the more familiar ones, involving fears that if the Bill became law, venereal disease would flourish, promiscuity would become rampant, more unstable relationships (a cliché applied to gay partnerships) would result, crime would rise and the rights of society would be infringed on. And to wrap up the churches' submission, homosexuality was described as 'a gross evil . . . worthy of criminal sanction', but which could be 'broken by the power of God'.

But was this castigation of homosexuality judgemental? Not according to some churches. They argued that 'the sympathetic condemnation of homosexuality is something which facilitates their release from that sin', although sympathy towards gay people by some churches in this period was in very short supply – especially with a few extremists even calling for capital punishment to be introduced for homosexuality.

It would be wrong, however, to align all the Christian churches in New Zealand with this anti-homosexual reform campaign. Some denominations, along with branches of others, demonstrated a more liberal and even a compassionate view on the issue, and held back from passing judgement on individuals. One of the most assertive churches opposing homosexuality, though, was also one of the country's largest: the Catholic Church. Homosexuality was openly condemned as a sin, and some Catholics feared that plans to remove discrimination against the nation's gay population were part of some secret 'undemocratic' plot which had as its ultimate end the destruction of Christianity and national sovereignty.

The other main religious group opposing the planned legislation was the interdenominational Coalition of Concerned Citizens, which preached the dangers of 'consensual non-procreative and recreational sexualities'. It argued that homosexuals were 'sinners' having 'no rights before God', and worse still, were acting in 'rebellion against the law of God'. The Coalition of Concerned Citizens portrayed legalised homosexuality as the enemy of traditional New Zealand family values – an argument that aimed to appeal to those in the country with a more reactionary view of society.

The Select Committee also got to hear submissions in support of the proposed legislative changes, although they were fewer in number. One of the more notable of these was that of the Human Rights Commission, which explained that criminal activity typically involved damage to property or people, and that homosexuality between consenting adults caused no such demonstrable harm. Moreover, the Commission argued that it was up to individuals and not Parliament to make decisions on moral issues.

As for the earlier suggestions coming from some churches that the legalisation of homosexuality would lead to an increase in the spread of disease, the Commission observed that one of the main contributors to diseases being spread in the gay community was the way in which the existing law encouraged 'homosexuals to conceal their sexual orientation'.

The main weapon which opponents to the Bill hoped would deliver them a victory began to be assembled within a few weeks of the Bill's introduction to Parliament. A petition was planned with the purpose of mobilising support behind the campaign to defeat the Bill, revealing to politicians the extent of opposition throughout the country to the legalisation of homosexuality. The efforts of opponents of Wilde's Bill were now invested in this petition. In a few months, organisers had amassed around 800,000 signatures, at a time when the country's population was 3.3 million. Even if there were some questions about the identity of all the signatories, there was no doubt that this was an unprecedented show of popular opinion on a social issue in New Zealand.

There was a growing sense of momentum in the opposition camp. All hope was now pinned on the enormous petition convincing MPs that supporting Wilde's Bill could cost them votes in the next election. In order to drive this message home, a special presentation of the petition was planned to take place at Parliament.

Yet despite the huge endorsement that the petition received, its delivery to the steps of Parliament was over-choreographed, with an element of contrived pageantry that for some people undermined the perception of the value of the petition. Supporters lined up, some waving New Zealand flags and others wearing sashes which read 'For God & Country & Family'. Box after box of petitions was passed hand to hand and delivered to the steps of the House of Representatives while some of those in attendance defiantly sang the national anthem. For possibly tens of thousands of New Zealanders, the country was indeed in need of saving at this hour.

The effect of this parade and presentation, though, was the opposite: 'it was a naïve and unsophisticated tactic, bereft of any consideration of the mechanics of the parliamentary process, and duly yielded no political result at all for its organizers, let alone the knockout blow that they hoped it would deliver for their cause'. It was an appeal to supposedly traditional national values in the face

March in support of homosexual law reform, May 1985.

REF: DOM/1985/0524/1/15A. ALEXANDER TURNBULL LIBRARY, WELLINGTON, NEW ZEALAND. HTTP://BETA.NATLIB.
GOVT.NZ/RECORDS/23251597

of an uncertain moral and social climate, but this reactionary plea failed to sink its roots into the country.

A gay writer later described the scene at the presentation: 'Sir Keith Hay led the supporters in prayer. The flag-bearers formed themselves into a cross. A Polynesian choir, bused in from Porirua, sang "Amazing Grace". A procession carried the 91 cardboard boxes of petition forms (each marked "THE PEOPLE HAVE SPOKEN"), one for each general electorate, up the steps to stack in front of Parliament's doors – an unprecedented use of the building. They were handed over by organisers Sir Keith Hay and Sir Peter Tait to MPs Norman Jones, Graeme Lee, John Banks and Geoff Braybrooke. Hay bizarrely told the crowd, "Beware! Beware! The grassroots are moving!"'

From the point of view of those campaigning to support the law change, this period had been both exhilarating and frightening, as one person involved recalled: 'It was sixteen months of hard, intensely stimulating work, physical and nervous exhaustion, and a certain amount of pure terror. The vote in Parliament at the end was finely balanced, but it was a victory, and as happy an ending as you get in real life. But there were casualties along the way. Homosexuality was the subject of intense debate and social polarisation, and bigotry got more violent than usual. Two people I knew had their lives destroyed by severe head injuries. Sometimes you wondered if it was worth it.'

The passage of the Homosexual Law Reform Act did not bring about an increase in the number of gay people in the country, and nor did it lead to public acts of gay sex – both developments that opponents to the legislation had predicted would come to pass if the law came into effect. On the contrary, acceptance of gay people and the removal of stigmas associated with homosexuality were gradual, and arguably never quite reached the point where there was no fear for all homosexuals of being openly gay.

Ten years after the passage of the Act, one gay woman described the personal inhibitions that remained as a consequence of over a century of criminalisation and moral condemnation of homosexuality: 'I didn't come out until after the passage of the bill. My coming out had much to do with how I felt and what I thought might be right for me. Like a lot of emancipatory legislation this Act might have entrenched my legal rights but it didn't make it any easier for me in the community. I have had many jobs where, although I thought it was wrong not to come out, I have remained in the closet. I have avoided talk about what I did on the weekend, and fretted about what personal details I should tell people. Sometimes I am still scared that people will judge me for what they think I am, rather than finding out who I am. This is a part of my life that I am always aware of. I always consider how much of it I am going to tell people.'

Undoubtedly the significance of the legislation was enormous for those directly affected by the legal status of their sexuality. 'Every teenager in New Zealand who was worried about his or her own sexuality, particularly every teenage gay male, knew that this was a debate about whether he had any worth as a human being,' one campaigner recounted. 'There were more gay-related suicides than usual. And we went on, presenting our side, pretending to be calm and rational. The debate brought about a change in the law, and a change in perceptions, and it's now easier to be gay or lesbian than it was. Much easier. So it wasn't a mistake.'

The change was not instantaneous, as one observer noted in 1996: 'in most ordinary, nice families in New Zealand there is still an undercurrent of homophobia, and the high schools remain poisonous places for young people with uncertainties about their sexual orientation, or with certainties which don't conform. New Zealand still has perhaps the highest youth suicide rate in the world, and sexual orientation contributes hugely to that figure.'

By the time that the law was passed, on 9 July 1986, no public debate in New Zealand in living memory had taken place with such acrimony, using such hateful rhetoric and engaging directly such large numbers of the population. One of the effects of the Bill was to advance, over a very short period of time, social attitudes in New Zealand. As a consequence, a group in New Zealand who had been socially ostracised and legally discriminated against was slowly accepted by a growing number of people. Ascertaining public opinion at the time is difficult. Against the 800,000-strong petition

Presentation of petition against homosexual law reform, September 1985.
REF: DOM/1985/0924/1/33-F. ALEXANDER TURNBULL LIBRARY, WELLINGTON, NEW ZEALAND. HTTP://BETA.NATLIB.
GOVT.NZ/RECORDS/23042977

signed by opponents of decriminalisation is the fact that some opinion polls showed a narrow majority of New Zealanders were prepared to accept that consenting adults could do as they chose, with the tacit proviso that it be done behind closed doors.

So while the vocal opponents of the decriminalisation of homosexuality feared that the Homosexual Law Reform Act would bring about a collapse in the nation's moral order, in fact the legislation came to be seen as a correction that enabled the law to once again line up with social expectations. It not only reflected the reorientation of the country's public morality but also heralded substantially greater acceptance of diversity in New Zealand society. Bit by bit the old confines of the rugby-racing-beer cliché of the nation's culture were breaking down. The Homosexual Law Reform Act was the single most dramatic example of this sea change in how New Zealand was coming to terms with its increasing diversity.

19

ROGERNOMICS

IT IS HARD TO know exactly what New Zealanders were hoping for economically when they elected a Labour Government in July 1984. For several years leading up to that point, the country's economic direction under the stewardship of Finance Minister and Prime Minister Robert Muldoon had been taking on an increasingly socialist tinge. Surely a Labour Government would offer more economic management in this direction? After all, Labour was the party that had been built on socialist principles.

However, to the surprise of many people, the incoming Labour administration embarked on a path of radical reform, sometimes leading and sometimes forcing the nation into a substantially new economic direction. What resulted was one of the most momentous turning points in New Zealand's economy – one which dismantled many parts of the existing economic structure. It generated the term 'Rogernomics' (named after the Labour Finance Minister Roger Douglas) to describe a particular ideological approach to managing the economy; and it left a legacy of 'restructuring' that remained long after the Fourth Labour Government was voted out of office.

Ironically, while Rogernomics was a severe ideological reaction to what was perceived as the failures of Muldoonism, Muldoon himself had embarked on his economic policies from the mid-1970s in reaction to another set of economic dangers. The oil shock of 1973, combined with Britain's entry into the European Economic Community, growing unemployment and an uncertain future for the country's exports, helped to form Muldoon's conviction about how the economy should be managed.

There were several characteristics of Muldoon's style of economic management, but at the forefront of these was his belief that the state had an obligation to involve itself directly in the running of the economy. Of course the very existence of a government implies some degree of interference in the workings of an economy, but Muldoon did not intervene simply to correct market failures or provide social services. Increasingly his intervention became a pronounced feature of his Government, and veered further away from the sort of free-market policies that had formed the backbone of National Party policy for decades. Muldoon was unapologetic about this new direction, arguing that 'intervention is what Government is all about'.

Muldoon's overriding concern was with preserving economic stability – a desire possibly nurtured by his experiences as a child during the Depression. This resulted in efforts to shape the contours of the economy to maintain the status quo, and when such efforts produced the inevitable distortions, more attempts at regulation were applied in an effort to maintain the semblance, if not the substance, of that stability. Muldoon employed devices such as exchange-rate controls, subsidies for the agricultural sector, export incentives, restrictions on foreign exchange dealings and foreign investment, and a highly regulated (yet fractious) labour market.

In a speech in 1986 his successor as Prime Minister, David Lange, summed up New Zealand under Muldoon: 'The government ruled through the corporate state. Vested interests prevailed . . . Monopolies improved their position . . . Regulation and control proliferated, culminating in an attempt to legislate inflation out of existence.' And it was not as though this approach to the economy was part of some visionary strategy. Instead, its reactionary essence produced a series of often arbitrary decisions.

The seemingly contradictory counterpoint to this desire for stability was a speculative approach to the future needs of the economy. The 'Think Big' strategy – mainly a series of energy schemes – was the most obvious example of this. Muldoon's initiative was 'to look for a new bonanza', as one analyst put it. However, many of these projects failed to reap the financial windfall that the Government expected, and as a result more regulation and tinkering were required in order to compensate for their adverse effects on the economy. Orthodox approaches to running an economy were starting to be dispensed with by the beginning of the 1980s – something that Muldoon justified by appealing to common sense: 'The New Zealand economy, as are many other economies, is unique, and the theories of economic management have to be tailored accordingly by practical experience and common sense.'

Such homilies ignored the deeper crisis that the country was facing by 1984 as a consequence of this highly individualistic style of economic policy. That year the Treasury published its own perspective on the state of the nation's economy. It was an assessment that made for grim reading: 'The economy is beset with serious structural difficulties, and . . . we have continually failed to make the best of the circumstances we find ourselves in.'

The biggest of all these structural difficulties was the wage–price freeze, which relied on regulating the price of all goods and services and of all wages and salaries in order to control rampant inflation. Such a ham-fisted method of managing inflation had only made matters worse, according to the Treasury: 'It is . . . fair to say that monetary, fiscal and exchange rate policies were all held hostage to the freeze . . . [The Government's] economic management has not displayed the essential balance seen in more successful countries'.

Yet Muldoon still refused to budge, and maintained his view that Treasury's opinion on the remedy the economy needed was misdirected. As Douglas later described the situation at this time, 'when the fourth labour government took office in 1984, New Zealand had been living in what could be described as a fortress economy for 50 years. A mentality bent on protecting us from the rest of the world reigned supreme.' In his view, something drastic was needed as a reaction to the effects that Muldoon's policies had had on the nation.

One of the more dispassionate assessments of the economic circumstances New Zealand was in during this period gives some sense of the extent of the problem that was looming. 'Economic conditions were not sustainable in New Zealand when the reform was initiated in 1984,' the economist Allen Schick wrote a decade later. 'The economy was in disrepair, and conventional remedies – more fiscal stimulus and more government intervention – had not worked . . . Doing nothing – or as little as politicians could get away with – was not a viable option.'

In August 1984, one month after its election win, the new Labour Government announced its 'Opening of the Books'. It was a slightly theatrical spectacle which aimed at both exposing the failures of the Muldoon administration and proposing a new direction in economic policy for the country. This was the beginning of Rogernomics. The clue to the ideological roots of this new economic direction lay in the name Rogernomics itself, which was an adaptation of Reaganomics – after United States President Ronald Reagan, who a few years earlier had begun to introduce a range of policies based on freeing up the workings of the market and minimising the interventionist role of the Government.

In New Zealand's case, such a philosophy represented a complete rejection of Muldoonism. However, what few people in the country had any inkling of in mid-1984 was the extent and the swiftness of the reforms Roger Douglas had in mind. They would turn out to be the most radical adjustment to the economic system that anyone had experienced in living memory, and would also lead to a fundamental change in the way New Zealanders saw the workings both of the economy and, to some extent, of society as a whole. And what made the changes even more rupturing is that in many instances they required a dismantling of many of the old and established systems in the country, before the introduction of new ones got underway. Guiding much of this drastic transformation of the economy was the concept of 'deregulation', which was regularly stated to be the philosophical basis supporting the subsequent reforms. It was a principle supported by Treasury, which worked hand in hand with the incoming Government on the plans to rescue the economy.

The prescription devised by Douglas, some of his fellow Cabinet colleagues and the Treasury was based on the advantages of competitive markets and economic liberalisation. While these concepts in themselves were hardly new in other developed countries, they were certainly radical in the context of New Zealand's heavily regulated economic environment. However, adopting what appeared to have worked overseas was not a guarantee that it would have the same effects in New Zealand. Some of the ideas were 'borrowed almost verbatim' according to one economist, and therefore had 'questionable relevance to New Zealand's historical and social context'.

What made the economic restructuring in New Zealand in the period from 1984 to 1989 an even harsher experience for many in the country was that it was carried out 'more extensively, more quickly and showed a degree of theoretical purity that was probably unparalleled anywhere in the world' up until that time. One of the consequences of the extent and the ideological purity of the reforms in the second half of the 1980s was that they set a standard for economic liberalisation which the rest of the world could emulate.

Hints of Douglas's free-market leanings were evident as early as the 1970s. In a speech in 1978 he warned that 'New Zealand is heading for bankruptcy. It's not going to happen overnight but by the end of next year, every economic indicator will be pointing in the wrong direction, unless radical new policies are implemented.' He suggested that the country was 'being strangled' by groups such as trade unions and certain branches of the public sector. In 1981 Douglas issued an alternative budget while in opposition. It was a further indication, albeit a subtle one, that the shadow Finance Spokesman was contemplating an alternative to traditional Labour economic policies.

When Labour came to power, Douglas was able to enact his programme for reform so quickly through two principal methods. Initially he relied on the fact that Muldoon had called a snap election in 1984, which meant that Labour's policies were not subject to the sort of scrutiny they would have received in a longer campaign. As a result, very few people had a clear idea what Labour's economic ideas were – something that Labour campaigners were not unhappy with. Douglas was also able to act swiftly by 'presenting his critics and doubters repeatedly with *faits accomplis* they could only complain about, not prevent or delay'. This tactic was employed on

Sir Roger Douglas, the
Finance Minister who led
major economic reforms
during the 1980s.
REF: EP/1985/4764-F. ALEXANDER
TURNBULL LIBRARY, WELLINGTON, NEW
ZEALAND. HTTP://BETA.NATLIB.GOVT.NZ/
RECORDS/22403766

the rationale that changes made rapidly were more likely to produce rapid results, and therefore achieve public acceptance much sooner.

Despite this speed (or perhaps, to some degree, because of it), the pace of the reforms was uneven. There is no doubt that in the first two and a half years, from July 1984, the restructuring of the New Zealand economy took place with an unprecedented velocity, but this affected only some parts of the economy. Other sectors had to wait their turn, with some reforms not taking place until the tail end of this reform era, in 1995 – long after Douglas had finished his tenure as Finance Minister.

Douglas adopted a series of principles which, in 1989, he explained as being his 'recipe' for implementing successful structural reform. These included introducing reform 'by quantum leaps' on the basis that 'moving step by step lets vested interests mobilise [while] big packages can neutralise them'. He insisted that 'Speed is essential. It is impossible to move too fast. Delay will drag you down before you can achieve your success.' Once the reform process was under way, Douglas declared that it was crucial to keep the momentum rolling and 'never let it stop'. Interruptions – like the crash of the sharemarket in 1987 – far from suggesting the need for restraint had only seemed to spur the reformers on.

The need for some sort of popular support for these reforms was a theme Douglas returned to repeatedly. He was adamant that 'Adjustment is impossible if people don't know where you are going. You have to light their path.' In a similar vein he observed that the type of reform was central to obtaining this sort of support: 'opportunity, incentive and choice mobilise the energy of the people to achieve successful change. Protection suppresses it. Get the framework right to help everyone act more effectively.'

After a concentrated focus on deregulating financial and goods markets almost immediately on assuming office, Labour began to work on the nation's taxation system. One of the lasting changes it brought about, and one which affected the entire country, was the introduction of an indirect taxation system: the Goods and Services Tax (GST). Introduced on 1 October 1986 at a rate of 10 per cent, GST was an attempt to balance taxation on income with taxation on expenditure. Practically all goods and services would have the GST rate added to them by the seller, and it would allow the Government to reduce personal income tax levels. Almost every business in the country registered for GST, effectively collecting this tax on behalf of the Government. The consequences were not as frightening as some people had predicted, and GST became an entrenched part of the nation's taxation system.

Attacking state monopolies, which had developed a popular reputation (even if it was not necessarily accurate) of being inefficient, was one of the next stages in Labour's campaign of deregulation. The Postal Services Act 1987 abolished the Post Office and replaced it with three separate entities that were owned by the state but which would be run as businesses. On 1 April that year, New Zealand Post came into being, dealing with mail; Telecom Corporation of New Zealand was formed to run the country's phone system; and Postbank took over the banking functions of the former Post Office.

Reforms in the name of efficiency inevitably brought some human costs with them. The first of these were redundancies, followed by a reduction in some of the services on offer. This certainly occurred with the restructuring of the Post Office. Ten months after the legislation separating the Post Office into three separate business entities was passed, New Zealand Post announced that 432 post offices around the country were to be closed. These post offices had been operating for decades, in some instances – not because they were necessarily profitable but because they were regarded as a public service. This massive closure, which affected mainly rural communities, was carried out on the basis that administration and delivery costs needed to be reduced. Public service was no longer the sole guiding principle for their existence.

There were protests in many smaller New Zealand communities in response to the closures, but the newly instilled profit motive meant that New Zealand Post had little alternative but to shut down its unprofitable outlets. Then, at the close of the decade, the second wave of reforms hit the former Post Office. Postbank was sold to ANZ Bank in 1989, and Telecom was privatised the following year. New Zealand Post remained state-owned, and entered the banking sector with the formation of Kiwibank in 2002.

The whole of the public sector faced some changes as a result of the Government's restructuring schemes. Douglas and his colleagues wanted to get the most value from government spending, and this entailed trying to make its departments as efficient as possible. Improved accountability, measurable outputs and the devolution of authority were all new remedies injected into the public sector in a bid to make it more agile and responsive to the needs of its two masters: the people and the Government. Some departments were now headed by chief executive officers, who were directly accountable to the relevant minister for their department's outputs and performance. It was an attempt to introduce the efficiencies of the business world into the more staid environment of the public sector.

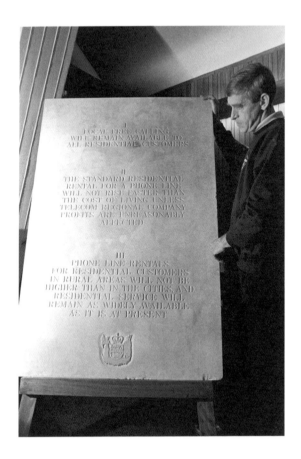

Telecom's pledges to the
New Zealand public,
June 1990.
REF: EP/1990/1916/7-F. ALEXANDER
TURNBULL LIBRARY, WELLINGTON,
NEW ZEALAND. HTTP://BETA.NATLIB.
GOVT.NZ/RECORDS/22824242

Sometimes, as in the example of the Post Office, government departments – or parts of them – were converted into a distinct corporate entity. And as the Telecom example demonstrated, this halfway stage could eventually lead to full privatisation. Efficiency in these state-owned enterprises (SOEs) was certainly improved when compared with their former incarnations as government departments. However, such transitions were not without their casualties. From the period of their creation in 1986 and 1987 through to 1992, the workforce of the country's SOEs was reduced by 40,000. In addition to these job losses was the fact that the services offered by some SOEs and some fully privatised former state departments now incurred a cost to the public. This was what was known as 'user pays' – a principle based on the idea that the state did not automatically have to provide all services without any direct cost to the person using them. Once introduced, the idea took hold rapidly and spread to other government departments, where many of the services they had previously offered to individuals now came with a cost to the user.

The Muldoon period was characterised by a period of increasingly militant trade-union activity which, when confronted with sometimes intransigent employers, resulted in a rash of strikes around the country. Strikes – and indeed the entire system of labour relations in New Zealand – were seen by free-market advocates as an impediment to greater productivity. Douglas had introduced ad hoc changes to labour laws from 1984, but these were mere harbingers of a much more far-reaching and fundamental alteration to the relationships between workers and employers that the advocates of economic restructuring were preparing. The Employment Contracts Act (introduced by a National Government in 1991) was very much in the spirit of Douglas's reforms. It aimed to give employees 'the freedom to choose whether or not to associate with other employees for the purpose of advancing their employment agreements with employers'. It allowed for individual bargaining, which meant the power of many unions was reduced and the labour market was deregulated to a greater degree than had existed for a century. However, the sequence of the labour market reforms at the tail end of this era of the restructuring was significant in that it did not allow for the lower costs of a deregulated labour market to have any influence on the performance of the economy during the Rogernomics phase of the restructuring.

When it came to government expenditure, one of the largest – and growing – areas was that of social welfare. The 1972 Royal Commission of Inquiry into Social Security had reasserted the previously held belief that 'The community is responsible for giving dependent people a standard of living consistent with human dignity and approaching that enjoyed by the majority, irrespective of the cause of dependency'; but the pressure that increased welfare spending was placing on the country's economy was something that Labour was eager to address in the following decade. When the Royal Commission's report was released in 1972, welfare spending amounted to 5.9 per cent of New Zealand's gross domestic product (GDP). By the time Labour was elected in 1984, this spending had nearly doubled to 11.6 per cent of GDP. Douglas was unable to arrest the growth in welfare spending as a proportion of GDP in Labour's first term in government, but his ideological commitment to reducing welfare spending was carried on by the National Government in the early 1990s, which eventually resulted in a small reduction in state spending on benefits.

Even after the first four years of swift and wide-reaching reform, Douglas was adamant that the Government had to keep its goals in sight. He stressed the importance of the quality of government decision-making; the need to 'identify the basic problems facing the economy, and then to deal with their root causes'; and the requirement to ensure that the nation's resources flowed 'to where the return is highest', which necessitated a more flexible economy in which there was a greater role for prices to reflect changes in supply and demand. And with all of these principles, Douglas emphasised that the adjustments to achieve an efficient economy would have to be pursued 'in the most efficient way possible'. The result of this speed (or haste, depending on your point of view) was 'one of the most notable episodes of liberalization that history has to offer', as one economic historian has described it.

After the first frantic three years of reform, Douglas claimed the credit for a number of changes in New Zealand's economy. Agriculture was less dependent on the state than it had been for several decades; import controls had been virtually abolished; the country's finance sector was now one of the most deregulated in the world; government monopolies had been whittled away; the tax system had been adjusted to become one of the 'least distorted' in the OECD; inflation was falling; and there had been an improving trend in the balance of payments deficit.

Apart from the Depression in the 1930s, there had never been a time in living memory when the country had been jolted so abruptly from one economic state to another. However, unlike the Depression, which was an aberration from the normal path of economic growth, the restructuring of the Labour Government from 1984 set in place a change not only in the economy but in the way the purpose and functions of the economy are viewed that remained well after other governments had come and gone. Many of the reforms were tinkered with in subsequent years, but their underlying principles remained intact. In less than a decade, New Zealand went from being 'a bastion of welfare interventionism to a liberal reformer's paradise'.

The Rogernomics period in particular (and arguably to some extent the period in the early 1990s when these reforms continued under National's Finance Minister Ruth Richardson) also demonstrated that while there was some popular appetite for radical economic reform, this tended to be short-lived. The desire for a return to some semblance of stability meant that any restructuring that was going to take place had to be done in a comparatively short space of time, as Douglas had acknowledged.

Yet despite the term Rogernomics becoming one of derision in some quarters in later years, the fact that the fundamental economic and structural changes introduced from 1984 have remained as accepted principles of the New Zealand economy suggests that at least some of the tenets of the restructuring era can be seen as a turning point in New Zealand's economic and perhaps even social organisation.

20

THE INTRODUCTION OF MMP, 1993–1996

I T WAS THE SORT of revolution that was perhaps typical of what would be expected from New Zealand society: ordered, non-violent, democratic and enduring. The introduction of the mixed member proportional (MMP) system of electing Members of Parliament and political parties was every bit as radical as the economic restructuring that immediately preceded it. It resulted in both the composition of Parliament becoming abundantly more diverse, and the need for cross-party alliances where previously the majority party had enjoyed the luxury of ruling almost like an elected dictatorship between elections.

The allegedly (often with good reason) autocratic style of rule that came to symbolise the Muldoon period became a powerful argument that was frequently put forward by the opponents of the country's existing first past the post (FPP) method of electing Members of Parliament. But was New Zealand's existing electoral system – which had served the country with occasional adjustments since the 1850s – really so faulty that it needed such a major overhaul?

Labour's landslide election victory in 1935, during the height of the Depression, heralded the beginning of the country's two-party system. Following Labour's watershed win in that election, opposition groups, most of which were in some state of disarray, coalesced the following year into the National Party. National and Labour were to dominate domestic politics for decades thereafter.

By the beginning of the 1980s, the FPP system seemed to have settled into a comfortable and steady rhythm of elections, with the public effectively given the choice of two parties from which to select a government. In 1979 political scientist Stephen Levine summed up this system using the metaphor of a pendulum: 'one party is elected, to be replaced, inevitably, by the other. So long as the electoral system and selection processes remain unaltered, a predominantly two-party system may be expected to endure.'

Within this system most MPs became little more than voting fodder, with their parties relying on a considerable degree of conformity. 'Party government,' Levine concluded, 'has ensured a stable base of majority support for an executive's legislative and financial programme, and the influence of the individual MP has been gradually but significantly reduced. It is no longer necessary for a government to manoeuvre to obtain a majority, and ministries in New Zealand since 1890 have been remarkably stable.'

Dull though it may have appeared, it was precisely this stability that made the existing system so attractive. Compared with the frequent eruptions of instability in so many other parts of the world, New Zealand's record of reliable, steady government was an achievement that was something the country could be proud of, and as the old maxim reminded people who speculated on the possibility of changing the electoral system, 'If it ain't broke, don't fix it.'

There was little enthusiasm among the ruling parties in the 1960s and 1970s for any material adjustment to the system, which was hardly surprising. Like many institutions of rule, they were at their most zealous when protecting their own prerogatives.

What proved to be one of the most effective aspects of the apparatus of FPP was its enduring capacity to exclude any significant representation in Parliament of third parties. National and Labour operated like a duopoly for most of the second half of the twentieth century. The Maori presence was guaranteed only on account of the four seats initially allocated in the nineteenth century, and in the post-war decades these were de facto Labour seats as a result of a long-standing relationship between the Labour Party and the Ratana movement. Otherwise only the Social Credit Political League (later just 'Social Credit') managed to secure seats in Parliament. But the FPP system typically distorted popular preferences: as an example, in the 1981 General Election, Social Credit secured just over 20 per cent of the vote yet secured only two seats in a Parliament of ninety-two seats.

Such a system proved to be a huge disincentive to the formation of new political parties. New Zealand may have achieved political stability, but at the price of the system looking increasingly static and stale. And what made the 1981 election result even more confounding for those interested in a more directly representative system of government was that while National won forty-seven seats to Labour's forty-three, Labour secured 39.01 per cent of the vote, compared with National's 37.88 per cent. The reliance on electorate seats as opposed to outright popular support allowed National to form a government even though it had not received the single largest share of the vote.

The dominance of the two main parties was attributable in part to the mass membership that they attracted, which in turn was spawned by the fact that Labour and National had a near-exclusive presence in Parliament. For this mass membership to be maintained, both parties had to ensure they remained committed to policies with broad appeal. The result was that during some periods, the policy differences between National and Labour often appeared to dissolve altogether.

The FPP system had been in place in the country since 1853 (with occasional modification when experiments were tried at the turn of the twentieth century with a variant of FPP). From 1903 the conventional FPP system was back in operation, with each registered voter able to vote for a candidate to represent the electorate that they lived in. The candidate in each electorate who won the most votes (they did not need to get an outright majority) would become the Member of Parliament for that electorate, representing the party that they stood for. In the 1970s Social Credit (understandably, given its disproportionately small number of seats in Parliament) launched a petition for New Zealand elections to take place based on a proportional representation basis, but there was little public passion for the idea at the time and it failed to gain traction.

Pro-MMP advertising, November 1993.
REF: EP/1993/3927/28-F. ALEXANDER TURNBULL LIBRARY, WELLINGTON, NEW ZEALAND. HTTP://BETA.NATLIB.
GOVT.NZ/RECORDS/23099027

In 1981 and again in 1984 Labour promised during the election campaigns that if elected to government, it would establish a Royal Commission to explore alternative systems of voting that would be more representative. Within a year of Labour winning the 1984 election, the Royal Commission on the Electoral System was assembled, and in December 1986 it presented its report to the Governor-General. The Commission had been guided by ten principles, which included the need for fairness between political parties, the effective representation of minority and special interest groups, the special role of Maori, recognising the role of the Treaty of Waitangi, and the need for a system that functioned fairly, effectively, with stability and in the interests of the voter. The Royal Commission was also charged with exploring the appropriate number of MPs Parliament should have, the basis of electorate size and population, and even the term of Parliament.

241

The Commission acknowledged that the existing FPP system was open for improvement in some areas and that to a certain extent it had inhibited the democratic process. The dilemma of how to choose who to vote for under the FPP regime, for example, had long been acknowledged as problematic: 'Is it "rational" to vote for the more competent candidate of a party for whom one may feel little sympathy? On the other hand, is it "rational" to vote for a candidate whom one regards as less able because of his membership in the party of one's choice? Is it "rational" to vote for or against a candidate because of one's attitudes towards the leaders of the major parties? Is it "irrational" to vote for a candidate, or a party, because of the strong preference for one of the policies in the potpourri found in any manifesto?' There were so many options – none of them absolutely ideal – that voters had to contend with under the FPP system.

The Commission's unambiguous preference was for New Zealand to adopt the MMP system of voting, in a variant of the sort that was being used in West Germany at that time. Its proposal was for a parliament of 120 seats, sixty of which would be elected through nationwide party lists and the other sixty as constituency MPs, with at least fifteen of the sixty constituency seats being in the South Island. The electoral boundaries would remain roughly the same as they were at that time, with the exception being that the boundaries would be required to take into account 'a community of interest among members of Maori tribes'. Prior to each election, every party would have to announce their lists, which could include constituency candidates who would be taken off the list if they won in their electorate.

In the MMP system, each voter would have two votes: one for the party list and one for the constituency representative. The risk existed, however, for the proliferation of minor parties in Parliament as a result of this list system, and so to prevent this from occurring the Commission proposed a threshold of 4 per cent of the combined list vote for a small party's eligibility to enter Parliament. When the MMP system was introduced this threshold was raised to 5 per cent.

THE INTRODUCTION OF MMP, 1993–1996

One of the more surprising recommendations of the Commission was that if an MMP system of voting was introduced, then the Maori seats ought to be abolished. The Commission regarded the existing FPP system of 'separate Maori representation with plurality to be seriously deficient in providing for the effective representation of the Maori people', and added to this view the assessment that 'separate representation works against the development of mutual understanding between the races' and was a potential impediment to political integration. Its recommendation for the proposed MMP system was that there would be 'no separate Maori constituency or list seats, no Maori roll, and no Maori option . . . All New Zealanders would vote in the same way for the party they wished to govern, and for a constituency MP'. However, the threshold for a party to enter Parliament would be waived in the case of parties which primarily represented Maori interests.

By putting Maori voters practically in the same category as general voters, the Commission believed that Maori could 'expect to enjoy a just and equitable share of political power'. The new system would 'foster and encourage the growth of understanding between Maori and non-Maori and the desire on the part of both to look to the common interest'. The rejection of separate seats for Maori was clear, and posed a challenge for the Labour Government, which had relied on the support of the Maori seats for decades.

With all the minutiae of the MMP system discussed in the Commission's report, its recommendation was that rather than simply having the system passed into law, the public ought first to have its say through a referendum, the results of which would be binding on the Government. However, Labour proved to be reticent on a change to the electoral system – something which the National Opposition saw as a weakness to be exploited. As the chief executive of the Electoral Commission noted in 2000: 'There was a widespread public perception that the Labour governments elected in 1984 and 1987 had deceived the voters by failing to carry out their election manifestos and by imposing new models of economic and state sector management against significant public opposition. Many people and groups began to look for ways to reassert popular and parliamentary control over governments. They saw the recommendation of the Royal Commission that there should be a referendum on a change to a proportional voting system as a means of doing so.'

Consequently in the 1990 election campaign National took the initiative in promising to hold a referendum on electoral reform, despite the fact that National was even more reluctant to change from the existing FPP system. Labour had little choice but to also declare its support for a referendum, especially as it had led calls since the early 1980s for a more proportional system of voting to be introduced. Growing public support for a change in the electoral system clearly encouraged the two main parties to be more than usually pronounced in their endorsement of the proposed referendum.

The first referendum (which would be non-binding) was held on 19 September 1992 – a date that resonated with historical significance for some as it was the ninety-ninth anniversary of women's suffrage. The purpose of this initial referendum was to see whether the New Zealand public wanted a change in the electoral system and, if they did, which option they preferred. The choices were to keep FPP or to opt for either MMP, STV (single transferable vote), SM (supplementary member) or PV (preferential vote). Provided that there was a majority for a change to the electoral system, the Government committed itself to holding a second and binding referendum the following year. This second referendum would give voters the choice of FPP or whichever of the other alternatives had received most support in the first referendum.

For such an important issue, voter turnout at just over 55 per cent was unexpectedly low. This was later attributed to a combination of the complex design of the referendum question and the difficulty of publicising all the options. However, of those who did vote in the referendum, almost 85 per cent indicated their preference for a change from the existing FPP system.

Of the alternatives listed, the clear favourite was MMP, which received around 70 per cent support. Mike Moore, the Leader of the Opposition, quipped when the result was announced that 'The people didn't speak on Saturday (the day of the referendum). They screamed.' It was a clear indication that a change in the electoral system was imminent.

The second referendum (which would be binding) was held in conjunction with the 1993 General Election. If the MMP option was nominated (as everyone suspected it would be, based on the results of the first referendum and subsequent opinion polling), the Electoral Act 1993 provided for the introduction of the MMP system of representation to be enacted for the following election. However, as a further safeguard, Parliament recommended that after two elections under the MMP system a review would take place and a referendum would once again be held in order to allow for the public either to confirm its earlier preference or to revert to the FPP system. The vote in 1993 for the referendum was narrower than the previous referendum, with only 54 per cent favouring the change to MMP. Voter turnout – at just over 85 per cent – was much higher, however, because it took place alongside the General Election.

Maori seats were retained in the new MMP system and increased proportionately. In the 1996 General Election (the first under the MMP system) there were five Maori seats, followed by six in the 1999 election and seven in the subsequent elections. In 2005 the recently formed Maori Party secured four of the seven Maori seats and formed what, for many, was an unlikely alliance with the majority National Government. This was important not only because it represented the ascent of a specifically Maori party but also because it revealed that despite its diminutive size a Maori party could have an influence in government under MMP – something that would not have been possible under the previous electoral system.

In the period between the 1993 referendum and the first MMP election in 1996, there was some uncertainty among all the political parties as to what tactics they should employ in the lead-up to the election. The election was held on 12 October 1996 and the results – while not unlike previous results for the two main parties under FPP – produced uncertainty under the new electoral system. National won forty-four seats, Labour thirty-seven, New Zealand First seventeen, the Alliance thirteen, ACT eight, and United New Zealand one seat.

Dissolution of the last first-past-the-post Parliament, 1996.
Ref: EP/1996/2600/32A-F. Alexander Turnbull Library, Wellington, New Zealand. http://beta.natlib.
govt.nz/records/23137433

Although National received the single biggest share of the votes (and, accordingly, the single largest number of seats in Parliament), it needed additional seats to achieve the absolute majority required to form a government. What followed was a protracted period of haggling between the parties, which soon boiled down to one objective: which of the two main parties could secure the support of New Zealand First.

In some policy areas, New Zealand First was closer to Labour than National, 'especially in the areas of monetary policy, asset sales, education, health, social welfare, immigration and Treaty of Waitangi issues'. However, the party was 'spatially closer to National on industrial relations and fiscal policy, and equidistant from the two parties on the controversial issues of compulsory superannuation and the re-purchase of the Crown's recently sold forestry assets'. Given this potential split in loyalties, it remained uncertain for weeks which way New Zealand First would tilt. It was also apparent that a reasonable number of New Zealand First's seventeen Mps had National-leaning sympathies, or at least had former associations with the National Party.

Ultimately National, for its part, was more willing than Labour to make the kind of concessions New Zealand First sought, and so for these reasons, plus the need – according to New Zealand First leader Winston Peters – for stability, the party aligned itself with National. It was not until 11 December 1996, however, that an agreement between National and New Zealand First was formally concluded, and the process of swearing in the new government could get underway.

This month of uncertainty involved the formation of a new government, but there were further episodes of instability during the first term of this inaugural MMP government. The relationship between National and New Zealand First broke apart, and some of the New Zealand First MPs split from their own party and became independents or formed new and short-lived parties. Yet it was solely with the support of these fledgling political entities that National was able to maintain its majority.

This was hardly what New Zealanders wanted from their new system of government. There had been a growing sense of frustration among the public at the convoluted negotiations that seemed to be an inevitable part of MMP government-forming. Subsequent wrangles within the coalition, almost leading to its collapse, caused a rise in popular dissatisfaction to the point that by the end of the decade there was an upsurge in support for FPP, which was seen as at least being a more predictable and stable system.

However, Parliament had become much more diverse as a result of MMP, with a greater number of women, ethnic minorities and other groups not previously associated with having a presence in the House of Representatives. This trend towards greater diversity continued in subsequent elections and was seen by MMP supporters as vindication of the new electoral system.

The change to the MMP voting system was the most momentous turning point in the country's electoral regime in one and a half centuries. Its importance lay not just in the fact that a change had been made for its own sake, but because the ensuing modification to the way that New Zealanders elected their government produced much more representative governments than had existed before and resulted in a much more diverse Parliament, with MPs from a greater variety of political parties taking their place.

And nor was this diversity merely token. One of the requirements of MMP was that unless a party received an outright majority, it was obliged to work with other parties in some form of coalition. The result was a series of trade-offs and compromises in policies in order to ensure a government could be formed. The mechanics of this were sometimes messy, with prolonged negotiations and courting of some parties. But it provided a further check and balance for the tendency towards autocratic rule which had sometimes been a feature of FPP governments, while also ensuring that legislation reflecting a wider range of the electorate's interests was enacted.

Parliament and the country's population enjoy (and occasionally suffer) a reciprocal relationship. Under the MMP system there was a sense from the outset that this relationship brought more voters into its fold, and that this no longer applied just to Labour and National supporters. Parties such as United Future, New Zealand First and the Greens owed their presence in Parliament after 1996 to the MMP system, even if that presence meant that they occasionally got to wield influence that belied their small numbers. No other political development in the country since the introduction of parliamentary democracy in the 1850s could claim to have had such a widespread impact on how New Zealanders chose their governments and, through that, on how they were governed. Despite its shortcomings, the MMP electoral system remains one of the most notable turning points in New Zealand history.

EPILOGUE

JUST HOW ARBITRARY THIS list of turning points has been is evident in the fact that if an entirely different set had been selected, they would provide an alternative but equally valid explanation of how New Zealand evolved into its present state. The purpose of the twenty turning points chosen for this publication has been to claim not that they are the definitive events in the progression of the country as a nation, but that they demonstrate that New Zealand's development has not been preordained by some inevitable flow of events. Rather, more often than not, major turns in the direction of the country have often been attributable to the actions of a small number of individuals. And even some of those mass movements, such as rise of the suffragettes, or convulsive events, such as the wars of the 1860s, have often had just a few people involved at their inception.

Another feature that the turning points included in this work reveal is the huge diversity of ideas, beliefs and courses of action that go to make up the history of a nation. For its entire period of human habitation, there was never a time when the country experienced a uniformity of opinion about its destiny. It is this pluralism which, although sometimes giving the impression of instability, has generated the forces that have shaped New Zealand's evolution. What these turning points suggest, in all their organic, unexpected and occasionally volatile forms, is that the patterns of the past are just as much the forms of the future, and that the uncertainty leading up to every turning point is an essential ingredient in this evolution.

BIBLIOGRAPHIC REFERENCES

The following is a select bibliography that lists the main sources used in each chapter. It does not include newspapers, journal articles, artworks, official reports, theses or legislation.

1 Discovery

Ballentyne, T., *Orientalism and Race: Aryanism in the British Empire*, New York, 2002.

Buck, P., *An Introduction to Polynesian Anthropology*, New York, 1945.

Buck, P., *Vikings of the Sunrise*, Christchurch, (1938) 1954.

Burney, J. (ed.), *A Chronological History of Voyages and Discoveries in the South Seas*, vol. 3, New York, 1967.

Curnow, A., 'Landfall in Unknown Seas', in *Collected Poems, 1933–1973*, Wellington, 1974.

Evans, J., *Nga Waka o Nehera: The First Voyaging Canoes*, Auckland, 1997.

Firth, R., *History and Traditions of Tikopia*, Wellington, 1961.

Golson, J. (ed.), *Polynesian Navigation: A Symposium on Andrew Sharp's Theory of Accidental Voyages*, Wellington, 1962.

Howe, K. R. *The Quest for Origins: Who First Discovered and Settled the Pacific Islands?*, Auckland, 2003.

Irwin, G., *The Prehistoric Exploration and Colonisation of the Pacific*, Cambridge, 1992.

Johansen, J. P., *Studies in Maori Rites and Myths*, Copenhagen, 1958.

Kirch, P. V. and Green, R. C., *Hawaiki, Ancestral Polynesia: An Essay in Historical Anthropology*, New York, 2001.

McNab, R., *From Tasman to Marsden: A History of Northern New Zealand from 1642 to 1818*, Dunedin, 1914.

McNab, R., *Murihiku: A History of the South Island of New Zealand and the Islands Adjacent and Lying to the South from 1642 to 1835*, Wellington, 1909.

Mead, H. M., *Tikanga Maori: Living by Maori Values*, Wellington, 2003.

Richards, C., 'The Substance of Polynesian Voyaging', in *World Archaeology*, vol. 40, no. 2, 2008.

Rusden, G. W., *History of New Zealand*, vol. 1, London, 1883.

Selwyn, G. A. *New Zealand*, London, 1847.

Sharp, A., *Ancient Voyagers in the Pacific*, London, 1957.

Slot, B. J., *Abel Tasman and the Discovery of New Zealand*, Amsterdam, 1992.

Sorrenson, M. P. K., *Maori Origins and Migrations: The Genesis of Some Pakeha Myths and Legends*, Auckland, 1979.

Suggs, R. C., *The Island Civilizations of Polynesia*, New York, 1960.

Sutherland, I. L. G., *The Maori Situation*, Wellington, 1935.

Thomson, A. S., *The Story of New Zealand: Past and Present, Savage and Civilised*, vol. 1, London 1859.

Tregear, E. R., *The Aryan Maori*, Wellington, 1885.

Von Hochstetter, F., *New Zealand: Its Physical Geography, Geology and Natural History*, Stuttgart, 1867.

2   Hongi's Visit to England, 1820

Ballara, A., *Taua: Musket Wars, Land Wars or Tikanga? Warfare in Maori Society in the Early Nineteenth Century*, Auckland, 2003.

Barton, R. J., *Earliest New Zealand: The Journals and Correspondence of the Rev John Butler*, Masterton, 1927.

Binney, J., *The Legacy of Guilt: A Life of Thomas Kendall*, Auckland, 1968.

Church Missionary Society, *The Missionary Register for 1820*, London, 1820.

Cruise, R. A., *Journal of a Ten Months' Residence in New Zealand*, London, 1824.

Hursthouse, C., *New Zealand, or, Zealandia, The Britain of the South*, vol. 1, London, 1857.

Smith, S. P., 'Wars of the Northern Against the Southern Tribes of New Zealand in the Nineteenth Century, Part III', in *Journal of the Polynesian Society*, vol. 9, 1900.

Strachan, A., *The Life of the Rev. Samuel Leigh*, London, 1870.

Urlich Cloher, D., *Hongi Hika: Warrior Chief*, Auckland, 2003.

Wakefield, E. J., *Adventure in New Zealand from 1839 to 1844*, London, 1845.

3   Appointment of James Busby as Resident, 1832

Carleton, H., *The Life of Henry Williams: Archdeacon of Waimate*, vol. 1, Wellington, 1948.

Craik, G. L., *The New Zealanders*, London, 1830.

Davis, C. O., *The Life and Times of Patuone*, Auckland, 1876.

Dumont d'Urville, J. S. C., *New Zealand, 1826–1827*, trans. O. Wright, Wellington, 1950.

Elder, J. (ed.), *The Letters and Journals of Samuel Marsden 1765–1838*, Dunedin, 1932.

FitzRoy, R., *Voyages of the* Adventure *and the* Beagle, *1826–1836*, Vol. 1, London, 1837.

Harrop, A. J., *England and New Zealand from Tasman to the Taranaki War*, London, 1926.

Hight, J. and Bamford, H. D., *The Constitutional History and Law of New Zealand*, Christchurch, 1914.

Leys, T. W. (ed.), *Early History of New Zealand*, Auckland, 1890.

McNab, R. (ed.), *Historical Records of New Zealand*, vol. 1, Wellington, 1908.

Montgomery, J. (ed.), *Journal of Voyages and Travels by the Rev. Daniel Tyerman and George Bennet*, vol. 2, Boston, 1832.

Moon, P. and Biggs, P., *The Treaty and its Times*, Auckland, 2004.

Moon, P., *Fatal Frontiers: A History of New Zealand in the Decade Before the Treaty*, Auckland, 2006.

Moon, P., *Te Ara Ki Te Tiriti, The Path to the Treaty of Waitangi*, Auckland, 2002.

Parkinson, P., *"Preserved in the Archives of the Colony": The English Drafts of the Treaty of Waitangi*, Wellington, 2001.

Ramsden, E., *Busby of Waitangi: H. M.'s Resident at New Zealand, 1833–40*, Wellington, 1942.

Rogers, L. M. (ed.), *The Early Journals of Henry Williams 1826–1840*, Christchurch, 1961.

Sharp, A. (ed.), *Duperrey's Visit to New Zealand in 1824*, Wellington, 1971.

Turner, J., *The Pioneer Missionary: Life of the Rev. Nathaniel Turner*, Melbourne, 1872.

Turton, H. H., *An Epitome of Official Documents Relative to Native Affairs and Land Purchases in the North Island of New Zealand*, Wellington, 1883.

Wakefield, E. J., *Adventure in New Zealand from 1839 to 1844*, London, 1845.

Webster, J., *Reminiscences of an Old Settler in Australia and New Zealand*, Christchurch, 1908.

Winks, R. W. (ed.), *British Imperialism: Gold, God and Glory*, New York, 1963.

Wright O. (trans.), *New Zealand 1826-1827 from the French of Dumont D'Urville*, Wellington, 1950.

4 Maketu Execution, 1842

Brodie, W., *Remarks on the Past and Present State of New Zealand: Its Government, Capabilities and Prospects*, London, 1845.

Clarke, G., *Notes on Early Life in New Zealand*, Hobart, 1903.

Horsman, J., *The Coming of the Pakeha to Auckland Province*, Wellington, 1971.

Lennard, M., *Motuarohia: An Island in the Bay of Islands, Sometime Known as Roberton's Island*, Auckland, 1959.

Marjoribanks, A., *Travels in New Zealand with a Map of the Country*, London, 1846.

McIntyre, W. D. and Gardiner, W. J. (eds.), *Speeches and Documents on New Zealand History*, Oxford, 1971.

Moore, D., et al, *Rangahaua Whanui National Theme A: Old Land Claims*, Wellington, 1997.

Ross, J. C., *A Voyage of Discovery and Research in the Southern and Antarctic Regions*, vol. 2, London, 1847.

Swainson, W., *New Zealand and its Colonization*, London, 1859.

Sweetman, E., *The Unsigned New Zealand Treaty*, Melbourne, 1939.

Umi Perkins, M., *Mana/'Ike: Maori and Native Hawaiian Education and Self-Determination*, Honolulu, 2004.

Wolfe, R., *Auckland: A Pictorial History*, Auckland, 2002.

Wolfe, R., *Hell-Hole of the Pacific*, Auckland, 2005.

5 New Zealand Company Settlements

Bidwill, J., *Rambles in New Zealand*, London, 1845.

Brees, S. C., *Pictorial Illustrations of New Zealand*, London, 1849.

Burns, P., *Fatal Success: A History of the New Zealand Company*, Auckland, 1989.

Heaphy, C., *Narrative of a Residence in Various Parts of New Zealand*, London, 1842.

Hursthouse, C., *New Zealand, or, Zealandia, the Britain of the South*, vol. 1, London, 1857.

Marais, J. S., *The Colonization of New Zealand*, Wellington, 1927.

Martin, S. M., *New Zealand in a Series of Letters*, London, 1845.

Morrell, W. P., *British Colonial Policy in the Age of Peel and Russell*, Oxford, 1930.

Mundy, G. C., *Our Antipodes, or Residence and Rambles in the Australasian Colonies*, vol. 2, London, 1852.

Petre, H. W., *An Account of the Settlements of the New Zealand Company*, 5th edn., London, 1842.

Renwick, W. (ed.), *Sovereignty and Indigenous Rights: The Treaty of Waitangi in its International Contexts*, Wellington, 1991.

Wakefield, E. G., *The British Colonization of New Zealand; Being an Account of the Principles, Objects, and Plans of the New Zealand Association*, London, 1837.

Wakefield, E. J., *Adventure in New Zealand from 1839 to 1844*, vol. 2, London, 1845.

6 The New Zealand Constitution Act

Adams, P., *Fatal Necessity: British Intervention in New Zealand, 1830–47*, Auckland, 1977.

Fenton, F. D., *Observations on the State of the Aboriginal Inhabitants of New Zealand*, Auckland, 1859.

FitzGerald, J. E. (ed.), *A Selection from the Writings and Speeches of John Robert Godley*, Christchurch, 1863.

Fox, W., *The Six Colonies of New Zealand*, London, 1851.

Fuller, F., *Five Years' Residence in New Zealand; or, Observations on Colonization*, London, 1859.

Moon, P., *Hobson: Governor of New Zealand, 1840–1842*, Auckland, 1998.

Moon, P., *The Edges of Empires: New Zealand in the Middle of the Nineteenth Century*, Auckland, 2009.

Porter, A., *The Nineteenth Century, The Oxford History of the British Empire*, vol. 3, Oxford, 1998.

Sinclair, K., *A History of New Zealand*, Auckland, 1988.

Swainson, W., *New Zealand and its Colonization*, London, 1859.

Thomson, A. S., *The Story of New Zealand, Past and Present, Savage and Civilised*, vol. 2, 1859.

Ward, A., *A Show of Justice: Racial Amalgamation in Nineteenth Century New Zealand*, Toronto, 1973.

7 Thomas Gore Browne's Waitara Purchase

Abraham, C. J., *Journal of a Walk with the Bishop of New Zealand from Auckland to Taranaki in August 1855*, London, 1856.

Clarke, G. *Remarks Upon a Pamphlet by James Busby Esq., Commenting Upon a Pamphlet Entitled the Taranaki Question by Sir William Martin*, Auckland, 1861.

Cowan, J., *The New Zealand Wars: A History of the Maori Campaigns and the Pioneering Period*, vol. 1, Wellington, 1955.

Cowan, J., *The New Zealand Wars: A History of the Maori Campaigns and the Pioneering Period*, vol. 2, Wellington, 1956.

Fargher, R., *The Best Man Who Ever Served the Crown: A Life of Donald McLean*, Wellington, 2007.

FitzRoy, R., *Remarks on New Zealand, in February 1846*, London, 1846.

Grayling, W. I., *The War in Taranaki, During the Years 1860-1861*, New Plymouth, 1862.

Kawharu, I. H., *Maori Land Tenure*, Oxford, 1977.

Martin, W., *The Taranaki Question*, 3rd edn., London, 1861.

Moon, P., *FitzRoy: Governor in Crisis 1843–1845*, Auckland, 2000.

Moon, P., *The Edges of Empires: New Zealand in the Middle of the Nineteenth Century*.

Rutherford, J., *Sir George Grey: A Study in Colonial Government*, London, 1961.

Sinclair, K., *The Origins of the Maori Wars*, Wellington, 1957.

Swainson, W., *New Zealand and the War*, London, 1862.

Thomson, A. S., *The Story of New Zealand: Past and Present, Savage and Civilised*, vol. 2, 1859.

Wells, B., *The History of Taranaki*, New Plymouth, 1878.

8 Maori Get the Vote

Dalton, B. J., *War and Politics in New Zealand, 1855-1870*, Sydney, 1967.

Jackson, W. J., *New Zealand: Politics of Change*, Wellington, 1973.

Lipson, L., *The Politics of Equality: New Zealand's Adventure in Democracy*, Chicago.

Moon, P., *Ngapua: The Political Life of Hone Heke Ngapua, MHR*, Auckland, 2006.

Orange, C., *The Treaty of Waitangi*, Wellington, 1987.

Scholefield, G. H. (ed.), *The Richmond–Atkinson Papers*, vol. 2, Wellington, 1960.

Sinclair, K., *Kinds of Peace: Maori People After the Wars, 1870–85*, Auckland, 1991.

Ward, A., *A Show of Justice: Racial Amalgamation in Nineteenth Century New Zealand*.

Wells, B., *The History of Taranaki*, New Plymouth, 1878.

9 Women Get the Vote

Briggs, A., *A Social History of England*, 2nd edn., London, 1994.

Brookes, B., Macdonald, C., and Tennant, M. (eds.), *Women in History: Essays on European Women in New Zealand*, Wellington, 1986.

Burdon, R. M., *King Dick: A Biography of Richard John Seddon*, Christchurch, 1955.

Devaliant, J., *Kate Sheppard: The Fight for Women's Votes in New Zealand*, Auckland, 1992.

Gillis, J. R., *A World of Their Own Making: Myth, Ritual and the Quest for Family Values*, Cambridge, Massachusetts, 1996.

Hutching, M., *Leading the Way: How New Zealand Women Won the Vote*, Auckland, 2010.

Lovell-Smith, M., *The Woman Question: Writings by the Women Who Won the Vote*, Auckland, 1992.

Murray, J. M. and Cocker, J., *Temperance and Prohibition in New Zealand*, London, 1930.

Reeves, W. P., *State Experiments in Australia and New Zealand*, vol. 1, London, 1902.

Simpson, H. M., *The Women of New Zealand*, Auckland, 1962.

Sheppard, K., in P. R. Fogarty, '"The Shrieking Sisterhood": A Comparative Analysis of the Suffrage Movement in the United States and New Zealand', MA Thesis, University of Canterbury, Christchurch, 1988, p. 9.

Tyrrell, I., *Woman's World/Woman's Empire: the Women's Christian Temperance Union in International Perspective, 1800–1930*, North Carolina, 1991.

Wood, J., *A Challenge, Not a Truce: A History of the New Zealand Women's Christian Temperance Union 1885–1985*, Wellington, 1985.

10   Recovery of the Maori Race

Ballara, A., *Iwi: The Dynamics of Maori Tribal Organisation from c.1769 to c.1945*, Wellington, 1998.

Cholmondeley, T.. *Ultima Thule; or, Thoughts Suggested by a Residence in New Zealand*, London, 1854.

Cowan, J., *The New Zealand Wars*, vol. 2, 1923.

Evison, H. C., *Te Wai Pounamu: The Greenstone Island: A History of the Southern Maori During the European Colonization of New Zealand*, Christchurch, 1993.

Fenton, F. D., *Observations on the State of the Aboriginal Inhabitants of New Zealand*, 1859.

Fox, W., *The War in New Zealand*, London, 1866.

Lange, R., *May the People Live: A History of Maori Health Development, 1900–1920*, Auckland, 1999.

Moon, P., *The Edges of Empires: New Zealand in the Middle of the Nineteenth Century*.

Nicholas, J. L., *Narrative of a Voyage to New Zealand*, vol. 2, London, 1817.

Polack, J. S., *New Zealand: Being a Narrative of Travels and Adventures During a Residence in that Country Between the Years 1831 and 1837*, vol. 2, London, 1838.

Pool, D. I., *Te Iwi Maori: A New Zealand Population, Past, Present and Projected*, Auckland, 1991.

Pool, D. I., *The Maori Population of New Zealand 1769–1971*, Auckland, 1977.

Sutherland, I. L. G., *The Maori Situation*, Wellington, 1935.

Terry, C., *New Zealand, Its Advantages and Prospects as a British Colony*, London, 1842.

Turton, H. H., *An Epitome of Official Documents Relative to Native Affairs and Land Purchases in the North Island of New Zealand*.

Yate, W., *An Account of New Zealand*, 2nd edn., London, 1835.

11   The First World War

Byrne, A. E., *The Official History of the Otago Regiment*, Dunedin, 1921.

Cowan, J., *The Maoris in the Great War*, Melbourne, 1926.

Efford, E., *Penalties on Conscience; an Examination of the Defaulters' Detention System in New Zealand*, Christchurch, 1945.

Hamilton, I., *Gallipoli Diary*, vol. 1, New York, 1920.

King, J., *Gallipoli Diaries: The Anzacs' Own Story Day by Day*, Sydney, 2003.

Moon, P., *New Zealand in the Twentieth Century: The Nation, the People*, Auckland, 2011.

Mulgan, J., *Report on Experience*, Auckland, 1947.

Phillips, J., et al., *The Great Adventure: New Zealand Soldiers Describe the First World War*, Wellington, 1988.

Pugsley, C., *Gallipoli: The New Zealand Story*, Auckland, 2008.

12   The Savage Government Elected

Condliffe, J. B., *The Welfare State*, London, 1959.

Firth, C., *State Housing in New Zealand*, Wellington, 1949.

Hanson, E. *The Politics of Social Security*, Auckland, 1980.

Hawke, G. R., *The Making of New Zealand: An Economic History*, Cambridge, 1985.

Paul, J. T., *Humanism in Politics: New Zealand Labour Party Retrospective*, Wellington, 1946.

Schrader, B., *We Call it Home: A History of State Housing in New Zealand*, Auckland, 2005.

Wood, F. L. W., *This New Zealand*, Hamilton, 1946.

13   The ANZUS Pact

Bell, R. J., *Unequal Allies: Australian–American Relations and the Pacific War*, Melbourne, 1977.

Evatt, H. V., *Foreign Policy of Australia; Speeches by the Rt. Hon. H.V. Evatt*, Sydney, 1965.

Hoadley, S., *The New Zealand Foreign Affairs Handbook*, Auckland, 1989.

McGibbon, I. (ed.), *Undiplomatic Dialogue: Letters Between Carl Berendsen and Alister McIntosh 1943–1952*, Auckland, 1993.

McIntyre, W. D., *Background to the ANZUS Pact: Policy-Making, Strategy and Diplomacy, 1945–55*, Christchurch, 1995.

Miller, T. B. (ed.), *Australian Foreign Ministers: The Diaries of R. G. Casey 1951–69*, London, 1972.

Schnabel, J., *The History of the Joint Chiefs of Staff. Volume 1: The Joint Chiefs of Staff and National Policy, 1945–1947*, Delaware, 1979.

Spender, P., *Exercised in Diplomacy*, Sydney, 1969.

Starke, J. G. *The ANZUS Treaty Alliance*, Melbourne, 1965.

Templeton, M. (ed.), *An Eye, An Ear and a Voice: 50 Years of New Zealand's External Relations, 1943–1993*, Wellington, 1993.

14   Maori Urban Migration

Else, A. (ed.), *Women Together: A History of Women's Organisations in New Zealand*, Wellington, 1993.

Grace, P., Ramsden, I. and Dennis, J., *The Silent Migration: Ngati Poneke Young Maori Club 1937–1948*, Wellington, 2001.

Hill, R. S., *Maori and the State: Crown–Maori Relations in New Zealand/Aotearoa 1950–2000*, Wellington, 2009.

Himona, R. in *Te Putatara*, Wellington, August 1989, p. 1.

Hunn, J. K., *Report on the Department of Maori Affairs*, Wellington, 1960.

Martin, J. E., *Holding the Balance*, Christchurch, 1996.

Metge, J., *The Maoris of New Zealand*, London, 1967.

Moon, P., *Victoria Cross at Takrouna: The Haane Manahi Story*, Wellington, 2010.

Myint, H., *Economic Theory and the Underdeveloped Countries*, New York, 1971.

Ropiha, T. T., 'The Place of the Maori in a Modern Community', in *Te Ao Hou: The New World*, no. 19, August, 1957, p. 10.

Sutch, W. B., *The Maori Contribution: Yesterday, Today and Tomorrow*, Wellington, 1964.

Walker, R., *He Tipua: The Life and Times of Sir Apirana Ngata*, Auckland, 2001.

Williams, D., *Crown Policy Affecting Maori Knowledge Systems and Cultural Practices*, Wellington, 2001.

15 Britain Joins the European Economic Community

Adam, J., *Twenty-Five Years of Emigrant Life in the South of New Zealand*, Edinburgh, 1874.

Beloff, N., *The General Says No*, London, 1963.

Bowler, I. R., *Agriculture Under the Common Agricultural Policy: A Geography*, Manchester, 1985.

Howard, A., *Rab: The Life of R. A Butler*, London, 1987.

Hursthouse, C., *New Zealand, or Zealandia, the Britain of the South*, vol. 1. London, 1857.

Jackson, K. (ed.), *Fight for Life: New Zealand, Britain and the European Economic Community*, Wellington, 1971.

Macmillan, H., *At the End of the Day, 1961–1963*, London, 1973.

Moon, P., *New Zealand Birth Certificates: 50 of New Zealand's Founding Documents*, Auckland, 2010.

Noakes, J. Wende, P., and Wright, J. (eds.), *Britain and Germany in Europe 1949–1990*, Oxford, 2002.

Swainson, W., *New Zealand and its Colonization*, London, 1859.

Williscroft, C. (ed.), *A Lasting Legacy: A 125-Year History of New Zealand Farming Since the First Frozen Meat Shipment*, Auckland, 2007.

16 The Maori Renaissance

Cox, L., *Kotahitanga: The Search for Maori Political Unity*, Auckland, 1993.

Kawharu, I. H. (ed.), *Waitangi: Maori and Pakeha Perspectives of the Treaty of Waitangi*, Auckland, 1989.

Moon, P., *Tohunga: Hohepa Kereopa*, Auckland, 2003.

Orange, C., *The Treaty of Waitangi*, Wellington, 1987.

Scrimgeour, F. and Iremonger, C., *Maori Sustainable Economic Development in New Zealand: Indigenous Practices for the Quadruple Bottom Line*, Hamilton, 2004.

Sharp, A. *Justice and the Maori: Maori Claims in New Zealand Political Argument in the 1980s*, Auckland, 1990.

Walker, R. J., *He Tipua: The Life and Times of Sir Apirana Ngata*, Auckland, 2001.

Ward, A., *An Unsettled History: Treaty Claims in New Zealand Today*, Wellington, 1999.

17 The Springbok Tour

Barlow, G., *All Blacks Versus Springboks: A Century of Rugby Rivalry*, Auckland, 1992.

Commonwealth of Nations, *The Gleneagles Agreement on sporting contacts with South Africa*, London, 15 June 1977, para 1, 3.

Gustafson, B., *His Way: A Biography of Robert Muldoon*, Auckland, 2000.

Meurant, R., *The Red Squad Story*, Auckland, 1982.

Richards, T., *Dancing on Our Bones: New Zealand, South Africa, Rugby and Racism*, Wellington, 1999.

Templeton, M., *Human Rights and Sporting Contacts: New Zealand Attitudes to Race Relations in South Africa, 1921–1994*, Auckland, 1998.

Thompson, R., *Retreat from Apartheid: New Zealand's Sporting Contacts with South Africa*, Wellington, 1975.

18 The Homosexual Law Reform Act

Brickell, C., *Mates and Lovers: A History of Gay New Zealand*, Auckland, 2008.

Guy, L., *Worlds in Collision: The Gay Debate in New Zealand 1960–1986*, Wellington, 2002.

Millett, T., 'Elusive Goal', *Friends of LAGANZ*, issue no. 10, Wellington, June 1996, n. p.

Moon, P., *New Zealand in the Twentieth Century: The Land, The People*, Auckland, 2011.

Robinson, R., *Survivors of Suicide*, New Jersey, 2001.

Weiner, M. (ed.), *Modernization*, New York, 1966.

19 Rogernomics

Boston, J., et al., *Public Management. The New Zealand Model*, Auckland, 1996.

Duncan, I. and Bollard, A., *Corporatization and Privatization: Lessons from New Zealand*, Auckland, 1992.

Garnier, T. and Levine, S., *Election '81: An End to Muldoonism?*, Auckland, 1981.

James, C., *New Territory: The Transformation of New Zealand, 1984–1992*, Wellington, 1992.

Kelsey, J., *Rolling Back the State: Privatisation of Power in Aotearoa/New Zealand*, Wellington, 1993.

Massey, P., *New Zealand. Market Liberalisation in a Developed Economy*, New York, 1995.

Moon, P., *Muldoon: A Study in Public Leadership*, Wellington, 1999.

Muldoon, R. D., *The New Zealand Economy: A Personal View*, Auckland, 1985.

Palmer, G., *Unbridled Power: An Interpretation of New Zealand's Constitution and Government*, Auckland, 1987.

Rudd, C. and Roper, B., *The Political Economy of New Zealand*, Auckland, 1997.

Schick, A., *The Spirit of Reform: Managing the New Zealand State Sector in a Time of Change*, Wellington, 1996.

Walker, S. (ed.), *Rogernomics. Reshaping New Zealand's Economy*, Auckland, 1989.

20   The Introduction of MMP

Boston, J., et al., (eds.), *From Campaign to Coalition: The 1996 MMP Election*, Palmerston North, 1997.

Harris, P., *New Zealand's Change to MMP*, Wellington, 2000.

Levine, S. (ed.), *Politics in New Zealand: A Reader*, Cheshire, 1975.

Levine, S., *The New Zealand Political System: Politics in a Small Society*, Sydney, 1979.

Miller, R., *The Public's Reaction to MMP and Coalition Government Data from the New Zealand Elections Studies 1993–2005*, Auckland 2006.

Robinson, A. D., *Notes on New Zealand Politics*, Wellington, 1970.

PICTURE ACKNOWLEDGEMENTS

All images have been sourced from the Alexander Turnbull Library, Wellington, New Zealand. Some images have been sourced from special collections, and these are acknowledged on the following pages: Schmidt Collection: 75, 99; G H Swan Collection: 78; S P Andrew Collection: 102, 127, 146, 157; Charles Morice Collection: 113; W J Harding Collection: 124; S C Smith Collection: 131; A P Godbear Collection: 140; Evening Post Collection: 151, 163, 173; War History Collection: 160; James McAllister Collection: 183; Peter Bromhead: 188; Dominion Post Collection: 192, 201, 208, 213, 222, 225, 231, 234, 241, 246.

INDEX

Note: Italicized page numbers indicate photographs or illustrations.